Planetary Improvement

Planetary Improvement

Cleantech Entrepreneurship and the Contradictions of Green Capitalism

Jesse Goldstein

The MIT Press
Cambridge, Massachusetts
London, England

This book was set in Stone Serif by Westchester Publishing Services. Printed and bound in the United States of America.

Library of Congress Cataloging-in-Publication Data

Names: Goldstein, Jesse, 1977- author.
Title: Planetary improvement : cleantech entrepreneurship and the contradictions of green capitalism / Jesse Goldstein.
Description: Cambridge, MA : MIT Press, [2018] | Includes bibliographical references and index.
Identifiers: LCCN 2017038810 | ISBN 9780262037822 (hardcover : alk. paper) | ISBN 9780262535076 (pbk. : alk. paper)
Subjects: LCSH: Entrepreneurship--Environmental aspects. | Capitalism--Environmental aspects. | Sustainable development.
Classification: LCC HB615 .G647 2018 | DDC 338.9/27--dc23 LC record available at https://lccn.loc.gov/2017038810

10 9 8 7 6 5 4 3 2 1

For Jack and Lillian Krayton

Contents

Acknowledgments

I have worked on this project for eight years amid an abundance of intellectual generosity, mutual aid, and genuine care. When I think about all of the people I have shared spaces and ideas with since my research began in 2009. I am overwhelmed by a deep sense of humility and respect for the collective nature of scholarship and the "pluripotent intellect" that has nurtured me on this journey.

This book began as my dissertation at the City University of New York (CUNY) Graduate Center, where I spent a few too many years learning, living, laughing…and adjuncting. My dissertation committee—Hester Eisenstein, Cindi Katz, and Ken Gould—were all excellent mentors and offered me invaluable support through this process. Hester introduced me to my field site and accompanied me at numerous historical materialism conferences; Ken introduced me to the world of environmental sociology and continues to provide valuable guidance and support; and Cindi, whose workful play and playful work has probably shaped my own thinking and doing more than anyone's, has been a most generous guide to life, to academia, and more specifically to the world of critical geography that I have been welcomed into as my intellectual home away from home (I'm technically a sociologist). And keeping with the geographers, I need to thank Vinay Gidwani for offering crucial guidance early on in my process.

My community at the CUNY Graduate Center irrevocably transformed the ways in which I think about the world. I want to thank Stanley Aronowitz, David Harvey, and most importantly my fellow students, who made the Graduate Center one of the most vibrant intellectual spaces I will probably ever experience. Seemingly endless conversations, analysis, and reflection with Elizabeth Johnson, David Spataro, Michael Polson, Justin Myers, John Boy, Paul Jackson, Christian Anderson, Amanda Huron, Stephanie Wakefield,

Steve McFarland, C. Ray Borck, Alyson Spurgas, Bradley Gardener, Malav Kanuga, Amanda Matles, Andrew McKinney, Stephen Boatright, and so many others have shaped how I see the world and challenged me in innumerable ways.

I have participated in a number of amazing collaborations through this period. The SpaceTime Research Collective has been a pillar of my intellectual community, and I feel an intellectual debt to all of its members, past and present. Organizing the first two Historical Materialism: New York conferences with Asher Dupuy-Spencer, FTC Manning, John Clegg, Kate Perkins and the rest of the HMNY organizing collective was a formative experience, introducing me to a broad world of historical materialist scholars, including many who have gone on to become important friends and collaborators. Thanks as well to Sebastian Budgen and the rest of the HM editorial group for patiently working with our organizing collective. I also want to thank my friends and collaborators Elizabeth Knafo, and Matthew Schneider-Mayerson, along with the rest of the team who produced the *Rare Earth Catalog*, which has given me a chance to translate some of the ideas from this book into other forms.

Friends and colleagues from New York City and beyond have also helped me through this process and transformed my thinking in important ways: Daniel Aldana Cohen, Heather Rogers, Brett Story, Laura Hannah, Gelvin Stevenson, Rosemary Collard, David Tyfield, Josh MacPhee, Paula Segal, Matthew Huber, and many others. At a material level, this work would not have been possible if Joe Ugoretz had not given me the opportunity to serve as an instructional technology fellow, which allowed me to stop adjuncting and focus on research and writing.

I want to thank Jessica Dempsey, Imre Szeman, Christian Anderson, Elizabeth Johnson, Geoff Mann, Martha Kenney, Matthew Schneider-Mayerson, Laura Portwood-Stacer and Damian White for their helpful feedback on portions of this work, and Jim Igoe for believing in the project from its earliest post-dissertation inception and providing me important mentorship along the way. My editors at MIT Press, Beth Clevenger and Marcy Ross, have been incredibly supportive, and Mary Bagg provided exceptional copyediting. Of course all the standard disclaimers apply and I'm ultimately responsible for errors and omissions, and for not heeding all of their sage advice.

My colleagues at Virginia Commonwealth University (VCU) were incredibly supportive as I finished this book, and I especially want to thank my current collaborator Victor Chen for his caring mentorship and keen editorial eye. The first-time book writer's group has been a tremendous support, and I want to thank Myrl Beam, Cristina Staniclu, and Chris Cynn in particular for their intellectual and emotional support. I've also worked with two exceptional research assistants (and friends), Caitlin Cunningham and Bryan Gorman, who I cannot thank enough.

I would also like to thank my community in Richmond, Virginia, where I've spent the last three years while at VCU: Julietta Singh, Nathan Snaza, Sean Doody, Chioke I'Anson, John Orth, Corin Hewitt, Molly McFadden, Claire Schoen, Kristin Reed, Orla McHardy, Nick Vanderkolk, Brooke Inman, Cara Benedetto, Evrim Dogu, and Tressie McMillan Cottom.

I have and continue to learn so much from my students at Baruch College, Brooklyn College, Parsons, and now VCU. Teaching really has shaped how I think about the world.

I wouldn't be where I am without my incredibly loving family: my parents Marcia and Ron, my sister Daria and her family, Andy, Alex, and Olivia. I am deeply appreciative of Molly Fair, who was by my side through this whole process. Her family members deserve thanks as well: Andy (who enthusiastically read and edited a very early draft of my manuscript), Ellen, Naomi, David, and Josephine.

It seems like a lifetime ago that I first pulled out my sports coat and headed to midtown Manhattan, where I found the NY Cleantech Funders Forum, and with it a network of warm and welcoming entrepreneurs, investors, and consultants whose candor and willingness to engage in discussion and debate made this work possible. (To further protect the anonymity of those I interviewed and identified by initials, and to respect the privacy of the group itself, I created a fictitious name for these events.) The many individuals I encountered through this research deserve my deepest gratitude for letting me into their professional lives and treating me with dignity and respect. I can only hope that they find this work, although critical, comes nonetheless from a shared commitment to bettering the world we live in, harnessing its creative potential for socially and ecologically productive ends.

Introduction: From French Fries to Planetary Salvation

Let's begin at the 88th session of the NY Cleantech Funders Forum.[1] It is 9 a.m. in a windowless conference room on the 31st floor of a skyscraper in midtown Manhattan. Fifteen cleantech professionals—investors, lawyers, entrepreneurs, brokers—sit around a large table, at the head of which stand two entrepreneurs, ready to make an investment pitch for their product, the Vegawatt. The Vegawatt is a waste-to-energy technology targeting small, fast food restaurants. It converts used fry grease into fuel for a combined heat and power diesel generator, which in turn produces hot water and electricity. Waste in, energy out. The graphic on the first slide in the presentation shows a green electrical cord plugged into a French fry, which is positioned next to their sales line: "Out of the deep fryer, into your pocket!"

During the pitch, the company's two founders explain several benefits that the users of their device will accrue: "saving money on utility bills, producing free hot water, reducing CO_2 emissions," and last and perhaps most important, "saving the planet." Their website lays out the entire progression:

Your Benefits When You Run Your Restaurant On Vegawatt™ Power
Save over $700 every month off your utility bills!
Produce Free electricity onsite
Produce Free hot water onsite
Save on Waste Vegetable Oil disposal fees
Reduce your Electricity Demand charges
Reduce the CO_2 emissions of your restaurant
Reduce the dependence on fossil fuels
Save the Planet[2]

The Vegawatt is a perfectly good technology that offers restaurants a solution to a costly problem: instead of paying to dispose of fry grease, turn it into a source of heat and energy. But what interests me here is the broader story these Vegawatt entrepreneurs told about their product's projected efficiency gains. They offered what I would come to recognize as a typical cleantech arc; begin with incremental gains (in this case monthly savings on energy bills and waste disposal fees), progress to incremental environmental savings (reduced CO_2 emissions), and present these incremental gains as the initial steps toward a major environmental transformation (reduced dependence on fossil fuels) that will ultimately help save the planet.

The environmental impacts of fast food production have been well documented—from factory farming and the production of massive amounts of disposable containers to a regular stream of food waste, and more generally to the promotion of an unhealthy diet that is incredibly energy- and chemical-intensive.[3] As you might expect, none of these industry conditions find a place in Vegawatt's pitch, which instead isolated one single waste stream, suggested a way to improve it, and left the matter at that. It makes you wonder, just what planet is being saved, and for whom?

From French fries to planetary salvation: this is easy enough to assert in a cleantech investment pitch, where the path connecting incremental gains to system-wide transformation speaks to a powerful imaginary about how the world could or should work, about how innovation, technology and economic growth could and should help us right all of our societal wrongs. This imaginary—what I call *planetary improvement*—infuses a sense of purpose, meaning, and thus legitimacy to an otherwise mundane and profit-motivated world of industry and work. In this regard, it functions as a new green spirit of capitalism.

The likelihood that technologies predicated upon recycling and burning oil will help to wean society from its addiction to fossil fuels may be somewhat of a stretch. Saving the planet is a noble goal, but if a company like Vegawatt wants to attract investors, it will have to prove that its primary focus is on making incremental gains in already established markets. As I watched the Vegawatt presentation, one of the lawyers in the room interrupted the CEO's pitch: "We're not here to save the planet. We're here to help you gestate something that can afford expensive New York City lawyers." (The words "like me" were implied.)

A complicated and contested politics of technological innovation has begun to underwrite the new, green spirit of capitalism. In this book

I examine the innovation of green technologies known as *cleantech* and the widespread investment—emotional as well as financial—in the promise of technological salvation. These investments mark a dynamic tension between capital and creativity that runs to the heart of the green economy, actively shaping the contours and trajectory of green technological innovation. The new green spirit of capitalism, or what I refer to as planetary improvement, enlists environmentally motivated efforts to shape the future into a project that ultimately aims to perpetuate much of the underlying ecological instability of the present. Instead of promoting forms of creativity that are capable of envisioning new and better worlds, planetary improvement marshals creativity into the process of innovating new and better commodities, whose value is measured in sales as opposed to an assessment of what living better—more equitably and more sustainably—might actually entail.

Here I use this broad term *creativity* to capture all of the many ways that imaginative, inventive, innovative activity exceeds the narrowing bounds of its entrepreneurial expression—and I could append so many more adjectives to this list, including poetic, analytic, experimental, artisanal. Being entrepreneurial is not, nor should it ever be, the only way in which one can engage in creative production. This broader, intergenerational, and inherently collective capacity to create and make and imagine represents a wild expanse of possibilities and potentials. However, in the green economy, this "wild" is regularly being tamed by the pressures of commercial success, which compel entrepreneurs to narrow their focus upon potentially marketable technologies that offer incremental improvements (slightly less wasteful, slightly more green or clean) to the status quo.

My exploration of these dynamics in the chapters that follow is based on three years of ethnographic research in the New York City cleantech startup and investment scene. From 2010 to 2013, I attended dozens of investment pitch sessions and networking events. I visited entrepreneurial incubators and met with scores of cleantech professionals, from entrepreneurs and inventors to lawyers and venture investors. I learned about fascinating new technologies and encountered a wide array of people who were genuinely interested in seeing these technologies succeed. Instead of following specific technologies or startups through their entire lifecourse, I was exposed to what felt at times like a revolving door of innovations and innovators, each a little bit different, yet also remarkably the same. Pitch after pitch, meeting after meeting, I began to focus less on the technologies being developed and the unique and often incredibly targeted problems they each aimed to address, and more on the general culture of cleantech entrepreneurship, innovation, and investment. This is a world forced to grapple with a complicated and often contradictory set of commitments, to "greening" the economy (and by extension the planet), as well as to developing business models that could reliably make some "green" for potential investors. In this double sense, I observed a world that was not-yet green; start-ups that are not yet profitable aiming to improve an industrial economy that is not yet environmentally sustainable.

Prior to conducting my fieldwork, I prepared by reading dozens of texts promoting one form or another of a green capitalist economy, thinking that this would be common ground in the cleantech space I was about to enter. To my surprise, even though I regularly heard echoes of the arguments contained in these texts, very few people I encountered during my research had read much from this genre. I found that these "big picture" ideas were important, but only in the abstract, and only insofar as these abstractions did not interfere with the more pressing needs of finding investors and becoming commercially viable. And so, while I began my research naively thinking that I would find a living extension of these texts and an expression of their worldview, what I actually found was a far more complex and far more interesting negotiation of environmental and economic logics.

My fieldwork, which began in 2010, was largely being conducted in the shadow of the Occupy Wall Street (OWS) movement, and my life was actually split between these two worlds—an occupation in Zuccotti Park, blocks from Wall Street, and cleantech meetings in corporate boardrooms high up in midtown skyscrapers. The discrepancies between these two spaces heightened my fascination with both. In one, I participated in a spontaneous outpouring of productively channeled anger and the pent up capacities of people who knew they could and should make the world anew. Together, we experimented with creating impromptu social infrastructure while taking on the rather Herculean task of publicly, collectively, and antagonistically existing in a rapidly gentrifying New York City. Meanwhile, in midtown, I mingled with (mostly) men in suits who were networking, pitching, and otherwise jockeying to commercialize clean technologies, and to make some money in the process.

Somewhat to my surprise, there was more overlap between these worlds than I expected. This is not to say that OWS resonated with the majority of cleantech professionals I met, but it did resonate with a very substantial minority, who would tell me about attending the marches and their reasons for supporting the movement. One evening at Zuccotti Park, I was browsing through the books in the OWS library, which had grown over the course of the occupation from one row along a marble embankment to thousands of books, organized in plastic bins marked with various topical headings: nonfiction, politics, poetry, and so on. In the bin labeled "environment and sustainability" there were only four books. I opened one, Joel Makower's *Strategies for the Green Economy*. Handwritten on the inside cover was this dedication:

To Occupy Wall Street: From my library to yours. Thank you for representing me. I am working for you at a cleantech company. I am a Wall Street Broker turned Cleantech exec. "Doing well by doing good," but doing good comes first. I am the 99 percent.

What does it mean to "do good"? This question—and the ways in which it is strategically not asked, cuts to the core of the green spirit of capitalism that I explore. A good deal of attention has been directed at the ways in which efforts to "go green" often function as an ideological veneer of corporate social responsibility and good public relations work.[4] While this is undoubtedly true, at another level these "green" discourses represent something more than just clever marketing. There are important ways in which people involved in the green or clean economy earnestly believe in what they are doing. Far from simply fooling a simple-minded populace with good public relations, there are those who actually see themselves working to create a better, more sustainable world. As will become clear below, many (but certainly not all) of the people I met during my research fall into this category. In many ways I wrote this book for them: environmentally committed entrepreneurs, investors, inventors, and service providers, as well as those considering such work. I mean to offer a constructive analysis that honors their environmental intentions while critiquing the market relations they operate within, relations which have become normalized and naturalized as simply the way things are.

My goal in exploring this world of early-stage cleantech entrepreneurialism is twofold, based on questioning each half of the term *cleantech*. Regarding *clean*, I want to understand what "green capitalism" means to the creative professionals who are actively trying to bring a sustainable world into being. What opportunities and possibilities do they see? What excites them about working on environmentally oriented projects, and why is it important for these projects to be profit oriented? What sort of imaginary does it require to envision how "non-disruptive disruptions" could make the sort of planetary-scale impact that they hope to achieve? Then, regarding *tech*, I want to understand how it is that in a room full of idealistic and creative producers who want to disrupt and transform our socioeconomic system in order to "save the planet," the seemingly iron laws of the capitalist market economy consistently shape what sorts of technologies are even worth considering in the first place. I want to understand the innovation ecosystem as a space in which creativity is, on the one hand, encouraged and supported, and on other hand, simultaneously disciplined, shaped, and enclosed.

Though it is common to conceptualize entrepreneurs as the creative vanguard of capital, *Planetary Improvement: Cleantech Entrepreneurship and the Contradictions of Green Capitalism* instead shows how capital, or the investors operating in its name, are primarily interested in working with entrepreneurs who are willing to relinquish direct control over their projects and instead become key employees, to be hired and fired as needed. While triumphant neoclassical economic arguments see innovation as something that capital spurs or actively encourages, here these narratives are turned on their head, as we see that capital captures, controls and contorts—as much as it creates—innovative visions of sociotechnical possibility and transformation.

In the pages that follow, I show that entrepreneurialism, writ large, need not be categorically dismissed by critics of capitalism, but can instead be seen as shorthand for forms of creative labor that can and should be reclaimed and redirected. How can we untether innovation from investors' responsibility to maximize profits at all other expense? Can we envision ways to produce socially, to be innovative, creative, and caring, while beholden to a different set of responsibilities altogether?

Cleantech in NYC: The Funders Forum

Although Silicon Valley provided an initial reservoir of excitement about cleantech, a number of other regions—both internationally and in the US—have been able to assert themselves as significant hubs of cleantech commercialization and development. New York State is a major source of innovation for energy storage, with the NY Battery and Energy Storage

Consortium leading the way. The New York State Energy Research and Development Authority (NYSERDA) helps coordinate research and development across the state through numerous granting programs, and by supporting proof-of-concept centers meant to rival those in Silicon Valley and Boston.[5] In conjunction with a sizable investment community (in 2013, New York ranked third in venture investing behind Boston and Silicon Valley) this has made the state an increasingly relevant space in US-based cleantech innovation.[6]

My decision to conduct research in NYC, as opposed to Boston or Silicon Valley, and even more specifically to focus on the Funders Forum, was grounded by the presumption that if, in fact, there is a new, green spirit of capitalism emerging, then I should not have to look only at high-profile or fantastically powerful and/or wealthy scions of a new energy economy, or speak only with its most prominent boosters. While the cleantech space may have been initially catalyzed by some major players on the West Coast, I am interested in showing how broader market participants follow suit: how they reinterpret, redefine, and reimagine the cleantech project in and through their everyday efforts to build, piece by small piece, a cleaner economy. And so I chose mainly to interact with a much more diverse, much less wealthy cleantech investment scene: the slightly less influential, slightly less kempt, slightly less important, slightly less connected sea of professionals that make cleantech more than an elite activity or buzzword of global governance, but who, as I show in the subsequent chapters, embody, perform, and rehearse cleantech as their market.

The Vegawatt was the first in a series of cleantech projects I observed at the Funders Forum, a monthly entrepreneurial pitch event, and one of the longest continually running cleantech events in the US. PL, as I will call the organizer, began this event in 2002 and has been running it continuously ever since on a monthly basis, with about 10 meetings per year. (Events are often suspended in the summer months.) I attended sessions regularly from November 2011 (the 88th meeting) through January 2013 (the 110th meeting), returning occasionally when I've had the chance. Anywhere from 12 to 30 people attend each breakfast meeting, most of whom pay the $50 admission fee (exceptions are made for some first time attendees and those experiencing financial difficulty, or as PL likes to say, "still waiting for a check"). This generates a few hundred dollars each month, the only money PL is paid. The event has since been held at a number of different locations: when I first attended it was hosted by a mid-town Manhattan law firm in the windowless conference room I described above; it later moved for half a year to the Times Square offices of a large accounting firm, and then to the midtown offices of a law firm on the West Side.[7]

Each month at the Funders Forum, an entrepreneur from an early-stage cleantech company addresses a room full of investors, service providers, and fellow entrepreneurs. Each presentation is intended as an investment pitch: an explanation of the technology, the commercialization strategy, the market opportunity, and then an overview of financial needs, projections, and investment opportunities.

I saw entrepreneurs pitch technologies ranging from aneutronic plasma fusion reactors (more on this in the chapter 6 and the coda) and novel waste-to-energy generators to energy efficiency software and fuel additives. Almost all of the presenting companies were at an early stage of development. Over 100 different companies have presented at the Funders Forum, representing a wide range of services and technologies, most of which are related to energy production, distribution, or storage in one way or another, and (almost) all of which could be considered part of the broader "cleantech space."

Despite the name, at any given Funders Forum meeting only a small number of actual funders shows up. The other attendees include a wide range of professionals, from academics and researchers (such as myself), to inventors and entrepreneurs (often past and future presenters), to lawyers and other service providers (broker-dealers, public relations specialists, accountants). It would be difficult to place all of the attendees into discrete categories—many of them function in multiple roles, and each has a somewhat unique story. There are retirees looking for a second career, attorneys looking for clients (whether to help broker a deal or to provide IP protection). There are professionals who work for larger companies as financial planners, researchers, and analysts. There are prospective presenters—entrepreneurs, engineers, inventors, and financial officers, for instance—who come to check out the event. The handful of investors I encountered at the event included one regularly attending angel investor and a few other assorted money managers of one form or another (representatives from small private equity firms, venture capitalists, private investors).

These professionals slip in and out of different roles depending on their current situation and the projects they encounter; an individual can operate as a consultant on one day and as an entrepreneur or inventor on the next. Even with the regular attendees, it is difficult to pin them down with one professional designation or another. This is especially the case with the strategic consultants. PL himself is a good example. In the two years that I regularly attended, during the round of introductions that began each breakfast meeting, PL's designation transitioned from "adjunct professor of environmental economics" to "board member of a solar company" to "working with an interesting engineering firm upstate" to "CEO of a modular farm business" to "I'm the guy hosting these events." Others provided a more stable identity. FG was a chemical engineer turned patent attorney. KL was a "solar financial analyst." LM was there to "bring clean technologies to Africa and the developing world." And MC regularly described himself as "a disruptive technology hunter." These professionals are, as Federico Caprotti suggests in his study of cleantech discourses, some of the diverse advocates and service providers that play a formative role in defining cleantech and policing its boundaries.[7]

What Lies Ahead…

I did not set out to write *Planetary Improvement* as an attempt to assess whether the greening of capital is viable or can "work." My hope is that we can set these debates temporarily aside while we attempt to understand a new green spirit of capitalism, along with some of its main presuppositions. There is a need to develop a more generous (albeit critical) analysis of the idea and the project—greening capitalism—for what it is and what it may become. If we rightly acknowledge that free markets have never been all that free, why should we presume that green capitalism would be all that green?

I open chapter 1 with an overview of the history of cleantech and an introduction to the core contradiction that I investigate throughout the book: while the professionals I met were excited about creating and commercializing "disruptive" technologies that might radically transform our lives, when it came to actually finding (and funding) commercially viable projects, considerations of anything disruptive quickly gave way to assessments of which technologies demonstrated potential to provide incremental gains in already established markets. Building from Luc Boltanski and Eve Chiapello's book *The New Spirit of Capitalism*, I argue that planetary improvement represents a new, green spirit of capitalism, one that mobilizes a seemingly radical, anti-systemic critique of capitalism in order to provide moral legitimacy and affective force for proposals that make the modern industrial economy less environmentally destructive—still capitalism, just a better, greener version. This new green spirit of capitalism allows entrepreneurs and investors to thoroughly indict industrial capitalism while simultaneously disarming their critique. The goal, ultimately, is to find "non-disruptive disruptions": in other words, technologies that can deliver "solutions" without actually changing much of what causes the underlying problems in the first place.

As a term, *planetary improvement* references the discourse of agricultural improvement that helped legitimize enclosure and colonial land grabs in the first centuries of capitalism's ascent. Agricultural improvement targeted so-called inefficient forms of agricultural production—from those practiced by European commoners to a wide range of indigenous agricultural practices throughout the colonized world. In a similar way, planetary improvement recasts "dirty" or wasteful forms of industrial production and consumer-driven lifestyles as a terrain of potential improvement. Instead of inefficient commoners or inefficient laborers, however, here it is capitalist society itself that is guilty of being wasteful.

In chapter 2, I place planetary improvement in historical context, connecting it to the rise of business environmentalism over the latter half of the 20th century. Through the recuperation and reformulation of well-established critiques of the waste-making industrial economy, planetary improvement is sanitized to remove any lingering anti-systemic or even anti-capitalist orientations (as well as any interest in appropriate technologies) and recast as creative, Schumpeterian entrepreneurialism focused on developing and deploying clean technologies at a planetary scale. I enter into this discussion by examining the surprisingly obtuse and difficult-to-define concept of *impact*, especially the ways in which its use reveals an emotional and aspirational force underlying the commitment that my respondents had to cleantech entrepreneurialism. *Impact*, as the term is used, refers both to the possibility of socioecological disruption, or the ability to make an impact-beyond-capital, as well as the possibility of market disruption, or the ability to make an impact-as-capital.

Using a series of vignettes from my fieldwork, startup entrepreneurs, consultants, and investors explain to me why they do what they do, how their work is entrepreneurial, and why they have not chosen to pursue four distinctly less impactful alternatives and the types of activity associated with them: (1) "boring" industries, (2) small businesses, (3) hippies and environmentalists, and (4) Wall Street. Boring industries support the status quo of business-as-usual—a not-clean, waste-making economy. Small businesses engage in a scale of operation that is inconsequential—a wasted opportunity to address planetary-scale problems. Hippies adopt the irrational excesses of idealistic environmentalism—a perspective detached from practical business sense. And Wall Street operates with a narrow focus on making money—a position that blinds people to nonfinancial considerations.

In explaining how to deal with inexperienced entrepreneurs, a senior investor at the Funders Forum offered a simple maxim: "kill the inventor!" To an unexpected degree, this became a refrain at the event—a way to acknowledge the need to rein in any overly idealistic commitments to technological (or social, or environmental) development in the process of shaping a start-up, and its founders, for the market. Accordingly, in chapter 3, I argue that the cleantech innovation ecosystem is built around attempts to manage and control creativity.

If the Schumpeterian dynamic of creative destruction typically envisions innovators destroying and replacing incumbent technologies and the industries they support, here we see an opposing tendency, whereby innovators (and their creativity) are disciplined by incumbent industries and the investment logics supporting them. The saying "capitalism spurs innovation" conjures a sense that capitalism promotes, accelerates, and encourages creative advance. However, spurs are also disciplinary devices, used for example to break in horses to make them comply with the will of their riders. Inventor-entrepreneurs are subjected to precisely this sort of "training" or discipline—what Henri Lefebvre refers to as *dressage* (another horse-related term), a process of bending and being bent.

In chapter 3 I explore how dressage operates through the expectations and formal legal agreements that accompany venture investments. Though it is common to conceptualize entrepreneurs as the creative vanguard of neoliberal capitalism, in *Planetary Improvement* I demonstrate instead that capital, or the investors operating in its name, are only interested in working with "doubly free" entrepreneurs. I introduce the term *doubly free entrepreneur* as an analog to Marx's conception of the doubly free laborer: free from the means of production and free to enter into the labor market. Doubly free entrepreneurs, once they are freed from their innovation, are free to become employees of the firm they had previously controlled, and therefore able to be hired and fired as needed.

Labor is always ultimately a social process, and entrepreneurial creativity therefore represents one small aspect of a broader, intergenerational, and inherently collective capacity to create, make, maintain, and imagine—what Marx referred to as the "general intellect." Dressage speaks to a more broadly understood enclosure of this creativity, subtly reinforced through the lionization of entrepreneurship as the pinnacle of creative activity. As a result, a wide array of possibilities and potentials are actively disciplined and reduced to the potential to create (green) capital.

Just as a good, investment worthy entrepreneur is one that is willing to be brought under control, trained, and disciplined by the mentorship of investors, in chapter 4 I explain how something similar can be said of venture investors themselves, who have to respond to their own set of disciplinary obligations, or fiduciary responsibilities. Just as entrepreneurialism can function as a more general subjectivity and orientation to the world that extends beyond the specific individuals at the helm of new businesses, the same is true of venture capital. As such, the gravitational pull of fiduciary responsibility extends far beyond specific investors, generating a general, pervasive and commonsense understanding of what projects, what futures, and, ultimately, what natures are possible in the first place.

Well-known investors such as John Doerr are able to make very public, very impassioned pleas for a collective commitment to planetary improvement. But the adjunct to these front-stage proclamations of the green spirit of capitalism occurs in spaces like the Funders Forum and similar pitch events, which can be considered "backstage" venues, where ideas are rehearsed and refined. Although there were not always a lot of investors present at the events I observed—or, for that matter, money to be invested—there was no shortage of money's "smarts." A wide array of strategic consultants—from brokers and financial advisers to boutique investment bankers and accountants—took on, experimented with and rehearsed the very distinct intelligence that it takes to be a venture investor. While venture investors were exalted as representing "smart money," this was in the context of strategic consultants proving to entrepreneurs, investors, and themselves that they could exhibit these same sorts of smarts—that they were smart-without-money. The scripts of smart money portray capital's abstract and abstracting logic as an unquestionable intelligence, ultimately demanding that all cleantech innovations, all attempts to make an impact-beyond-capital, accept the market's gravitational force. This is the force, we might say, that tethers the green spirit to capital.

I show in chapter 5 how the green spirit of capitalism emerges through efforts of cleantech entrepreneurs to hold on to aspirational ideals of large-scale ecosocial transformation while still accepting the market imperatives endemic to the commercialization process. A series of conceptual separations between economic and political realms of activity allows cleantech proponents to gesture vaguely toward world-making ambitions, while at the same time insulating these visions from their day-to-day business activities and short-term financial projections. I go on to explore four such examples in particular: (1) a separation between personal and professional commitments; (2) the difference between thinking (about climate change) and doing (something profitable); (3) the disparity between abstract and concrete concerns, only the latter of which can be modeled and acted upon; and (4) the distinction between short-term (fundable) solutions and long-term visions.

Planetary improvement is less about improving the planet in some objective, "natural" sense than it is about improving and sustaining a very distinct mode of inhabiting this planet, of making natures and organizing lives (human and nonhuman alike). As such, the persistence of the very set of social relations causing environmental problems at a planetary scale—the excesses of mass consumer life and the industrial capitalist system underlying it—is accepted as a natural, unquestionable condition of working in the cleantech space. What emerges is a way of seeing the world as not-yet clean, and of seeing the future as a forever-receding horizon of possibility, whose radical transformation is preserved in people's minds while the perpetuation of an unsustainable status quo is preserved in reality.

Throughout my research, I found a general unwillingness to engage with the implications of these presuppositions, a deliberate and socially constructed process of not-knowing. Building on Kari Norgaard's *Living in Denial*, which explores the everyday practices of climate change denial and the ways people process uncomfortable information—things that they know they don't want to know—I argue that planetary improvement entails a related process of green capital denial. Cleantech entrepreneurs envision themselves transforming the capitalist economy into a green economy bit by bit, and refuse to see how the capitalist economy is actually transforming their visions and ideas, molding any new technologies or the possibility thereof into a commodity form that primarily serves the needs of capital.

I look in chapter 6 at a number of recent and ongoing proposals for technologically mediated environmental transformation. Whether advanced nuclear, or wind, water, and solar, at the core of each proposal lies strikingly similar visions of a sustained abundance of cheap energy, unburdened by CO_2 emissions or any of the other pernicious externalities that are destabilizing the biosphere. Yet the demand for this abundant energy, which powers the very industrial economy that is causing so much environmental harm, is never meaningfully addressed. This is not to suggest that we should categorically reject clean technologies just because they are currently mobilized to provide incremental gains to the status quo, but that we do need to question whether we can afford—collectively, socially, environmentally— to place so much focus on developing solutions that are predicated upon the perseverance of the very problems that need to be solved in the first place.

The sociotechnical capacity is out there to transform the world in any number of ways, but realizing some of the more emancipatory (socially and environmentally) visions may require that instead of "killing the inventor," we "kill the investor," thereby liberating our imaginations, our sciences, and our technologies and innovations from the narrowing logic of capital.

In the book's coda, I look towards a critical politics of environmental technology and innovation that moves beyond simplistic binaries that peg all technology and all innovation—or even, for that matter, all entrepreneurship—as inherently good or bad. We must find ways to evaluate sociotechnical systems within what decolonial scholars would call a pluriversal context, one in which modern technological knowledge is considered one of many legitimate ways of knowing and engaging with the world. To the extent that investors, entrepreneurs, and businesspeople—or anyone else who has internalized the smarts of smart money—act as representatives of our collectively creative capacities, then new technologies, and perhaps even new policies and forms of governance, will be oriented around greening what a very privileged *we* already have—improving *our* lives and *our* planet—without ever questioning whether it is precisely these lives in possession of this planet that need to be challenged and ultimately transformed.

I conclude by asking whether there may be a green spirit that goes beyond capitalism—a recognition that we are more and better than the relatively simplistic, inward-looking and self-obsessed logic of capital's expanded reproduction. Liberating this spirit will require hard work, political struggle, unexpected alliances, and a deep sense of humility. We face a messy and uncertain future as we engage with the long and hard work of transforming our socioecological lives. It is my hope that in this book I have set out some of the terms of this struggle.

1 Non-disruptive Disruptions: Cleantech and the New Green Spirit of Capitalism

Despite a growing concern about global climate change, which continues to accelerate at a terrifying pace, and despite the substantial growth of renewable energy and other less environmentally impactful technologies, there is little that can truly be considered "green" about our planetary society—not now, and not in the foreseeable future. Excitement around renewable energy technologies like solar and wind power is warranted, but also needs to be put into context; fossil fuel combustion, the main contributor to climate change, shows little signs of relenting despite this growing renewable sector, not least due to steadily increasing aggregate energy use globally.[1] The overwhelming consensus of the scientific community, as expressed in documents such as a series of Intergovernmental Panel on Climate Change (IPCC) reports, offers a chilling prognosis for our future.[2] This is not the place to rehash the IPCC's grim findings, nor will I dwell on the direct material effects of climate destabilization—they have been and continue to be well chronicled. We can instead jump to the key take-away: the climate has changed and our time is short. Our time was likely short two decades ago, and with the unabated growth of the fossil fuel–based, techno-industrial system that lies at the root of our environmental problems, matters have only intensified.

By now, there is little question, except in the rhetoric of reactionary billionaires and the faux populism they fund,[3] that ecological disasters will continue and that they are a direct result of industrial capitalism. On this point, very little separates those seeking to transform capitalism and those seeking to supersede it. Calls to "green" the economy range from the proliferation of new green markets and jobs, the funding of new technological innovation, and initiatives targeting recycling, reuse, and regulation to more radical critiques calling for degrowth, or even an outright end to the capitalist mode of production.[4]

Technological innovation—or more broadly the creation, development, production, and distribution of new (and old) technologies—has become, within the broad contours of environmentalism, of paramount importance in the struggle to mitigate or reverse climate change. Technology is increasingly cast as a driving force of human history and a key element of progress, which allows for any of its overtly political and social roots to be subsumed by matters of economic efficiency and material productivity.[5] As such, the politics of innovation, understood as a historically contingent process at the intersection of technological capacity and social organization, remains largely overshadowed by a pervasive and ultimately uncritical embrace of whatever new technologies are currently under development, so long as their promoters assure us of their socioecological or "green" virtue.

The presumption that new green technologies are both necessary and necessarily profitable anchors visions, in many shapes and forms, of a new green capitalism that can and must be brought into existence. Luminaries of the modern environmental movement, from Amory Lovins and Gustave Speth to Fred Krupp and Lester Brown, have embraced this vision and for over two decades have been attempting to establish the conceptual and ideological viability of a happy marriage between environmentalism and capitalism, or as Thomas Friedman (2008) puts it, between "Mother Nature and Father Profit."[6]

On the one hand, scientific evidence presents an unending litany of planetary-scale processes that at this point are likely to be irreversible and accelerating: melting permafrost, the near complete loss of ice coverage at the North Pole, droughts causing massive unrest and turning farmers into migrants who are increasingly being met by militarized borders. The scale of environmental problems is almost impossible to truly apprehend. And then, as if spawned from an alternate universe, consumer culture is filled with "green" solutions to a whole different set of problems: eco-efficient light bulbs, canvas tote bags, energy-efficient appliances, and the ubiquitous promise that the unnecessary packaging safeguarding your new product on its path from the factory to your home was made out of partially recycled materials. Personally, I find the most humorous of these efforts in the tourism industry—hotels asking their guests to forego extra towels and sheets in the name of the environment, but never to forego those extra flights—one of the most carbon-intensive forms of transportation that modern civilization has normalized and promoted—that got them there in the first place.[7]

Whether you agree or not, we know the line: every little bit helps; you have to start somewhere. While some of these green solutions may be small, incremental, and even largely inconsequential, doing something is surely better than nothing, and further, getting people to do what they can must be a necessary step toward socioecological transformation. In the face of such enormous, species-threatening problems, how has the horizon of possibility for what can be done been so thoroughly reduced to such minor gestures—most of which essentially amount to choosing a slightly less-bad technology (better light bulbs, better packaging) while otherwise continuing to perpetuate a largely unchanged, unsustainable set of material and energetic practices?[8]

In this book I focus on the central role that technology plays in visions of green capitalism—or more specifically, in the belief that "clean" technologies, known as *cleantech*—can and should figure centrally in any socioecological transformation of the capitalist economy: solar power instead of coal; biodegradable materials; energy-efficient machines, and the software to manage them; or wind farms, electric vehicles, and waste-to-energy contraptions in every conceivable form. There are so many possibilities for improved (cleaner, greener) machines, materials, and fuels to be integrated into and ultimately displace currently used products and technologies. Toward these ends, gains have surely been made. For instance, solar and wind power have established themselves as a viable growth industry, and meeting the standards of green building codes has become an almost unquestioned element of world-class architecture and construction.[9] While conducting the research for this book, I have explored scores of fascinating technologies, many of which do seem to offer potential for a marked improvement over the environmentally destabilizing status quo.

Although few question the need for better, greener technologies, how this translates into environmental politics remains an open question. Here is where fault lines begin to emerge—between those who see in these new or newly applied technologies an alternative to prevailing models of economic organization and those who see instead the potential for a greener variant of the same economic forms.[10] While the former perspective is more likely to interpret capitalism as a fundamentally environmentally destabilizing social formation, the latter perspective is more likely to dovetail with theories of ecological modernization that maintain faith in the rise of an ecological rationality that will subsume capitalism within a broader and more humane orbit.[11] At stake, then, is an assessment of whether a ceaselessly expanding and crisis-prone global capitalist economy, along with the nation-states invested in its perpetuation, can ever adequately address an environmental crisis that is largely of its own making. That said, it would be oversimplifying matters to reduce this split to a binary of reform versus revolution. Wide-ranging approaches to environmental politics engage with the complexities and hybridities of the present crisis, offering nuanced proposals that eschew categorical rejections of the present economic order while still proposing radically transformative visions of another possible world.[12]

Prominent technology billionaires such as Jeff Bezos, Bill Gates, and Richard Branson have thrown their weight (and money) behind visions of green growth in support of entrepreneurial innovation aimed at tackling global climate problems. Even Peter Thiel, who publicly castigated cleantech at the 2011 TechCrunch Disrupt conference, has since invested in a clean nuclear energy startup called Helion Energy.[13] These efforts resonate with the market-oriented environmentalism of the Breakthrough Institute, which has been publishing white papers since 2003 that castigate environmentalists for focusing on regulatory fixes essentially meant to control existing technologies, as opposed to engaging with a politics of innovation. As Breakthrough cofounders Ted Nordhaus and Michael Shellenberger warn: "Climate change will not be solved with end-of-pipe solutions, like smokestack scrubbers and sewage treatment plants that worked for past pollution problems. Rather it will require us to rebuild the entire global energy system with technologies that we mostly don't have today in any form that could conceivably scale to meet that challenge."[14] In the Breakthrough Institute's *Ecomodernist Manifesto*, matters are left in a somewhat simplified form—you are either for or against technology. Those who are against it are reactionary and irrelevant radicals, unable to see the writing on the wall: leaving technology behind is not an option, and we must therefore put our efforts behind those engaged in developing the new technologies that we can and will need as we face the challenges presented by this new climatic epoch, what many are now calling the anthropocene.[15]

While there is truth to their indictment of an underdeveloped politics of technology and innovation in critical environmentalism, it is quite possible to reach somewhat different conclusions. The politics of technology and innovation are—as Breakthrough suggests—essential to developing a critical environmentalism. But this means developing a critical analysis of the social and political dynamics that shape innovation as a process; seeing it as a form of creative production and therefore subject to a range of institutional, social, and political pressures. In many ways the Breakthrough Institute does just this, building off of the historical sociology of Fred Block, whose work shows just how important state funding has been to US innovation throughout the 20th century.[16] Accordingly, Breakthrough advocates for active state involvement in the funding of new energy technologies, whether in its early proposals for a new Apollo project, or subsequent calls to develop a Clean Energy Development Authority.[17] Although institute fellows and affiliates readily question where funding for new technologies comes from, they seem less able to assess how the structural logic of technology funding, or investment capital, operating within broader circuits of accumulation, may itself impose a discrete, environmentally destabilizing logic upon the trajectories of technological innovation.[18] Their assessment of which technologies matter is predicated upon the unquestioned necessity and desirability of continued economic growth as well as the maintenance and even expansion of resource intensive (industrial, mass consumerist, militarized) lifestyles.

Critical sociological analyses of technology have traditionally focused on the role that technological development plays as a mediating factor between capital and labor, specifically in terms of the labor-saving and labor-disciplining aspects of industrial technologies.[19] A somewhat less-developed but growing perspective, the cultural political economy of research and innovation, analyzes the process of technological development itself, and the connections between the needs of capital and the contours of entrepreneurial innovation.[20] This perspective helps push back against any general sense that innovation is somehow directly associated with capital—what capital wants, its engineers create—and instead sees innovation as a conflict-ridden process of social and creative production, in which any attempts to control and coordinate technological advance are always incomplete.

Accordingly, in this book I offer a corrective to the Breakthrough Institute and other like-minded environmentalisms, by going beyond the refutation of environmentalism as an anti-technological foil used to justify an uncritical embrace of already-existing technological trajectories. Perhaps it is obvious, but still worth repeating: simply being for or against technology will not suffice. Instead, environmentalists must develop a politics of technology and innovation that can provide grounds for productive critiques of the specific sociotechnical systems emerging out of specific innovation agendas and the ways they are being shaped by the global economy—whether venture capital firms, philanthro-capitalist foundations, or even state-led efforts to spur innovation through the funding of a vibrant entrepreneurial ecosystem. It is with this in mind that I have chosen to focus my analysis on the innovation of new green technologies—cleantech—and the widespread investment, emotionally as well as financially, in this very specific vision of planetary improvement through technological innovation.

From Mother Earth to the Mother of All Markets

As a term, *cleantech* was first coined in the early 2000s by venture capitalists looking to brand their interest in alternative energy, distinguishing it from a slew of nearly identical failed commercial projects and appropriate technology initiatives of the 1970s. Much of the initial excitement surrounding cleantech emanated from Silicon Valley, where a dense network of entrepreneurs, funders, industry-focused research centers (Stanford University in particular), and a wide range of service providers have come to form a vibrant innovation ecosystem that has become nearly synonymous with high-tech entrepreneurialism.

It is no coincidence that Silicon Valley's turn toward cleantech occurred in the early 2000s. The 1990s represented the height of the venture capital industry, with returns rising steadily over the decade until finally spiking with the dot.com boom of 1999–2000. As this speculative bubble burst in 2001, venture capitalists found themselves sitting on hundreds of millions of dollars raised for new investment that could no longer target internet startups. Alternatives needed to be found. The September 11th attack on the World Trade Center and subsequent military intervention in Iraq put energy security into the spotlight. From 2002 to 2008, rising natural gas prices drove the price of electricity in the US up 38 %. The price of gasoline increased four-fold over that same period, and analysts were predicting that the price of oil would continue to rise—at the time, Goldman Sachs anticipated a flattening of the curve at $200 a barrel.[21] This heightened sense of energy insecurity dovetailed with environmentalist concerns regarding carbon dioxide emissions and global warming. Out of this confluence of events, interests, and fears, the scions of Silicon Valley saw energy and the environment as a new world-shaping (and profit-making) opportunity. They embraced cleantech as a third pillar of their technology space, joining biotech and infotech, which had been their primary foci for the past three decades.

As Federico Caprotti explains, over the first decade of the 21st century, cleantech as an idea spread far beyond the venture capital industry and eventually came to stand for an entirely new technology sector.[22] Cleantech serves as an umbrella category for a wide range of services and technologies that claim to have some environmental benefit over existing alternatives—hence making them relatively cleaner. The cleantech "space" (how business people refer to new markets or sectors) focuses on energy technologies—renewable energy, improved efficiency of nonrenewable energy generation, energy-use monitoring, and energy storage. That said, it is not limited to energy, and any technologies or services that increase the efficiency of material or energetic throughput of a process—whether production, consumption, or distribution, can be considered a clean technology. One report from 2005 defined cleantech as "any knowledge-based product or service that: improves operational performance, productivity or efficiency; while reducing costs, inputs, energy consumption, waste or pollution."[23] The Cleantech Group, largely responsible for popularizing the term in 2002, distinguished cleantech from earlier terms such as greentech and envirotech, which "represent the highly regulatory driven, 'end of pipe' technology of the past with limited opportunity for attractive returns."[24]

Cleantech began to take off in the early 2000s with a few key venture capital firms, such as Khosla, Kleiner Perkins, and Vantage Point, which largely defined the space through their investments. While environmental technologies were only 1% of venture capital (VC) funding in 1996, by the early 2000s they had increased to 6% of VC investment dollars, a percentage greater than semiconductors, financial services, or media.[25] The fate of Idealab, a Silicon Valley tech incubator, offers a paradigmatic example. Through the 1990s, Idealab helped launch internet companies such as eToys, NetZero, and PetSmart.com, but in 2000, it was forced to raise additional funds with a $300 million initial public offering as the dot.com boom melted away. Shortly thereafter, Idealab reemerged in the cleantech space, promoting companies such as Energy Innovations, which developed solar panels for commercial buildings. Idealab's founder Bill Gross explained this transformation: "Reinventing energy is a multitrillion-dollar opportunity. It's the next big disruption.... It dwarfs any business opportunity in history."[26]

This first wave of cleantech investing brazenly announced that a new energy economy was imminent, inevitable, and immeasurably profitable. Cleantech boosters took inspiration from Carlotta Perez's 2002 book, *Technological Revolutions and Financial Capital: The Dynamics of Bubbles and Golden Ages*, in which she identified information technology as the fifth industrial revolution. It was only fitting then, that cleantech would be the sixth.[27] Algae, wind, solar, smart grid, batteries, nano-materials—all found their places in investors' new cleantech portfolios. Venture capital was ready to pronounce cleantech as their sector, one in which they would, as with digital technologies, lead the way. The market potential was (and is) huge. Electricity was the third-largest industry in the US, with a value of $300 billion annually at the time. Furthermore, many of the distributed renewable technologies under consideration were well suited for the over two billion people in the world without reliable access to electricity. China and India were immediately pegged as potential markets of unimaginable proportions.[28] At the 2006 Cleantech Venture Network conference, Kleiner Perkins's John Doerr (who made his fortune investing in companies such as Netscape, Amazon, and Google) explained:

This is the mother of all markets.... As those Asian economies rise, people will move from rural to urban settings. All those people will want the same things that you and I want: clean water, power and transportation.[29]

Elsewhere, John Doerr argued that comparisons with the Apollo program or the Manhattan Project were not appropriate. Such comparisons "fail to capture the magnitude of what we face. This cuts across all human behavior. This is like re-industrializing the whole planet."[30]

Cleantech's boosters framed their mission as the technological heart and soul of a "smart" industrial revolution, one in which design and manufacturing processes would be reinvented with "lighter, smarter, and stronger" technologies that are "less expensive to manufacture and operate."[31] Cleantech remained a firmly economic endeavor—any possibilities of utopian technosocial advance were overshadowed by relentless market pragmatism. As the cleantech venture capitalist James LoGerfo explained, cleantech would promote technologies that are "ecologically sustainable, or at least less harmful."[32]

"At least less harmful." The phrase encapsulates the efficiency-maximizing "cleanliness" of cleantech and its promotion of any technology that is less bad than existing alternatives. Even that might be an exaggeration. If, as we will see in the chapters to follow, prior notions of environmental technologies associated with the appropriate technology movement were about producing technologies that were good enough for local and particular needs, cleantech transforms this goal into producing technologies that are good enough for the market. Ira Ehrenpreis, an early cleantech venture capitalist and cochairman of the Cleantech Venture Network's advisory board, explains: "The reason we're allocating dollars to this sector is we think we can deliver attractive returns.... It's not because we want to do great things for the environment or great things for the world," though to his credit, he does go on to admit that this would be a "great byproduct."[33]

Energy Miracles

When I began my fieldwork in 2010, cleantech still seemed to be a proud buzzword. At events that I attended businesspeople of all stripes would confidently proclaim that what they do, whether brokering, consulting, lawyering, or venture investing, was in and of the cleantech space. In hindsight, it is now clear that my research was being conducted during a period of transition. Initial venture capital excitement in cleantech had been unraveling since the 2008 financial crisis, which was around the time that the earliest venture investors were looking to find "exits" for their cleantech investments, only to find a somewhat inhospitable environment. Since its height around 2006, cleantech has been marred by over a decade of disappointing venture capital returns, along with the spectacular failures—accompanied by equally spectacular partisan vitriol—of US-government supported cleantech firms such as Solyndra and MiaSole.[34] At the same type of events, "cleantech" is now only uttered when necessary, emptied of its triumphalism and colored by a knowing sense that this project, or at least one iteration of it, may have slipped away.

The reason that cleantech innovation has been so ill suited for venture funding is the lengthy time it takes to develop energy technologies. It is a slow-moving field, on the technology side at least, relative to the pace of expected returns on capital investment. Many of the largest venture capital firms have taken a serious beating with their cleantech holdings, and have had to reevaluate their investment models—looking for longer time horizons and more patient capital. This idea, that patient capital (capital willing to forego liquidity for longer periods of time, and therefore willing to increase the risk of lower annualized rates of return) is the missing ingredient in cleantech's innovation ecosystem, has led to a renewed interest in active state involvement in supporting the commercialization and development of new technologies.[35] For instance, Bill Gates has assembled a network of billionaire investors through his Breakthrough Energy Coalition, with the promise to supply patient capital to innovative cleantech projects. At the time of this writing, Gates is currently excited about research into solar fuels being conducted at CalTech by Nate Lewis. Gates emphasizes the importance of government funding for projects like this, which hold the potential to discover "energy miracles." As he explains, "Most breakthroughs that improve our lives—from new health interventions to new clean energy ideas—get their start as government-sponsored research like Nate's. If successful, that research leads to new innovations that spawn new industries, create new jobs, and spur economic growth. It's impossible to overemphasize the importance of government support in this process. Without it, human progress would not come as far as it has."[36]

Silicon Valley certainly stokes the perception that the high-tech innovative fields they fund are constantly evolving and ever changing—operating at the speed of money—but this is only partially true. Yes, funding models change, as do policy frameworks, and there are even occasionally important new technologies and production facilities that come online. But at the same time, there is also a lot that stays the same. There may not be another algae company promising to revolutionize the fuel market anytime soon, but as we see with Gates, there are still similar hopes for clean technologies to deliver "energy miracles" that can help solve our global environmental problems.

Regardless of terminology, a broad commitment to finding technological solutions to environmental problems persists, and is in no risk of subsiding. New funding models are being explored, including crowdfunding applications for venture investment allowed by the 2012 JOBS Act, and new networks of "super-connectors" are attempting to connect promising start-ups with well-intentioned investors.[37] Total investment in clean technologies continues to grow, both in the US and globally, even as the portion of that funding devoted to earliest stage technologies has diminished. There has also been a shift away from technologies requiring large infrastructural investments and toward software- and computer-based projects, or those that focus on innovative sales and business models as opposed to new and commercially unproven technologies.[38]

In some ways, the call for various forms of patient capital can be read as an admission of the failure of venture capital as a cleantech investment model. But as we will see, many are still committed to venture investing as an ideal—where visionary investors remain the driving force behind innovation, tasking themselves with selecting the most promising firms to fund and support— and they interpret these failures as a technical matter (the investments were simply structured incorrectly). As will become clear in the pages to follow, I argue that there is a broader structural problem; that built into the logic of venture investing—whether traditional venture capital or some other form of patient capital—there is a focus on technology (narrowly defined) as the means to fix our environmental problems without actually making any substantive changes to the way sociotechnical-environmental life is organized. To return to Gates's belief in energy miracles, what excites him about Lewis's research is the possibility of preserving a piece of the status quo: "We could continue to drive the cars we have now. Instead of running on fossil fuels from the ground, they would be powered by fuel made from sunlight."[39]

And so, even as these funding models change, the sociotechnical imaginary of capital remains firmly in place—develop new technologies that can disrupt markets while leaving all of the trappings of mass consumer life in place. This logic, which I call planetary improvement, is not a passing fad. It is an extension of centuries-old discourses justifying capitalist expansion, colonialism, and development that are now focused on a new object—the planetary environment—in need of salvation.

A Green Spirit of Capitalism

At an evening cleantech event hosted by a local law firm, I watched an entrepreneur pitch a fuel-injection technology that promised to greatly increase the efficiency of diesel engines. After explaining the basics of the technology, he confessed to the audience, "we think there is potential for real disruption." Though in the end, he continues, "we want to deliver a solution without changing the world."

During my research I watched dozens of early-stage cleantech pitches whose presenters grappled with the contradiction between an investment in cleantech as an idea, and the very specific investment logics that prevailed in the cleantech space. On the one hand, the professionals I met were excited about creating and commercializing disruptive technologies that might radically transform our lives. But when it came to actually finding (and funding) commercially viable projects, disruption quickly gave way to assessments of which technologies demonstrated potential to provide incremental gains in already established markets. It seemed as though a new technology's affective force derived from the possibility that it could be truly disruptive, yet its commercial viability most often depended on the exact opposite; limiting novelty to incremental changes within existing markets. FG, a patent lawyer, explained to me:

FG: I think it's great to have disruptive technology, that's what we need to move forward and hopefully get out of these economic doldrums that we're in right now. But the way things are going to innovate, going forward you're not necessarily going to have those, those are rare, and most of the things that are successful are the things that are just slight increments on what already exists, where it's innovative enough to overcome obstacles that were not overcome with the original concept...but only making that minute improvement.

FG went on to explain that disruptive technologies are simply "ahead of their time" and society is not yet ready to accept them, hence their tenuous commercial viability.

The term *disruptive technology* is derived from the Harvard Business School professor Clayton Christensen's 1997 book *The Innovator's Dilemma*, in which he coins the term *disruptive innovation*.[40] For Christensen, this refers to a product or service that initially takes root in smaller markets with lower gross margins, but that once established, can eventually displace more established competitors by providing a more efficient or desirable means of addressing a broad need. In the cleantech space, the term was largely taken out of context, and instead used to refer more generally to technologies with the potential to radically transform, or disrupt, prevailing market patterns. Through month after month of fieldwork, as almost every cleantech project was described by one person or another as disruptive, or at the very least potentially disruptive, it became clear that these disruptions could mean almost anything, from seizing market share in a well-established market to radically transforming how urban transportation systems function.

In other words, who or what is disrupted was left relatively unspecified, allowing the concept to shift, as I explain in the next chapter, between distinct and often ill-defined conceptions of "making an impact."

Regardless of its presumed referent, the concept of disruption betrays a techno-fetishistic belief that the right new technologies can both radically transform industrial society while simultaneously capturing a massive share of existing markets—those very markets that depend upon the maintenance of the industrial society being disrupted in the first place. There is a certain pragmatic resignation to the current state of the market, which largely determines what is actually (financially and commercially) viable, as opposed to the far broader sense of what is potentially feasible in technological and social terms.

For critical environmentalists, this description of cleantech—as an opportunistic, profit-focused engagement with new technologies—would sufficiently indict this project and accuse those promoting it of being opportunistic parasites, or peddlers of false consciousness, who see in climate change a new source of profits and little else.[41] Environmental social theorists have made powerful arguments about the irreconcilability of a capitalist economy predicated on constant growth as well as ever-intensifying forms of extraction and wastage with the possibility of achieving ecological sustainability at a global scale. Some regard the suggestion that ecological disruptions can be slowed down while maintaining necessary economic growth as an impossibility.[42] Others dismiss green capitalism, in toto, as little more than an extension of capital's underlying tendencies.[43] Or, more cynically, others see it as an ideological facade allowing business as usual to proceed apace.[44] Hence the marketization of carbon emissions, the shift toward clean technologies, and the interest in large-scale organic food production, to take a few key examples, all become subsumed under a relentless drive for growth. This "treadmill of production" pervades the global capitalist economy, making green capitalism, as a project, either a technological fetishization imbued with naïve optimism, or the calculated emergence of new markets and the "greenwashing" of old ones.[45]

For instance, one presenter at the NY Cleantech Funders Forum, a chemical engineer, presented a new technology for producing biodegradable plastics (specifically disposable utensils), which promises to be far more efficient and cost-effective than existing alternatives. Of course, without any viable infrastructure to actually compost these goods after their initial, one-time use, they promise to have little effect upon the scale and persistence of the waste stream that is being targeted. Another inventor I met, who also happened to be a chemical engineer, told me about a technology he was developing that would capture flare gas and convert it into electricity; his anticipated target market would be offshore oil rigs, which regularly waste their flare gas and could instead use this energy to provide electricity to their platform. The irony of a "clean" offshore oil rig seemed completely lost on him.

It is hard to deny the allure of technophilic visions of green modernity and of a geo-engineered, technologically saturated planet that allows for the indefinite expansion of industrial excesses, or at least for us to keep open the possibility that smartphones, server farms, and the other innovations that have become necessities of modern life might not be irreconcilable with a sustainable global economy. Instead of simplistically castigating green capitalism as an ideological subterfuge or dismissing those who believe in such a project as peddlers of false consciousness, in what follows I explain how the cleantech project and those invested in it (again, emotionally as well as financially) are developing a logically coherent, emotionally charged (and often self-justifying) legitimizing discourse, the basis for what we can call a new green spirit of capitalism. This new green spirit mobilizes a seemingly radical, anti-systemic critique of capitalism, which provides moral legitimacy and affective force for proposals to irrevocably transform capitalism into a more environmentally virtuous economy; still capitalism, just a better, greener version.

Boltanski and Chiapello's *The New Spirit of Capitalism* (2007) explores how capitalism has, throughout its brief history, been accompanied by a set of non-capitalist values that motivate the bearers of wealth and set limits on the appropriate bounds of accumulation. They reenergize Max Weber's classic analysis of the Protestant work ethic, examining the ways people justify why their actions are "good, right, and plausible." People do this not only for themselves (this was Weber's focus: how individuals justify their individual actions with recourse to an individual relationship with God) but also for their sense of social value.[46] Despite the bald necessities (whether culturally constructed or not) of wanting to provide for oneself accordingly to existing social standards, there is beyond this a dual sense that one still needs to feel good about what it is that one does, and that what one does furthers the common good—whether by relishing the money-making pursuit, or by accepting on some level the social responsibility and mission of a firm, or by plugging into some general sense that capitalism actually does benefit society at large.

In a departure from Weber's assessment of the Protestant ethic as "the" spirit of capitalism, Boltanski and Chiapello argue that capitalism's spirit does not stay static, but constantly adjusts to cultural and economic conditions.[47] They explain these adjustments through a dialectic tension between capital and its critique. At any given moment during capitalism's development, specific critiques inevitably emerge, some of which are so powerful or convincing that they threaten to delegitimize and destabilize the system. It is at these moments of conflict between capital and its critique where a new spirit of capital forms, absorbing key dimensions of this critique and molding them into a new legitimizing discourse.

The New Spirit of Capitalism demonstrates how much of the anti-authoritarian cultural tropes of the late 1960s and early 1970s came to be repurposed in management texts of the following decades, no longer presenting an alternative to capital, but now an alternative capitalism—one better able to meet the challenges of a changing economy. In their telling, entrepreneurial culture represents a recuperation of the radical, countercultural critique of capitalism into a new spirit that embraced the entrepreneur as a symbol of individuality, freedom, fluidity, and flexibility. This entrepreneur is a self-made, self-directed, and creative individual, making a new world day in and day out, and bringing the revolutionary spirit to bear on the extraordinary potential of capital's growth imperative.[48]

The rise of modern environmentalism largely coincides with these same countercultural movements of the late 1960s and early 1970s discussed by Boltanski and Chiapello. This is not to reduce the one to the other, but to acknowledge that by the 1970s—and especially in the shadow of the oil embargo and related energy crisis—there was a strong anti-industrial, anti-capital environmental critique circulating, and this critique was largely recuperated into a new expression of what became business environmentalism—no longer concerned with saving the planet from capitalism, but instead committed to saving the planet with capitalism.[49]

Throughout the 1990s and into the 2000s, proponents of green capitalism in one form or another prefaced their aspirational works with a critique of capitalism as an inherently anti-ecological system, only to then fall back upon impassioned calls for an enlightened, ecological capitalism that could leave behind these toxic legacies and be reborn as a new, "clean and green" economy. For instance, Paul Hawken, Amory B. Lovins, and L. Hunter Lovins open their foundational text, *Natural Capitalism*, with a categorical denunciation: "Capitalism, as practiced, is a financially profitable, non-sustainable aberration in human development."[50] They continue to offer a utopian vision of a world entirely transformed, socially just and environmentally sound. The book promises to explain the simple steps necessary to bring forth this natural capitalism, which will no longer be a "non-sustainable aberration" but instead, an environmentally and socially progressive panacea.

I cannot claim in these pages to offer a comprehensive assessment of this new green spirit of capitalism, but I do hope to explore one centrally important dimension of it: the ways in which the innovation of "clean" technologies requires that one's aspirational ideals of a large-scale ecosocial transformation, such as the one presented in a text like *Natural Capitalism*, be insulated from the profit-maximizing market imperatives and necessity of perpetual growth that are endemic to capitalism, whether "green,", "natural" or otherwise constituted. As I will suggest in chapter 5, there is a way in which the climate change denial espoused by conservatives is met, by advocates of cleantech specifically and green capitalism or ecological modernization more broadly, with a liberal form of denial that might best be described as "green capital denial." In Naomi Klein's 2015 book *This Changes Everything* she argues that while climate deniers dismiss scientific consensus, they actually do understand the magnitude of social and political implications that addressing climate change adequately would entail—were they to concede that it was a problem worth addressing. In many ways green capital denial is about an equally important and far less acknowledged opposing phenomenon; a liberal acceptance of climate science matched with a refusal to accept the social and political implications of any adequate response.[51]

Planetary Improvement

These contradictions lie at the heart of a new way to ground this emerging green spirit of capitalism, which I am calling *planetary improvement*. I chose the term rather intentionally, so as to make connections with a much earlier history of agricultural improvement that first ushered capitalism into world history.[52] From the 16th century on, thinkers such as Thomas Petty and John Locke attempted to demonstrate that modern European farmers, engaged in practices of improved agriculture, were able to extract far more value out of a given parcel of land than the natives of unimproved lands, such as Ireland (for Petty) or the New World (for Locke).[53] They argued that it was morally and economically imperative to free up these lands (through acts of enclosure and/or colonial dispossession), thereby "increase[ing] the common stock of mankind" by making "wasted" land available for others to deploy in a more efficient manner.[54]

Those who did not yet embrace the new standards of improvement, such as commoners in England and most of the indigenous peoples of colonized lands, were castigated as slothful, lazy, and insubordinate in their failing to fulfill a God-given directive to be (maximally) fruitful. Enclosures and colonial dispossessions were justified accordingly—in the name of an abstract sense of maximum efficiency in producing goods for the market.[55]

Much of the revolutionary fervor associated with agricultural improvement had to do with the process of enclosure, by which non-capitalist spaces (including common lands and land not under cultivation) were brought into the orbit of the capitalist economy. Through acts of enclosure, any preexisting forms of land tenure, such as by common right, were effectively eliminated by law, separating the land (as private property, or real estate) from those who had previously had a more complex and interdependent relationship with their grounds of production and reproduction.[56]

Through enclosure, common lands were, on the one hand, closed off from local and particular uses—hence the symbolic and political power of fences and hedges that marked this transformed landscape.[57] And on the other hand, newly enclosed lands were opened up to increasingly global markets and flows of capital, which exerted its influence on those few left in possession of this parcelled land, and by extension those able (or coerced) to remain as laborers, working for wages as their sole means of survival.[58] Commoners were not simply being evicted from their land, they were also being given admittance to a "community of money" within which they could compete for their survival.[59]

Agricultural improvement was the legitimizing face of this otherwise ruthless and violent process of dispossession. At the crux of this process, an ontological transformation was taking place, a "production of nature" in which a landscape of fragmented and diverse potentials was being newly apprehended as a singular, *whole* world. This unified territory of potential improvement existed alongside a newly emergent sense that this whole world was populated by an endless supply of disposable wage laborers. Through this uniquely capitalist gaze, a decidedly not-capitalist world was reenvisioned and newly produced as a world that was not-yet capitalist.[60]

We can use this history of enclosure and agricultural improvement to make sense of cleantech entrepreneurialism and the new green spirit of capitalism. Debates about waste and efficiency are not limited to this early form of agricultural improvement, but have persisted throughout the development of capitalism, taking on numerous forms. Labor and industrial relations is perhaps the most obvious place where a war against wasted time has been waged—from Ben Franklin's famous adage that time is money to Frederick Taylor's scientific management of industrial work flows.[61] The 19th and 20th centuries saw a wide range of public health crises met by municipal improvement efforts aimed at eradicating urban wastes, from disease vectors and filth to homelessness and crime.[62] One could interpret the early 20th-century transformations underpinning mass consumerism as an attempt to minimize wasted sales opportunities through the creative use of marketing, disposability, and planned obsolescence to decrease turnover times.[63] Justification for the shareholder revolution of the 1980s was largely framed as a confrontation with managers who were wasting short-term profit-maximizing opportunities in their stubborn commitment to nonfinancial matters (such as production and provision of actual goods and services).[64]

Likewise, at the core of this new discourse of planetary improvement is an embrace of technological and organizational changes meant to maximize efficiency and minimize waste. Agricultural improvement targeted "inefficient" forms of agricultural production—such as those practiced by commoners and the wide range of indigenous agricultural practices throughout the colonized world. Planetary improvement instead targets "dirty" or "wasteful" forms of industrial production, aspects of the industrial economy that are not-yet green.

The parallels between agricultural and planetary improvement are striking. In 1793, the British Board of Agriculture's first director, Sir John Sinclair, wrote of improvement as a national imperative:

We have begun another campaign against the foreign enemies of the country, ... Why should we not attempt a campaign against our great domestic foe? ... Let us not be satisfied with the liberation of Egypt, or the subjugation of Malta, but let us subdue Finchley Common; let us conquer Hounslow Heath, let us compel Epping Forest to submit to the yoke of improvement.[65]

In 2008, Fredd Krupp and Miriam Horn wrote of planetary improvement in an almost identical register:

To save the planet from calamity, innovation and deployment of known technologies must occur now at a pace as intense and a scope as vast as the settlement of the western frontier.[66]

Planetary improvement's injunction to "save the planet" is fundamentally an extension of this longstanding colonial imperative to develop upon and profit from a productive landscape considered misused and abused. The implied expectations for what an improved—or in this case greened and cleaned—landscape is to look like emerge from the unquestionable modernizing imperative of the improvers themselves, who take it for granted that their way of living in and upon the world is not only good and right, but even more so, that it is precisely this way of life, *this* planet for *these* people, which needs to be saved, sustained, and expanded in the first place. It is in this sense that planetary improvers apprehend a whole world that is not-yet green; an industrial landscape of waste and excess that is available to be made more efficient, to proliferate in cleaner and greener ways, without ever having to be fundamentally transformed. Or, as the solar power developer Jim Rogers tells Thomas Friedman, "I look out on the rooftops of my customers and I see future power plant sites."[67]

The energy- and material-intensive production processes and consumer-driven lifestyles that have come to define 20th-century capitalism serve as a terrain of potential improvement. Their excesses, inefficiencies, toxicities, and wastes are cast, as with the wastelands targeted by Sinclair and the early agricultural improvers, as opportunities to go green. Interestingly then, inefficient commoners or inefficient laborers are not the one's being accused of wasting society's collective potential; now capitalism itself is guilty of being wasteful. As Peter Barnes, in his text proposing a variant of green capitalism, writes: "Capitalism as we know it is devouring creation."[68] Instead of targeting an external realm that is not yet integrated into the capitalist economy, planetary improvers look to improve an already capitalist economy that is simply not-yet green.

As we will continue to explore in the chapters to follow, this creates a complex set of contradictions underlying this new green spirit of capitalism.

Whereas Max Weber presented the Protestant ethic as a spirit of capitalism in which hard work became a means to save one's soul, planetary improvement, or this new green spirit of capitalism, calls for innovation (and the hard work of entrepreneurship) to be the means through which we collectively save the planet.[69] Expressed as a commitment to planetary improvement, this new green spirit of capitalism simultaneously calls for perpetuating the sociotechnical (and environmental) conditions that have undergirded past centuries of wealth accumulation, while at the same time hoping to forge new value relations that might ground a more ecologically stable regime of accumulation. Planetary improvers must therefore embrace a critique of capitalism (which has created this industrial world in need of improvement) while simultaneously bracketing and disarming this critique, so as to allow for the realization of commercial "solutions" to proceed unencumbered.

Though in the chapters to follow I focus specifically on cleantech entrepreneurialism, the compounding effects and implications of this new green spirit of capitalism ripple far beyond this one field. With the green moniker becoming an almost de rigueur addition to any new product or service circulating in the developed world, a deeper understanding of the contradictory tension between *green* as a cultural construct and *green* as a contested product of entrepreneurial practices is an essential aspect of understanding capitalism in the 21st century. This is not to suggest that planetary improvement and this new spirit of capitalism can provide an exhaustive or universally applicable assessment of green economies and their related environmental politics, but only that planetary improvement represents a very recognizable and repeatable pattern, expressed and reproduced to varying degrees in a diverse range of business-friendly environmental perspectives and projects.

2   Making an Impact: Entrepreneurial Approaches to Environmentalism

When DG first attended the Funders Forum in 2009, he was working for a cleantech startup that was attempting to create an algae-based fuel. The company's initial research had been promising, garnering interest from venture investors and a fair amount of publicity. But things did not work out as hoped. The technology was not scaling rapidly, the inventor did not see eye to eye with his investors, and eventually the project was abandoned. At the time, DG's job had been to develop investment leads in the Northeast, which is what initially brought him to the Funders Forum. When I met him, however, he was at the Funders Forum as a strategic consultant, looking for new opportunities in cleantech while he supported his family with a house-painting business. I asked DG to reflect on his time with the algae company and explain his reasons for leaving his more stable job (working for a large corporation) to pursue this cleantech startup.

DG: The thing with biofuels, the thing with algae, is people want to believe...that there is a panacea out there that will allow us to live the way we live and drive the way we drive and fly the way we fly and be great and have no global warming or take us off of foreign oil. And algae, you know, has the potential to do that. Obviously that's what attracted me to the algae industry, and as well, obviously, was money.... I said I'd rather be in a cleantech company that fails then sit in a back office function in a mailing company and watch the mailing industry slowly die a long death.

Cleantech was more than just another business opportunity for DG. It was a chance to make a meaningful impact, not just by making a lot of money, but because, as he said, "you think you can change the world." He explained further: "You know, you're not agnostic about it. It's not like I'm in the cup business and its cyclical and so you get out of cups and get into paperclips. It's not like that; people want this stuff to work."

During my time at the Funders Forum, startup entrepreneurs, consultants and investors all proudly explained that they were in the cleantech space because they wanted to make an impact, yet it was much harder for them to articulate what exactly this impact would (or could) be. Cleantech was "good for the country," "a noble place," or simply "crucial." But how, why, and in what ways? In this chapter I show how the green spirit of capitalism is often expressed through an unyielding commitment to making an "impact," without clearly distinguishing between two often contradictory senses of the term. Making an *impact-beyond-capital* is about changing the world, whereas making an *impact-as-capital* is about making a lot of money in the process; each has its place. Cleantech entrepreneurialism is not "just making money" like Wall Street bankers, or "just crying for nature" like pesky hippies and environmentalists. Between these two extremes, there are targeted opportunities to wage a war against waste, leaving behind "boring" industries embedded within a 20th-century economy of material and energetic excess by developing large-scale solutions that introduce, promote, and deploy clean technologies.

Cleantech's impact-beyond-capital speaks to an embrace of entrepreneurship as a creative, world-making practice (invoking here the work of the economist and political scientist Joseph Schumpeter), in which the accumulation of money is often seen as a measure of success, more so than as an end unto itself. If Max Weber described a spirit of capitalism in which people accumulated wealth so as to prove their worth in the face of God, in the cleantech space people instead seek to make money, or an impact-as-capital, so as to prove that they are helping to solve environmental problems, doing their part to clean a not-yet-green world.

Two Approaches to Entrepreneurship

To understand the distinction between making an impact-beyond-capital and an impact-as-capital we must first differentiate Schumpeter's account of entrepreneurship, along with its central role in capitalism's dynamic of creative destruction, from the neoclassical conception of the entrepreneur as a profit-maximizing risk taker.

The neoclassical conception of entrepreneurship focuses on profit-maximization through market arbitrage, and considers the entrepreneur to be a heroic example of economic man, or *homo economicus*, the rational economic actor who populates their theoretical universe.[1] According to this perspective, the entrepreneur is simply an individual who exhibits a rational, opportunistic, and acquisitive response to disequilibrium. As a result, market arbitrage, or the practice of finding a need that the market has not yet optimally met (or priced), becomes the central, risk-taking orientation of the neoclassical entrepreneur, who is, as the economist Israel Kirzner explained, simply an individual alert to profit-making opportunities.[2]

This neoclassical vision runs up against an alternative Schumpeterian vision of the entrepreneur as first and foremost a creator and disruptor.[3] Schumpeter critiqued neoclassical economic theory, specifically figures such as Léon Walras and Alfred Marshall, for understanding the economy as a system that tended toward equilibrium.[4] Their "marginalist revolution" held that all economic decisions could be understood as the product of rational decision makers, calculating the marginal utility of all available alternatives so as to always arrive at an optimal allocation of capital.[5] The entrepreneur's exploitation of existing disequilibria was a prime agent of this equilibrating tendency and the entrepreneur was therefore an exemplary specimen of *homo economicus*, the only actor necessary to explain the functioning of the capitalist economy and its price-setting markets.

Schumpeter fundamentally disagreed with this neoclassical approach, arguing that it failed to account for the possibility that the entrepreneur was in fact a market disruptor, responsible for pushing the economy out of equilibrium, and in so doing, initiating the process of creative destruction that was fundamental to the dynamism of the capitalist system.[6] Whereas the neoclassical economists simply understood entrepreneurship as an extension of economic rationality, for Schumpeter entrepreneurship was defined in distinction to this narrow logic, which meant that it had to be motivated by a different set of principles altogether.[7]

Schumpeter proposed a set of three primary motivations that factor into entrepreneurial activity. First is "the dream and the will to found a private kingdom." This refers to the accumulation of private property, social wealth, and the power that accompanies its possession.[8] Second is "the will to conquer." This entails a motivation to distinguish oneself, to prove one's superiority or social worth. As Schumpeter explains, the entrepreneur aims "to succeed for the sake, not of the fruits of success, but of success itself." Here, Schumpeter suggests that there is a nonfinancial motivation underlying the process of entrepreneurialism. As he elaborates: "The financial result is a secondary consideration, or, at all events, mainly valued as an index of success and as a symptom of victory." He then goes a step further with his third and final motivation, "the joy of creating, of getting things done, or simply of exercising one's energy and ingenuity." With this, Schumpeter suggests that entrepreneurship can be first and foremost an act of creative labor, more about making something, or solving a problem, than about making money.[9] Importantly then, to the extent that these last two motivations prevail, the entrepreneur exists in direct contrast to the neoclassical conception of a rational, profit-maximizing, economic agent.

This Schumpeterian description of entrepreneurship, as the motive force of capital's creative destruction, presents the entrepreneur as an innovative hero, unfettered from the narrow rationality of *homo economicus*. As such, entrepreneurship can provide, as Luc Boltanski and Eve Chiapello discuss, an affective force—a spirit—justifying excitement for the creative possibilities of market activities, insofar as they can lead to innovations that exceed or disrupt the present state of affairs.[10] Accordingly, entrepreneurship can be seen as a noble, socially meaningful engagement—a means by which one can effect change in society, or as we will now explore, a way for someone to "make an impact."

Impact

Let's examine this word *impact*. It is an abstract and thoroughly aspirational concept. From increasing energy efficiency and repurposing waste products to reducing emissions and ultimately "saving the planet," all of the hopes, beliefs, and assumptions that weave these diverse imaginaries together coalesce into this single concept: *impact*. It can be a noun, an adverb, and an adjective: impact, impactful, impacting. It can signify a direction, an intention, a promise. All of the people I spoke with in the cleantech space, from a socialist inventor to a climate change–denying angel investor, want to help build a world that won't just run itself into the ground, a world that will be around for their kids and their kids' kids. They all want to make an impact; most of them will tell you so explicitly. This one simple term revealed an emotional, affective, and aspirational force underlying their commitment to cleantech entrepreneurialism. It embodied the something-more-than-money that makes the pursuit of money worthwhile. It allowed individuals without much personally at stake (financially at least) to believe in the processes of capital accumulation, and in the collective socioecological good of their work.

In this sense, impact encapsulates the spirit of this field, a supplemental ethical and moral commitment that helps justify engagement with the cleantech project. Here I use the word *project* in a double sense. On the one hand it relates to Boltanski and Chiapello's diagnosis of a "projectionist city" in which work is fragmented into discrete projects that entrepreneurial subjects flow between.[11] Individual cleantech projects certainly operate in this way, with entrepreneurs, investors, and service providers all moving between and balancing any number of projects. But in another sense, taken all together, cleantech represents a general project, one perhaps more akin to the structure of missionary sentiment than entrepreneurial culture, in which all of these discrete gigs add up to a general and collective effort to promote cleantech—and in doing so, to orient or project out toward some form of collective, planetary salvation. In this latter sense, *impact* gestures toward a commitment to more than individual, self-interested goals or personal aspirations of innovative or financial success. It represents a general and generalizable, social and universally applicable desire to make a difference, to transform the economy, to "save the planet" with successful (therefore profitable) entrepreneurial enterprise.[12]

As collective and inclusive as this project may appear, there is of course a darker side to universalizing gestures such as this, insofar as they tacitly accept and reproduce the normalization of social and political exclusions. In other words, specific interests can easily come to stand in for general interests, leaving unspoken who or what the planet is being saved for. As the threats of climate change mount, *our* so-called collective well-being and collective survival appear at face value to be incontrovertible and seemingly inclusive goals. And yet, without interrogating the specifics of who is and is not considered part of this collective subject, universal ideals such as saving the planet can not only serve to normalize the exclusions and inequalities of the present, but can as well shape the way environmental problems are framed in the first place. Keep this in mind whenever you see this phrase emerge in the pages to follow. What exactly is the planet being saved from?[13]

To return specifically to the concept of *impact*, I found that it was hard for individuals to describe what this idea meant to them without recourse to tautology. For instance, one makes an impact by being impactful. In this regard, *impact* functioned similarly to terms such as *sustainability* or more recently *resilience*, which conjure a generally positive sense that good is being done, while leaving undefined what exactly will be sustained, or who exactly will exhibit resilience and adapt to new conditions.[14]

Since 2007, "impact investing" has become a buzzword of the socially and environmentally conscious investment community, and here too the exact definition of impact remains elusive. Wikipedia offers this definition: "Impact investments are investments made into companies, organizations, and funds with the intention to generate measurable social and environmental impact alongside a financial return."[15] There are impact-investing networks, such as Investors Circle and Toniic, the latter offering testimonials on its website. As Maximilian Martin, a social entrepreneur and financial strategist, explains, "To improve the state of the world in ways that matter, we need to make impact the common denominator of our investment and real economy activities."[16]

But what is impact? Measurement is meant to bring clarity to the term. Typically the "impact" of impact investing entails some quantifiable increase in social or environmental metrics, or at least the promise thereof. The Global Impact Investing Ratings System (GIIRS) was one proprietary tool developed to meet this need. Its promoters explain, "The impact investing industry is facilitating investments that are not only socially responsible, but which also actively create positive social and environmental impact."[17] Their ratings measure performance in categories such as governance, workers, community, and environment, essentially measuring how well the company treats all of its stakeholders, human and nonhuman alike.

GIIRS rates companies according to the social and environmental implications of their internal operations, but I found that cleantech entrepreneurs use the word *impact* mainly to refer to the social and environmental implications of external effects. A cleantech project is impactful if it transforms their customers' operations, or those of society more broadly. As a number of entrepreneurs (very self-consciously) explained to me, this often entails environmentally unfriendly internal practices, such as flying executives and salespeople across the globe and engaging foreign manufacturers with unclear environmental standards. Their hope is that eventual success, at a meaningful enough scale, will more than make up for the unfortunate climatic footprint endemic to their process of doing business.

It was easier for people to provide me with examples of their non-impactful past, or with examples of non-impactful paths not chosen, than it was for them to explicitly name the impact of their present work in the cleantech space. I have organized the following discussion around four distinctly non-impactful foils that help establish just what this elusive concept means: boring industries, small businesses, hippies and environmentalists, and Wall Street. I review each in turn, but to summarize: Boring industries represent participation in the status quo of business-as-usual, a not-clean, waste-making economy. Small businesses represent too inconsequential a scale of operation, a wasted opportunity to address planetary scale problems. Hippies represent the irrational excesses of too much environmentalism and are too detached from practical business sense. And Wall Street represents too narrow a focus on money making that is blind to nonfinancial considerations.

Taken altogether, these four foils allow us to trace the green spirit of capitalism, through a recuperation and reformulation of well-established critiques of the waste-making, industrial economy—removed from any lingering anti-systemic or even anti-capitalist orientations (as well as any interest in "appropriate technologies")—and then reasserted as part of a creative, Schumpeterian entrepreneurialism focused upon clean technologies suitable for deployment at the planetary scale. And here, considering the above critique of universal aspirations such as "saving the planet," *planetary* should be read not only in terms of scale, but also as a very specific way of envisioning the reproducibility of industrial (and commercially profitable) technologies as the only conceivable way to "scale up" to meet global problems such as climate change.[18]

Aluminum Foil and Video Games Are Boring

In 1934 Lewis Mumford published *Technics and Civilization*, a critical study looking not only at the development of machinery but also at the moral, political, and economic choices we have historically made regarding its use. Critiquing the way that modern capitalism structures work around the reproduction and expansion of an alienating and wasteful industrial order, he concludes, "there is no form of cruelty for a rational human being worse than making him produce goods that have no human value."[19] In speaking with people about the impact that they desired to have through their work, I found an implicit acceptance of Mumford's assessment. As we will see, this would often emerge through the many ways people explained their entrance into cleantech, and out of industries that they found to be far less meaningful.

During my fieldwork I visited a number of local entrepreneurial incubators. These places offer shared workspace for early-stage startup entrepreneurs. Some of them felt like a communal lab, with prototypes in various stages of production, while others were dominated by cubicles or open-concept computer workstations, conference rooms, whiteboards, and what have become some of the regular trimmings of creative office space (candy, couches, quirky games and distractions, and young people staring at their laptop screens with headphones on to compensate for the lack of walls). Companies selected to join an incubator typically get access to cheap or free cubicle space, conference rooms and other business amenities, and perhaps most importantly, a range of professional services, invitations to events, introductions to investors, and other networking opportunities for early-stage entrepreneurs.

I went to one of the New York City incubators to check in on a company that had recently presented at the Funder's Forum, and to interview the incubator's director, TW. After a brief wait in the reception area, TW took me to a central seating area surrounded by pods of cubicles where incubating startups were housed. Each could be identified by a large vinyl banner, laminated placard, or other such display intended for trade fairs or public tabling events, which protruded out of its space and served as de facto office decor. For my benefit, TW pointed out the cleantech companies scattered among the lot.

Prior to being interested in cleantech, TW was in the video game industry, which he described as "part of the waste economy." Making video game apps, he reflected, was essentially participating in a market for time-wasting software. Taking off from that point in our interview he explained his move into cleantech:

TW: I wanted to do something meaningful, where I could really make a dent.
JG: What does that mean to you?
TW: I'm not sure. Where I was at, I mean, basically before, I was helping people waste time. And I wanted to ultimately leave the world a better place than I found it and do something that had more impact—so that was job creation and it was making the place I grew up in and love and live in now a more livable place for my kid and our kids' kids.

TW distinguished his current work and the impact that he could make by supporting cleantech startups from the "waste economy" of mindless entertainment. Unlike video games, cleantech was not a waste of time. It was a chance to make the world a better place.

After meeting with TW, and checking in on the Funders Forum presenters, I spoke with some of the other cleantech entrepreneurs at the incubator. CN was a member of the incubator working on a cleantech project, but he only worked there part-time. The incubator could not offer enough space for his whole team, so he situated them at an office nearby. He maintained his membership, paid his cubicle rent, and tried to work there at least one day a week, to keep a connection to the space and all of its networking opportunities. At the time, CN was 24 years old, a recent graduate of a prestigious business school where he met his business partner, an engineering student at the same institution. While in school, he told me as our conversation began, he and his partner knew they wanted to create a large company together, though they had not yet figured out that it would be in cleantech.

CN: I am a serial entrepreneur—my dream was to do or to create something that hasn't been done or created before that would have a very positive impact globally.

JG: What does it mean to make a positive impact?

CN: It can be energy reduction. Less carbon emissions, less coal power plants.

JG: But at the time you weren't committed to cleantech, so what was positive impact then?

CN: It is an interesting contrast. At the time I was consulting for Reynolds Wrap. I was literally talking to CEOs and COOs about aluminum foil gauge, and you know I was giving great advice, I understood the market very well. But I said *what the hell am I doing?* Then this opportunity to save energy in buildings by 20% to 40% came along. I said, *this makes sense—I can have fun and develop great technology but I can also have an impact.*

In business school CN knew that he wanted to make an impact, before he was even sure what that meant. In the professional world, he discovered that doing so would require entering an industry that he believed in. For CN, being an entrepreneur was not enough; making or working for a profitable business was not enough. In order to feel impactful, CN wanted to be part of a larger project, in his case this became a collective effort to create the clean economy.

The impactfulness of cleantech entrepreneurialism is about changing the world—how, and in what ways is not always clear, though there is a clear sense of what sorts of industries and endeavors will *not* change the world. Better paper clips, mailing services, video games, aluminum foil: producing the basic commodities that allow for the perpetuation of mass consumer society and the production of waste, disposability, and distraction are decidedly not impactful pursuits. JR, a cleantech professional in his late 20s, explained his shift from real estate to cleantech.

JR: I just decided that I did not want to be in an industry that I didn't give a shit about. . . . It just wasn't a good atmosphere for me. I just didn't feel like they were adding much value to society—I mean obviously they are, they are enhancing wealth, but for who? The wealthiest of the wealthy?

SC, who is a broker as well as a hedge fund manager, translator, and researcher, explained how he left a job in finance, where he was employed to sell boring companies.

SC: My heart was not in it. I was so bored I couldn't give a damn. This wasn't changing the world.

Dissatisfaction and even disgust with the so-called boring status quo of mass consumer society provides a foundational pillar of the green spirit of capitalism: a world of waste denounced as an outmoded and unsustainable variant of capitalist modernity. These sentiments are reminiscent of Thorstein Veblen's critique of conspicuous consumption and the pecuniary interests that allowed "wastemanship" to overtake "workmanship" in modern capitalist society.[20] Veblen was writing during the first decades of the 20th century, when industrial mass production was beginning to make the conveniences of life available to ordinary people on an unprecedented scale. Over the ensuing decades, major sociotechnical developments, including those associated with World Wars I and II, the green revolution in agriculture, the rise of the automobile, and a suburbanized landscape of consumption and disposability irrevocably transformed the world.[21] This era initiated what the sociologists Allan Schnaiberg and Kenneth Gould call the "treadmill of production" and what others have described as the "great acceleration."[22] It was during this period that the American way of life was irrevocably "fossilized," making it synonymous with technologies from cars and airplanes to refrigerators and televisions, all of which depended upon an ever-increasing stream of energy, plastics, and extraction.[23]

This golden age of capital and consumption was a golden age of waste and pollution. At the time, Vance Packard's *The Waste Makers* gave popular voice to what was becoming an increasingly obvious inefficiency built into the economy: economic efficiency had become untethered from material and energetic efficiencies; disposability and waste were good for business.[24] Packard focused on the cultural, social, and psychological adulterations that planned obsolescence and excessive disposability had on an otherwise productive US society, arguing that contrary to corporate beliefs and growing profit margins, natural resources were being unnecessarily squandered.

In many ways the spirit of green capitalism is built upon a reprisal of Packard's (and by extension, Veblen's) indictment of the waste-making economy. Whether discussing products such as paper clips, mailing services, aluminum foil, or video games, during my research I found a widespread dissatisfaction with the everyday trappings of mass consumer life. Woody Tasch, author of the green capitalist text *Slow Money*, offers an expanded litany of these material and cultural wastes, which for him include "the building of nuclear weapons, the waging of wars in distant lands, the selling of cigarettes, the flying of trillions of air miles, the commodification of leisure, urban and suburban sprawl, gated communities and favelas, toxins in the food and water, and kids who watch an average of four hours per day of TV, paying more attention to it and to instant messaging than to people in the room."[25]

There is an irony to these sentiments: producing the basic commodities of mass consumer life and perpetuating the industrial system of waste and disposal (here, not in those "distant lands") is deemed boring, neither impactful nor socially valuable; yet producing greener varieties of these same products, or renewable energy technologies that will ultimately serve to power this same lifestyle—cleantech in its various instantiations—somehow represents a positive, impactful change.

If we think of technology in terms of multiple and often contradictory potentialities, we can begin to understand a complicated relationship with waste and efficiency that lies at the heart of cleantech and this new green spirit of capitalism. On the one hand waste and the industries producing it are reviled and rebuked, and yet on the other hand these same industries, the products they sell, and the lifestyles they support represent a vast sea of opportunities to green or clean production. To return to the discussion of improvement in chapter 1: just as agricultural improvers saw a world that was not-yet, but potentially subjected to modern agricultural practices (and regimes of wage labor), planetary improvers see a world of boring industries that are potentially, but not-yet, green.

Perhaps the most well-cited example of this appears in the work of Ray Anderson (1934–2011), whose modular industrial carpeting company, Interface, represented one of the most commercially successful, deeply environmentally conscious success stories of the green capitalist era.[26] Anderson claims to have found his inspiration in Paul Hawken's 1993 book *The Ecology of Commerce*. After reading this text, he subsequently redesigned the production and distribution of Interface's commercial carpeting, eliminating toxic and energy-intensive materials and production processes, and most importantly switching to a modular installation process, which meant wear and tear could be replaced as needed at a micro scale, avoiding wasteful replacement of entire floors. Anderson's modular carpets have been canonized as the pinnacle of industrial ecology and the greening of manufacture, and a wide variety of cleantech firms have followed suit, each in their own way, by promising to radically transform the provision of basic consumer and/or industrial goods and services.

Similarly, a number of the startups presenting at the Funders Forum offered technological solutions that promised to clean otherwise boring industries. One company was developing a packaging material made out of mushrooms. Another produced a clean fuel that can substitute for most industrial uses of acetylene in metal cutting. Another chemist-inventor presented a novel approach to producing low-cost, biodegradable disposable utensils. From technologies that repurpose used grease (such as the Vegawatt) to new forms of anaerobic digestion that promise to turn everyday trash into energy without incineration, finding ways to reduce or reuse waste streams is a major focus of clean technologies. Though boring industries may not be impactful, clean technologies largely rely upon their persistence.

Go Big or Go Home

When I first met CN, friends and family were the primary funders of his company; one family member in particular had put up $500,000. Recently however, the company attracted its first angel (an angel is a private investor who operates individually, or sometimes as part of an investment network, and is willing to make relatively small seed investments in a start-up). This well-known Boston-based investor put up $50,000 for CN's company, only a tenth the size of their familial patron's. But the angel's investment is what excited CN. This was the company's first installment of "smart money," and therefore its first true market legitimization. CN explained the significance of this investor to me.

CN: He invests in founders that are so passionate about their businesses that they will do anything to see them through. Cutting-edge technologies, people who want to make a vast difference on a global scale—major impact. When we talk to him about revenues of hundreds of thousands he wants to talk about billions.

CN and his team were scouting AngelList, an investor matchmaking site, trying to make connections with venture capital firms to see where they could get more smart money. "We need smart money as opposed to just cash," CN said. As I explain in greater depth in chapter 4, smart money comes from venture investors with useful relationships, or with experience in the specific field that a new firm is entering. Venture capital is, according to this narrative, the ultimate form of smart money. When I asked CN what he thought it would be like to have a venture investor, he told me that he was excited to have the opportunity to grow quickly. But, he said, "It can be a bit daunting.... Having somebody breathing down your neck is certainly not what any founder wants while running their business." However, he continued, without this sort of investment it will be difficult to scale their business. Instead, he said, "You're going to have a lifestyle business."

He explained that a lifestyle business would provide a couple million dollars in revenue, but something was missing:

CN: As a founder you have a nice salary, you have a comfortable life but you don't have systems that are deployed nationally in buildings from coast-to-coast. [Our angel investor] was the first to sort of introduce us to that. He said, "Guys, do you want a lifestyle business or do you want to grow this business into a big business?'
JG: What is it about the bigness that appeals to you?
CN: [My partner] and I have always had this dream where you could be making really cool products and manage really big teams and have a profound impact—and having a profound impact by our definition is to have your technology touching as many people as possible.

CN's entrepreneurialism, and his sense of impact, displays a world-making impulse, expressed within an economy (and culture) that primarily relies upon quantitative measures of success. The logical progression is quite straightforward: business is impactful, so more and bigger business means more and bigger impact. Smaller businesses therefore represent, by contrast, a wasted opportunity.

CN's aversion to small-scale, lifestyle business and its inability to make a "profound impact" represents a stark departure from the local and prefigurative projects that trace their legacy back to the countercultural environmentalism of the 1960s and 1970s, and which saw both beauty and transformative potential in small and appropriately scaled technologies.[27] This anti-establishment culture—from war resistors to communards—has generally been associated with a radical political and economic worldview, a systemic critique of "the colonization of technological rationality by commercial interests."[28]

At that time, Lewis Mumford was a vocal critic of the dominant sociotechnical system. Mumford argued that knowledge making had become authoritarian, thoroughly dominated by a commercial ethos and its hierarchical logic, threatening more democratic forms of making and thinking.[29] Instead of simply rejecting technology as an inherently anti-social and anti-ecological force, Mumford offered a more positive vision. He wrote:

A good technology, firmly related to human needs, cannot be one that has a maximum productivity as its supreme goal: it must rather, as in an organic system, seek to provide the right quantity of the right quality at the right time and the right place for the right purpose.... The center of gravity is not the corporate organization, but the human personality, utilizing knowledge, not for the increase of power and riches, or even for the further increase of knowledge, but using it, like power and riches, for the enhancement of life.[30]

During the 1960s, new social movements emerged that were committed to pursuing an alternative approach to technological development and knowledge making, often along lines sympathetic with Mumford's vision. The social ecology of Murray Bookchin, and in particular his vision of liberatory technologies, offered countercultural communities a way to understand the political salience of technological infrastructure and the ways in which technological decisions can help radically reshape social and ecological life.[31] A clear sense was emerging that alternative technologies, embedded within an alternative set of social relations, could be viable at a small scale, and conducive to a more meaningful, less alienating modern existence.[32] In the US, experimentation with alternative building forms, renewable and distributed energy systems, as well as new means of coordinating social life and new venues for sharing and disseminating knowledge, all proliferated in and through the relatively autonomous (though loosely connected) counter-cultural communities (and communes) that emerged during this time.[33] Sites such as the New Alchemy Institute, which occupied a small dairy farm in Cape Cod, became centers of experimentation for the burgeoning investigation into appropriate technologies. The following explanation comes from a 1970 institute bulletin:

Our programs are geared to produce not riches, but rich and stable lives, independent of world fashion and the vagaries of international economics. The New Alchemists work at the lowest functional level of society on the premise that society, like the planet itself, can be no healthier than the components of which it is constructed. The urgency of our efforts is based on our belief that the industrial societies which now dominate the world are in the process of destroying it.[34]

As the work of the Stanford University communications professor Fred Turner shows, this anti-establishment culture contained its own seeds of business-minded, libertarian-leaning techno-optimism, a world-making self-confidence that eventually eschewed its anti-systemic roots and transitioned into the entrepreneurial culture of Silicon Valley and its gospel of technological innovation.[35] Instead of continually opting out and forming small enclaves of good living, there were those who eventually chose to opt back in, with aspirations to support the development of new technologies—such as clean technologies—that would bring their conception of the good life to the entire world.

Today, within the broadly defined and self-proclaimed green economy, there are two distinct approaches to the issue of scale. The first is perfectly happy with small, local projects: *lifestyle businesses*, as CN described them. This entails visions of locally self-sufficient economies, small businesses doing good green work and supplanting the large industrial waste-making firms that have caused our environmental problems. Just as Silicon Valley represents an alternative to Wall Street, small business represents a similar alternative to big business and the waste-making economy that it supports. The work of Bill McKibben, Rob Hopkins' Transition Towns Movement, and Woody Tasch's *Slow Money* are all prominent examples of a discourse of revived localism at the heart of a green economy, which values small projects for their ability to demonstrate and incrementally build toward a more virtuous way of life.[36]

Cleantech however, primarily falls into a second category where bigger is better. More product, more impact. From the sense that ecological problems are planetary in scale, it follows that solutions must be as well. This scalar shift, from appropriate technologies to clean technologies (and from hippie to entrepreneur), is well illustrated in the work of Gary Hirshberg, the CEO of the yogurt manufacturer Stonyfield Organic.[37] Stonyfield began as a darling of the Slow Money movement, an example of small, local, and ecologically sound business that could help reclaim the food system from large, wasteful agribusiness concerns. However, as Stonyfield began to grow, its claims to being local and organic were stretched thin. In 2001 the global food conglomerate Group Danone bought a 40% stake in the company, which then increased to 85% in 2003. Stonyfield Organic subsequently became one brand out of many in a multinational's lineup. In 2017, the company was again sold, this time to another multinational, Lactalis.[38]

Hirshberg's personal narrative of becoming a green capitalist, which he chronicles in *Stirring It Up: How to Make Money and the Save the World*, begins with his exploits as a "windmill-building hippie."[39] He worked at the New Alchemy Institute, which had been one of the centers of the appropriate technology movement in the US during the 1970s, even becoming its executive director in the early 1980s.When Hirshberg was there, he worked on the institute's greenhouse, which was capable of feeding 10 people for a year. Good, but not good enough.

Everything changed for him in 1982, when on a visit to the Epcot Center in Florida he happened upon a pavilion that envisioned the future of farming. The exhibition included, "rivers of chemical fertilizers, herbicides, pesticides swooshing around the naked roots of anemic looking plants grown hydroponically in plastic tubes. In this paean to fertility, there was not a single grain of actual soil."[40] The problem, Hirshberg realized, was that 25,000 people went through this Kraft Foods–sponsored pavilion on a daily basis, more than the number of visitors to the New Alchemy Institute in an entire year. Hence, his epiphany:

I [had] to become Kraft.... To change anything, we needed the leverage of powerful businesses like Kraft. If we had their cash and clout, people would listen and change would begin.[41]

Hirshberg's argument bears summarizing: change requires power, large corporations have power, and therefore we need to become a large corporation in order to make change. He artfully avoids the alternate conclusion: in order to make change we have to take power away from large corporations. Hirshberg wants to sell a local product at the global scale, and he sees no contradiction with this effort to both honor family farms and to "think like Kraft." As he writes:

If I go on and on about the soil saving, health giving, life enhancing practices of family farmers, it's because I don't believe we can continue to exist on this earth without them. I am emotionally as well as intellectually committed to saving family farms. But business runs on hard numbers, not emotion, and I'm also sure that Stonyfield hasn't lost any of its virtue as it has become bigger. If anything, the larger we grow, the more good we can do.[42]

These are complicated sentiments—on the one hand mass production is seen to lead to excessive lifestyles and therefore to waste at a societal level. Yet on the other hand, to produce efficiently and effectively at this mass scale is lauded as a necessary capacity to effect widespread change. As with many forms of industrial-scale organic food production that fall back into environmentally unsustainable practices, with such a logic there is a danger of quantitative increases substituting for (as opposed to magnifying) qualitative transformations.[43] Simply being big, in whatever capacity, tends to signify one's impact, regardless of what that big impact actually happens to be. Or I suppose we could ask: At what point does the mass production of sustainably sourced organic yogurt packaged and shipped in disposable, single-serve plastic containers with a tear-away foil lid become just another boring industry?

Not a Hippie, an Environmentalist (or a Communist)

For Hirshberg, thinking like Kraft was another way to name the embrace of making an impact-as-capital. By contrast, the anti-establishment and often the (to some extent) anti-capitalist ethos of the appropriate technologies movement might better be characterized by that other form of impact, an impact-beyond-capital aimed at creating another world entirely. It is worth putting this transition, and the rejection of "irrationally" radical and anti-systemic environmentalism (castigated as either too hippie, too environmentalist, or even too communist) into some historical perspective. While countercultural movements of the 1970s experimented with appropriate technologies, mainstream culture—and mainstream environmentalists—became increasingly concerned with limits. In October 1973, members of the Organization of Petroleum Exporting Countries (OPEC) proclaimed an oil embargo against the US in retaliation for their support of Israel during the Yom Kippur War. The ensuing fuel shortages and sudden price rise brought energy production, consumption, and distribution into the limelight. The domestic supply of petroleum in the US was on the decline, and the increasing reliance on foreign sources of oil became painfully clear.[44]

Around the same time, Paul Ehrlich's *The Population Bomb* provided an alarming neo-Malthusian account of coming resource scarcities due to impending overpopulation of the planet. In the 1972 report *Limits to Growth*, the global think tank called the Club of Rome applied systems theory to questions of planetary ecology based on the results of their computer-based model, which predicted a future of instability and resource scarcity.[45] Coupled with the acute problems caused by the oil crisis, environmental concerns moved from the periphery to the center of political and economic life. When Jimmy Carter took office in 1977, he formed the US Department of Energy and established the importance of national energy policy. Alternative energy—referred to at the time as solar energy— was a core element of Carter's vision.[46] He took the threat of looming resource scarcity seriously, and presented a grim picture to the American public, warning that procuring sufficient energy sources would be a challenge marked by sacrifice and difficulty. Under the guidance of the newly formed Department of Energy and with the support of Congress, the Carter administration created tax incentives, grants, and regulations to support the development of solar power and other sources of alternative energy. They formed a new national research laboratory, the Solar Energy Research Institute, appointing Denis Hayes—who had helped create the first Earth Day in 1970—as its first director. In 1979, Carter held a press conference on the roof of the White House, dedicating a solar hot water heating system, and proclaiming, "No one can ever embargo the sun."[47]

Over the ensuing decades, Carter's agenda, focused on "harnessing the power of the sun," would come to be displaced by a business agenda, focused instead on harnessing the power of the market. Just weeks after this rooftop spectacle, amid the second oil crisis and the Iranian revolution, Carter's commitment to solar energy waned, and he switched his focus to synfuels made out of coal or oil shale, before losing in his reelection bid to Ronald Reagan in 1980.[48] Backed by the traditional energy- and extraction-based industries, and emboldened by an ascendant neoliberal ideology, the Reagan administration directly countered Carter's fixation on limits and sacrifice, offering instead an upbeat message of abundance and possibility. The sociologist Daniel Bell's vision of post-industrial society inspired a number of thinkers and futurologists who foresaw the emergence of an innovation-based economy that would supersede the material limits predicted by the Club of Rome.[49] As an explicitly anti-Malthusian economist Julian Simon asked, "Why shouldn't the boundaries of the system from which we derive our resources continue to expand in such directions, just as they have expanded in the past?"[50]

In response to what was becoming a hostile political climate, environmental organizations became increasingly professionalized, and developed non-confrontational, collaborative relationships with the business community in an effort to insure that they maintained their "seat at the table."[51] In order to maintain their legitimacy as level headed, business-savvy environmentalists, their critiques of industrial society would now have to be couched within a reassuringly pro-capitalist worldview. We can return to Stonyfield's CEO, Gary Hirshberg, who explicitly reminded his readers that capitalists, not hippies, will save the world—and that he is definitively the former:

Lest you dismiss my enthusiasm as nothing more than the delusional rants of a child of the 60s, I hasten to remind you that I am a passionate capitalist who has created thousands of jobs and millions of dollars of capital appreciation for hundreds of investors in Stonyfield Farm.[52]

Similarly, Woody Tasch doesn't want to "[run] the risk of seeming naïve, as well-intentioned but ineffectual as an old hippy at an annual shareholders meeting of Intel."[53] And Auden Schendler, the director of sustainability at Aspen Mountain Resort, writes that modern environmentalism is "pragmatic, businesslike, collaborative, and climate-focused" and has been "hamstrung by historical environmentalism, which was often shrill, exclusionary, irrational, and microfocused."[54] Schendler then makes fun of a woman who says at a meeting "I cry for the earth every day." He wants nothing to do with her:

Being mischaracterized as a tree-hugger is something that makes my job, and the jobs of others in my field, much more challenging than it would be otherwise.[55]

Turning back to the Funders Forum, LD, a broker-dealer and independent consultant, offered a similar sentiment.

LD: There is a blindness, which is that the environmentalists on the most part are such pains in the ass; they are easily dismissed because they are considered anti-industrialist. They are considered anti-progress, they sell shame and impose their morality on other people, and the reality is it's just a function of the numbers.

The 106th Funder's Forum was held in a small, corner conference room on the 21st-floor offices of a major law firm in midtown Manhattan, where it had been held for over a year after relocating from the accounting firm on Times Square, and before that from a different law firm, in a different sky-scraper on the other side of midtown, where I had attended my first meeting, the 88th. I arrived early, and in the half hour or so before the program formally began, I had a chance to talk with EN, the day's presenter. I asked him if he considered his business—software that helps plant managers increase the efficiency of their operations—to be cleantech. He grimaced:

EN: Saving the world is a noble cause, no one would argue with that. When speaking with my team I can tell them, "Hey, let's make a difference." However, when I go to speak with potential clients, I have to put on a different hat.
JG: You jumped from cleantech to saving the planet. Is that what cleantech is about?
EN: Oh yes, definitely. But that's the problem. If you talk too much about cleantech, people will think you're some sort of out-there hippie or something like that.
JG: Has this ever happened to you?
EN: No, because I don't use that kind of language.

EN's perception of what cleantech is, or stands for, is much different than the definition presented earlier—where saving the world or even far more modest environmental gains are at best a welcome side-effect of creating a new industrial sector. However, impressions matter. The affective force behind the cleantech project, whether explicitly acknowledged or not, has to do with the possibility of planetary salvation. But if you admit that this is what you care about first and foremost, you risk being discredited as a hippie environmentalist, interested only in making an impact-beyond-capital and unsuited for the hard work of making an impact-as-capital. As one investor and consultant explained to me, there are two types of green: the tree hugger idealist who wants to save the world and the realist who sees a new money-making opportunity; the latter will always win.

MQ, an angel investor who regularly attended the Funders Forum, saw hippies and environmentalists as unproductive actors, the privileged excrescence of formerly productive wealth. MQ's career began as a Wall Street analyst, in an era—he is quick to point out—where analysts actually had to know something about the economy, about the industries and the companies they were responsible for. For the last few decades he's been an independent agent—brokering and investing in deals that ranged from the sale of an offshore oil rig to the acquisition of a deceased author's estate (and the collection of unpaid royalties). When he was not looking for a cure for cancer (which sadly claimed his life in 2014) he was looking for the energy source of the future. The latter is what brought him, month after month, to the Funders Forum. For MQ, small-scale politics were not just ineffective, but thoroughly unproductive. They represented a waste of time and resources, and a luxury—such as organic farmers markets and other green lifestyles—primarily reserved for a wealthy elite that has "given up a life of being productive."

I never actually saw anyone at the Funders Forum or elsewhere in the cleantech space directly labeled and disparaged as a hippie or environmentalist. For the most part, these rhetorical figures were meant to provide a foil against which properly business-minded engagements with cleantech (and with making an impact-as-capital) could be situated.

If You Want to Make Money, Go to Wall Street

Entrepreneurs, consultants, and investors regularly told me that entrepreneurship was far from a sure thing, economically speaking. The risks involved—and the likely failures—are simply too great to prudently invest one's time and energy into a startup, especially if making money was your primary concern.[56] As one venture capitalist, PQ, explained to me:

PQ: It's hard for me to think of a case where someone has set out to be an early-stage cleantech entrepreneur solely because they're driven by the profit motive. If you're solely driven by the profit motive it seems to me you should go straight to Wall Street.

Wall Street is where you go to make money, whereas entrepreneurship is where you go to make an impact. In the wake of the 2008 financial crisis the Occupy movement chose the symbolic and very real location of Wall Street as its prime target, and their critique of Wall Street as a location of unbridled (and insatiable) profit-seeking resonated with a broad audience. As Karen Ho's ethnography of Wall Street investment bankers and their culture of expertise, hubris, and self-righteous acquisitiveness suggests, these cultural stereotypes of the wolves of Wall Street are far from unfounded.[57]

During my research, I encountered a common refrain pitting Wall Street as a generally nefarious foil against the innovation, creativity, and socioecological mission of cleantech entrepreneurialism. In many respects, Wall Street as an ideal was pitted against entrepreneurialism, which has come to be seen as an almost universal and unquestioned good, the purest expression of an enterprising self.[58] As Eric Schurenberg, editor of the magazine *Inc.* writes, "If you want to change the world for the better, in other words, you have to start with entrepreneurs. It's their job. ... All [of them] are changing the world for better, whether they set out to do so or not."[59] Entrepreneurs, whether in the field of cleantech or otherwise, are cast as producers, in contrast to the rest of us, who at best innocuously follow orders and keep the system running (classes taught, latte's poured), and at worst present a parasitical drain on the economy.[60] Wall Street—especially in the wake of the 2008 financial crisis—has increasingly been accused of the latter.[61]

There are clear connections between this most recent anti–Wall Street fervor and a much longer tradition of populism in the US, pitting producers against parasites and identifying the financial sector as an enemy of an otherwise capable and productive social body. As Thorstein Veblen put it, the "pecuniary interests" on Wall Street are centrally responsible for the wasteful, morally vacuous—and we would now add environmentally destructive—status quo that is produced by the boring industries that they finance and publicly trade.[62]

Though my research was based in New York City, the cleantech professionals that I met who voiced this anti–Wall Street sentiment had centered their financial imaginary on the other coast, in Silicon Valley, the home of innovation (as opposed to Wall Street, the home of securitized mortgages and financialized chicanery). Of course it is not as if all profit-maximizing, aggressive financial speculation and dispossession actually emanates from one particular street in Manhattan, nor is it the case that all technological innovation actually flows through the venture capital firms and research centers in Silicon Valley. These places are best understood as economic imaginaries, situated not only in concrete or absolute space (on their respective coasts) but as well in what the geographer David Harvey calls a relational space-time of symbolic valence. These places mean something, and these meanings exert a real influence on the world, far beyond their geographically bound locations. Accordingly, we could say that finance is to Wall Street what innovation is to Silicon Valley.[63]

We can read the division between Wall Street and Silicon Valley in terms of the contrasting ideals of the investment banker and the entrepreneur—the master of the universe versus the maker of the universe.[64] The former may make money, an impact-as-capital, but it is the latter that is also focused on transforming society, on finding disruptive technologies and making an impact-beyond-capital.

This distinction between Wall Street and Silicon Valley, or even between financialization and innovation, maps to the distinction between neoclassical and Schumpeterian conceptions of entrepreneurship discussed at the beginning of this chapter. While the former is squarely focused on profit maximization, the latter is more expansively committed to a creative process, where money is a means to other ends. At the Funders Forum and throughout the cleantech space, this Schumpeterian conception of entrepreneurship was proudly expressed, and the neoclassical entrepreneurship of finance, or specifically of Wall Street, was the single most important boring (and therefore less-impactful) industry that my respondents positioned their impact against. Money was of course centrally important for cleantech entrepreneurs, but it was not *just* about the money. By contrast, they would explain, on Wall Street it *is* just about the money. CN explained to me the difference between his community of cleantech founders and his peers who work on Wall Street:

CN: From what I have seen these are guys who don't necessarily love their jobs but go in there day in day out with their suits on just to make money. I have been working investment banking hours for years without making investment banking dollars—because I am more concerned about impact and changing the world and doing really cool things than having a nice house and a boat. You hope that eventually there is an overlap between having an impact and developing new technologies and starting cool companies and capital—but making a lot of money is not the only driver. It is part of the big picture but it is not the only thing. Plus I want to enjoy what I do. I never want to get anxiety on Sunday evenings because I have to go to work on Monday.

For the cleantech entrepreneurs I met with, financial success was as much, if not more, a measure of nonfinancial impact as it was a goal in and of itself. JQ provides a good example. He was trained as an engineer, after which he ended up being the CFO of a market research company, until one day deciding to leave it all behind.

JQ: I very much wanted to do more entrepreneurial and creative things than debits and credits—but really I was just looking at a bunch of paper on my desk one day and I said, "Oh, I've got to get out of here!"

This means, according to JQ's own definition, that he is not a "true" capitalist: "If you are a true capitalist you should make all the money that you can and tell them how to make all the money that they can."

After leaving his market research job, he started his own energy efficiency company, helping medium-sized institutions (such as small colleges) save money and energy with "low-cost, no-cost solutions." The model is simple: he self-finances modest improvements to his client's physical plant, making simple adjustments to the operations of large heating and cooling systems, which often entail—as he proudly boasted to me—inexpensive components bought at Radio Shack. In return he receives a percentage of the estimated savings from reduced energy use for a specified number of years.[65] He loves what he now does, and wouldn't ever consider returning to his old career. As he explained, "I am less interested in stuff like how to sell cornflakes."

JQ continued to explain to me his relationship with money. Everything he does professionally is aimed at saving money for his clients, and since he shares in these savings, the more he saves for them the more he earns for himself. And yet:

JQ: I think I am extremely not in it for the money, ironically, except for the fact that the money is a signal that I'm doing it right.... I have to sign an agreement with them that says I'm going to save them money, so ethically I have to do that, but I do think money is a good signal. It gives me a rush because it means I was successful, not because I'm going to take the money and go out and spend it.

As JQ understands it, although his creativity is rewarded financially—it is the creativity and not the money that justifies his pursuits. Money may be the medium and measure of social wealth, but there still remains a sense that as an entrepreneur he is working for something more.

If for Max Weber, writing about the Protestant spirit of capitalism, financial success signaled one's predestination for salvation, here we see financial success signaling a more secular success, born of creative achievement (or what Veblen might have called the "instinct of workmanship"). Instead of being directed toward a shared notion of God and godliness, this creativity is oriented toward and legitimized by a different sort of project, one that seeks planetary, as opposed to (or as a form of?) spiritual salvation.[66]

This leads to an important question, which I grappled with throughout my research. Are entrepreneurs like JQ just telling me what they think I want to hear? In numerous conversations with entrepreneurs and inventors, discussion would often begin with statements of impactful aspirations beyond "just" making money, but eventually it would revert to the details of financial and commercial strategies, how to maximize income, how to avoid dilution as an investor/owner, and so on. I found myself on multiple occasions interjecting:

JG: But I thought you said it wasn't about the money?
VG: It's not. It's not only about the money.

When these sorts of exchanges first occurred I would say to myself "gotcha!" thinking I had just revealed that my interviewee's seemingly altruistic commitments were not, in fact, as important as he or she made them out to be. Only after a fair bit of reflection have I come to see things differently; that I had been reducing these exchanges to something like a hunt for false consciousness. There is no point in trying to deduce whether impact or personal gain is the "true" or dominant motivator; or whether a stated desire to save the planet is simply what one is expected to say and not an honest commitment. This misses the point entirely. The key—and this is what defines cleantech's green spirit of capitalism—is that these two motivations are not mutually exclusive. In fact, one cannot be impactful in the cleantech space without both. As FJ, a consultant (who is also an internet radio producer, an entrepreneur, and an entrepreneurial coach) explained:

FJ: The entrepreneur who's just doing a business to make money will never truly be great. The really great entrepreneurs are the ones who are out to change the world, to create something beautiful and amazing and tremendous that has never been seen before. Almost any entrepreneur who is really, really, really successful is so because they had a dream that they were pursuing, they were making a gift of the passion—it was not about the money. Not that some aspects weren't about the money, but the dream wasn't about the money.
JG: Help me understand this. You can't be an entrepreneur and succeed without at least making some money?
FJ: It is not about that. The thing is the *focus* is not about making money. The *focus* is about doing things the most efficiently, the most effectively, about changing lives, about creating something new and different.... In the process of doing that you need to be a good business person, which means you need to keep an eye on the bottom line.

Cleantech entrepreneurialism is both energized and haunted by the traces of this contradiction between the possibility of making an impact-beyond-capital while at the same time remaining committed to making an impact-as-capital. Something of a dialectic synthesis seems to emerge—what

Hegel might call *aufheben*—a synthesis that is at the same time a negation, preservation, and supersession.[67] The cleantech entrepreneur is both a negation of the hippie/environmentalist and a supersession of this form, realized at a new "higher" level: the green or clean entrepreneur, saving the planet by selling her wares, or as the cleantech executive wrote inside the cover of that book I found at the Occupy Wall Street library: "'Doing well by doing good,' but the doing good comes first."

As I continue to demonstrate in the chapters to follow, throughout my experiences in the cleantech space it was not altogether clear that "doing good" always came first. The cleantech project may be about creating an impact-beyond-capital, but only insofar as this desire can be insulated from the far more prosaic necessity of making an impact-as-capital. The promise that cleantech can and will deliver more than mere profits has to be kept at a distance, simultaneously gestured at and kept at bay. Accomplishing this requires work; one does not simply embrace an impact-beyond-capital and an impact-as-capital without developing and internalizing a number of strategies for reconciling and redirecting their inherent and often contradictory implications. In the next chapter I explore this same division, between impact-beyond- and impact-as-capital, as a tension between investors and the creativity that they actively attempt to discipline, shape, and control. As I discovered, the best (most fundable) entrepreneurs in the cleantech space are the ones who are most willing to submit to the reigns— pun intended—of capital and the investors operating in its name.

3 Kill the Inventor! If Capitalism Spurs Innovation, Who Is the Horse?

There are so many banal and seemingly benign aphorisms that regularly fly under the radar, receding into the everyday rhythms of polite company. And yet they have the potential, once we acknowledge, pick apart, and examine them, to reveal much about the lives and relationships they pattern. One in particular has always stuck with me: *Capitalism spurs innovation.* Indeed it does. But what exactly does this mean?

During the past few hundred years of capital's relatively brief period of global dominance, there has been an unimaginable explosion of scientific, cultural, and technological developments. In the face of seemingly insurmountable environmental problems, it makes perfect sense to hope that this powerful engine of economic growth and sociotechnical transformation might somehow become our best chance at planetary salvation. Here, the planet takes center stage as an object of concern: a knowable, manageable, and controllable entity centering an ascendant regime of geological governance, or what historians Christophe Bonneuil and Jean-Baptiste Fressoz call geopower. This regime treats the environment as a global system to manage and control in the name of an undifferentiated *anthropos*, or humankind, whose problems are increasingly seen as solvable only via technological solutions, industrially produced and deployed at a planetary scale.[1]

The fact that a global system of industrial growth and military and consumer excess is largely to blame for the planet's most pressing environmental problems need not deter one's faith that greener and cleaner innovation, emerging out of this very same system, can undo the damage done. This premise runs to the core of planetary improvement: since innovation is "spurred" by capitalism, we must need more capitalism to accelerate a green technological transformation, forging that alliance, as Thomas Friedman puts it, between "Mother Nature and Father Profit."[2] Auden Schendler offers a succinct version of this argument in his text, *Getting Green Done*:

> If business is in large part the cause of the planet's problems, then it can also be the solution.... Business is designed to make money, and making money means creating more carbon emissions, often through growth.... Business is always going to default to profit at the expense of the atmosphere, because it costs nothing to pollute.[3]

After what sounds like a searing indictment of capitalism, he then takes a somewhat unexpected twist:

> This doesn't mean business is bad. Quite the opposite. Business gives people the prosperity to thrive and provides communities with the tax base to protect the local environment, and anyway, it's not going away. It's one of the oldest human endeavors, perhaps second only to love. What we need to do is find a way to make business a positive force across the board.[4]

Let's be clear on the structure of this argument:

A has caused B.

A is not going away.

Therefore, we need more A to create not-B.

This peculiar logical form is predicated, we have to assume, upon the idea that not all business is created equal. Although some businesses are fossil-fuel driven, industrially scaled, polluting, and unsustainable, this need not imply that all new businesses must necessarily follow suit. Another approach to business is possible: alternative technologies (not, it is important to note, alternative cultural, social, or economic relations) can and should be deployed by cleaner businesses. And these cleaner businesses should still be focused on making money—because that is what businesses do. In the process they should be making incremental gains toward a totally transformed future that will look very much like the present, only greener. This model fuels a somewhat quantitative approach to environmental transformation: planetary improvement requires more innovation, which therefore requires more dedicated funding, including more venture investment in clean technologies. Yet as Bonneuil and Fressoz ask, are not these entrepreneurs, investors, and the states supporting them the "bearers of a relationship to the world that has precisely produced the danger that they warn us of and offer to save us from?"[5]

As of this writing, investors continue to make calculated investments in various cleantech projects. As I mentioned in chapter 1, Bill Gates initiated his Breakthrough Energy Coalition, mobilizing private wealth (backed by governmental resources), to support the innovation of new "energy miracles," by which he means new technologies that can provide cheap, abundant energy to all of the world's population at a price cheaper than dirtier alternatives like coal.[6] Gates envisions a world of freedom in which even the poorest of the poor have been liberated from energetic deprivation, and given the opportunity to thrive. Here energy, just like the *anthropos*, is reduced to a single grid of intelligibility, a uniform and uniformly desirable commodity central to the basic necessities of living in this world. As the environmental scholars Larry Lohmann and Nicholas Hildyard explain, this historically particular conception of energy "posits an eternal scarcity of a kind that can only be relieved by industrial production, the destruction of commons and subsistence, and the rule of experts."[7] In other words, framing the world's problem as a scarcity of this one particular form of globally produced energy—predominantly consumed as electricity—already prefigures very specific forms of industrially scalable, technological solutions that can meet this planetary need.

That said, even some of capital's most vociferous critics have held out hope for a similar realm of freedom, an abundance for all that might result from precisely the sort of energy miracles that Gates seeks. For these critics, a technological acceleration through (and ultimately beyond) capitalist modernity would create the social, scientific, and technological infrastructure of capital's own supersession.[8] History of course, is a far messier affair; the liberatory potentials of sociotechnical progress were (and are) constantly subject to political struggles in which capital has enormous structural advantages to ensure that its interests remain dominant. As a result, the liberatory potentials of sociotechnical advance are largely (though never completely) subsumed by capital, which channels, orients, and ultimately shapes these collectively creative powers, mobilizing them toward industrial efficiencies and the expanded reproduction of capital itself.[9]

Increasingly, the entrepreneur figures central in this narrative of technological advance, taking on an almost mythic status as the fount of innovation and creativity.[10] As a process central to neoliberal commonsense, entrepreneurship has come to stand for a tight-knit collection of practices of constant self-improvement and personal branding, a creative and self-motivated orientation towards constant improvement and market-mediated success.[11] The founders of technology startups stand at the apogee of entrepreneurial culture, providing some of the most exalted and hyper-masculine examples of this pervasive form. These individuals, or at least the stories told of them, viscerally embody the new spirit of capitalism outlined by Luc Boltanski and Eve Chiapello, a culture of work in which autonomous, self-directed individuals channel untold reserves of inner strength and creative vision, casting off the constraints of hierarchical structures and encrusted bureaucratic forms to forge new, dynamic—disruptive—paths into the future.[12]

Popular business periodicals such as *Fast Company, Inc.* and *Entrepreneur* have helped create this well-rehearsed narrative of self-made, independent, and maverick entrepreneur-heroes. And yet, despite the ubiquity of these tales, there is another side of the story that gets significantly less attention: at the end of the day, the fundable entrepreneur is the one who is willing to be managed. In order to receive venture funding, entrepreneurs must relinquish much of their control and be willing to subject themselves to an employment relationship in which they can easily be replaced.[13]

In this chapter I explore a dynamic tension between capital and creativity that underlies the cleantech economy. While the analysis to follow is centered upon a process of managing, training, and disciplining individual entrepreneurs, it is important to think beyond the immediate experiences of this one relatively privileged segment of the workforce. We must come to understand how, at a broader level, our collective, social imaginary and capacity to create narrows when reproduced through the lionization of entrepreneurship as the pinnacle of creative activity.[14] The emergence of possible innovations, possible ecologies, and possible futures depends upon how we envision and empower this production of collective creativity. Only by looking beyond questions of whether the world needs more or less clean technology, or more or less green innovation, can we begin to ask how we understand the bounds of which technologies and which innovations are possible and desirable in the first place. We need to question whether and how this enclosure of a collectively creative capacity to think, make, and transform the world results in a limited assessment of just what forms of creative world making are tolerated, pursued, and considered viable contributions toward the production of better futures.

First, let's turn back to the Funders Forum, where entrepreneurs perform their pitches for investors—"smart money," as CN called them—who in turn must assess whether or not these entrepreneurial innovators represent smart investments.

Mad Entrepreneurs

Over the course of my fieldwork I saw scores of entrepreneurs present their startup pitches. Some were seasoned veterans of the business world, "serial entrepreneurs," and others were polished business school graduates, clearly able to articulate the how and why of their commercialization strategies. For all involved, mastering the pitch would be central to their success as a startup founder. This entailed a delicate balance between selling oneself and one's innovation (along with the business it will anchor). In terms of the former, one must exude just the right sort of confidence, charisma, and control. In terms of the latter, one must demonstrate the right balance of technological novelty, intellectual property/propriety, and commercial viability.

If we were to call the investment pitch an art form, it would not be the artistry of a singular creative genius—a Da Vinci, Picasso, or Van Gogh—but of a master craftsman, built upon repetition and the perfection of pre-established forms. Ultimately, there is a script that investors more or less expect the entrepreneurs to follow (these expectations are also shared by those who've internalized the investor's gaze, but that's a topic for the next chapter). Professors, consultants, coaches, and mentors prepare startup founders to master this script, and to make it their own. Here is a summary of how such a script might go:

Identify a problem that your product solves and the already-massive market available for capture. Provide a brief snapshot of the incredible team that you have assembled, perhaps offering some meaningless quantification of experience (e.g., we have 43 years of combined experience in the industry, or 27 collective years of research into our specific technological field). Provide enough technical details or at least pop-scientific analogies to help the audience understand what your product actually does—but not too much, lest you be seen as overly committed to the technology as opposed to the business. Explain the value proposition: how this product will represent a cheaper and more effective alternative for customers. Name a few inconsequential shortcomings of your product (sort of like owning up to the "tell me about your weaknesses" part of a job interview) so that you seem more credible—nothing is perfect. Differentiate your product from your main competitors, both incumbents and other startups like you. There is usually no need to mention the environmental benefits of your product or service except in passing, unless these are directly related to revenue streams or the above-mentioned value proposition. End with an overview of financial projections and your anticipated capital needs, while offering a clear sense that you know what to spend this money on. Don't ask for too much money, or too little; you need to show that you are lean and mean and able to efficiently use your capital, but also that you are willing to go big, and spend other people's money in order to make investors a hefty return.

The Funders Forum attracted presenters with a wide range of experience making a pitch. Some were well prepared, their pitch well modeled and well rehearsed. Others however, arrived with much less polished performances. For a good number of presenters, the Funders Forum was actually one of their first attempts to present to investors (or people who at least appear and act like investors). For these founders, *entrepreneur* was still a somewhat tenuous, and even at times unwelcome, designation. Many of them were, for lack of a better term, inventors: scientists, engineers, and tinkerers who had been focused on the physical and material science of making a new technology, as opposed to the dismal, economic science of making money. GF, a regular attendee at the forum, himself a "boutique investment banker" and consultant, referred to this latter group of presenters as the "mad entrepreneurs." They were scientists and engineers first; hype men, businesspeople, and salespeople second, if at all. They may have great technologies and ideas, but "they don't want to give up their first child, so that is why they never become anything other than a great idea." He explained further:

GF: The mad entrepreneur or the mad scientist is somebody who has a great idea and they may be onto something very good but they don't have the capital. They've got their second mortgage going; they have tapped out their friends and family; they think it's a great idea but they're never going to get it to market because they don't want to give up control. ... If I put them in front of an investor, that investor's going to be mad at me and I've had it happen. ... It doesn't take long—a couple of wrong answers from the mad scientists ...

These fears were corroborated and explained to me by OG, a venture capitalist.

OG: Let's say you sit down on week two of looking at a possible investment, you sit down with the scientist and talk about the management, and you know that they are the wrong guy just from the personality—but they are insistent that they be the guy to run it—then you probably don't make the investment.

The science of making *money* and the science of making *stuff* operate by quite different sets of standards, expectations, and (most significantly) temporalities. Take for instance the presenter at the 104th Funders Forum, a chemical engineer cum inventor cum entrepreneur who presented a technology that captures flare gas and transforms it into liquid fuel using a novel regenerating liquid catalyst instead of the standard Fischer-Troupe technique. While the Fischer-Troupe technique is incredibly efficient at large scales, his process is incredibly efficient at smaller, distributed scales—opening up a wide range of applications that the prevailing technology cannot support. The audience was intrigued at the prospect of this untouched, potential market; small flares everywhere, available to be transformed from waste into fuel. One of the venture capitalists in attendance—a regular at the Funders Forum—asked how much time and money he would need to produce a demonstration-scale prototype. After a momentary reflection, the presenter confidently explained that it would take $6.6 million and 22 to 24 months to create a fully functional, full-scale machine. Most of the time and money needed was not due to the difficulty of the process, he explained, so much as to the safety precautions that all chemical engineers must deal with.

Consensus in the room seemed to think that was too much money and too much time. Trained to always look for efficiencies, the curious venture capitalist asked, "How much would it cost and how long would it take without the safety concerns?"

The chemist grinned. "I can't do that, my kids want a dad to come home to."

The audience responded with polite, modest laughter, seemingly unconvinced that these were actually necessary costs, and not—as they've come to expect—the foot-dragging perfectionism of a "mad entrepreneur" who had yet to fully embrace the realities of commercialization.

Frustration with the inefficient entrepreneurialism of creative innovators like this chemist became a recurring theme throughout my fieldwork. JB best summed up the sentiment. As a lawyer and investor whose firm was hosting the Funders Forum at the time—and as the previous head of project finance for a large Wall Street firm—JB's authority filled the room: when he spoke, others listened (and eventually repeated) what he had to say. When dealing with entrepreneurs such as this chemist, he explained, it all boiled down to a simple maxim: "One of my first rules when dealing with small business is 'kill the inventor!'"

During my time at the Funders Forum, *kill the inventor* was an unexpected refrain—endlessly repeated in various iterations, and not just by JB. At times it would be invoked quietly as an aside to a familiar face, castigating the presenting entrepreneur. Other times it would be more publicly expressed in conversations with fellow attendees, as a shared piece of wisdom that confirmed one's ability to think as and with smart money.

For JB, *kill the inventor* encapsulated a number of important lessons about succeeding as a startup, and about making the sort of pitch that will actually attract the attention of investors. He put this into simple terms for me (as well as anyone who would listen, especially the younger attendees at the forum, whether entrepreneurs, service providers, journalists, or researchers): you have to get to commercialization as fast as possible; inventors often slow this process considerably. In business circles, he would continue, this is often called the "better mousetrap" problem, referring to innovators that continue to work on refining their technology or product well beyond what's necessary for commercialization. At one session, during the 45 minutes or so of networking after the formal presentations, I was standing in a small circle with JB along with one of the presenting entrepreneurs and a strategic consultant. The conversation turned toward this principle. JB reached over to the table and picked up a paperclip. "You know what's important about this paper clip?" he asked, rhetorically. "It's good enough. Not perfect. But it doesn't have to be. Just good enough."

The "inventor" was meant both literally and figuratively. On the one hand, there are real people involved with creating the technologies at the heart of cleantech startups. On the other hand, the word *inventor* evokes an excitement about the disruptive potential of new technology, a commitment to careful, patient, and rigorous development of said technology, and a constant expansion of its potential applications. The inventor may see a thousand possible applications in a new technology, but the entrepreneur needs to focus on taking only one of these applications to market.

There is nothing all that new about inventiveness, or an unbridled creativity that is willing to experiment with thought and action. In fact, as we saw in chapter 2, inventiveness, or the "joy of creation," was one of Schumpeter's defining, noneconomic motivations of entrepreneurship.[15] For Schumpeter, this creativity and willingness to take risks distinguishes the entrepreneur from the typical, profit-oriented businessperson, and provides the necessary spark of innovation that enables capital's dynamic of creative destruction. Typically the Schumpeterian conception of this dynamic envisions creative innovations destroying and replacing incumbent and less efficient technologies or industrial sectors. Here I suggest we reconsider Schumpeter's concept by entertaining the possibility that these incumbent industries—or at the very least the incumbent markets, consumer preferences, and financial logics supporting them—may in an equal and opposite manner, "destroy" the creativity meant to disrupt them. *Kill the inventor* can be read in just this light, as a countermovement to Schumpeter's description of entrepreneurs as the agents of creative destruction. Entrepreneurs, or more importantly the world-making creativity that they marshal, are themselves disciplined into economic conformity by a process that deemphasizes inventiveness, or the joy of creation, while focusing instead on market opportunities and profit maximization.

To be clear, *kill the inventor* is not meant to convey blood lust. It is simply a matter of economic prudence. As I would be repeatedly told (by everyone except, of course, inventors themselves), the problem is that inventors, or entrepreneurs being castigated for acting like inventors, care more about making things, and making them well, than they do about making a successful business. One entrepreneur explained as much to me after his presentation, exasperated by his partner, the inventor of the technology that they were trying to commercialize: "He just wants to make things.... He doesn't care about the money, that's why it took him so long to make the first prototype!"

Bending and Being Bent

Let's go back to that aphorism I opened the chapter with: *capitalism spurs innovation.* A lot hinges on the subtleties and implied meaning of the verb *to spur.* It is most commonly defined as providing an incentive or encouragement, or from the *Merriam-Webster Dictionary,* "to cause or promote the development of; stimulate." This leads to a first, and most common, interpretation: capitalism stimulates the development of innovation. There is certainly truth to this and certainly no need to rehearse the advances made in labor-saving and life-transforming technologies at the core of capital's dynamic rise. Silicon Valley's embrace of cleantech as their foray into a multitrillion dollar energy market was meant to be a case in point.

And yet, while a good portion of modern technological development and the resources to fund it has been either initiated or accelerated by profit-driven market competitors, a large portion of this creativity has been (and continues to be) developed by nonmarket means: in universities, as a result of government funding, or even out of the serendipitous and chaotic creativity of inventors and tinkerers who've been afforded the space and time to create.[16] The former venture capitalist William Janeway, in his theoretically informed memoir, *Doing Capitalism in the Innovation Economy*, refers to this creativity, in the aggregate, as "Schumpeterian waste," a necessary remainder that provides the raw innovative material for investors like him to identify, nurture, fund, and sell.[17] This waste must, Janeway argues, be adequately supported through forms of Keynesian public spending, so as to be made available to investors seeking new ideas to bring to market.[18] Thomas Friedman offers a similar vision, of "10,000 innovators, all collaborating with, and building upon, one another to produce all sorts of breakthroughs in abundant, clean, reliable, and cheap electrons and energy efficiency."[19] He asks us to consider this field of innovators as if they were a garden. "You have to intelligently design and fertilize them—with the right taxes, regulations, incentives, and disincentives, ... preparing all the soil, so the market and venture capitalists can pick off whichever sprouts look most likely to make the difficult transition from drawing board to marketplace."[20]

For Friedman, this harvesting implies a natural growth of innovative ideas, plucked by investors without much direct influence over what there is to be plucked in the first place. In actual fact however, this process—this gardening—entails a quite active process of "preparing the soil" so as to produce a garden that can yield one's desired crop. This intentional effort to make specific, promising innovations available relates to a second common definition of the verb *to spur*, again from *Merriam-Webster*: "urge (a horse) forward by digging one's spurs into its sides." For many, steeped in US popular culture, spurs are not everyday objects, but instead an iconic emblem of a mythic frontier culture, a Wild West where small metal spikes affixed to the heels of cowboys' boots dramatically clink to announce the presence of a valiant gunslinger. Their purpose beyond that is never made quite clear. In fact, spurs are quite common devices used to train, discipline, and domesticate horses. They figure central to the practice of dressage, or the historic art of breaking an animal in, physically and mentally subduing its active and creative energy so as to produce a docile and obedient creature that is ready to serve and perform.[21]

Henri Lefebvre uses the idea of dressage to make sense of the ways in which bodies are made, trained, and patterned according to the rhythms of society:

To enter into a society, group or nationality is to accept values (that are taught), to learn a trade by following the right channels, but also to bend oneself (to be bent) to its ways. Which means to say: dressage. Humans break themselves in like animals. They learn to hold themselves.[22]

Donna Landry's equine history of early modern English culture provides some colorful detail on the ideal form that this process can take.[23] She quotes an English gentleman named Sir Phillip Sidney, who in 1579 explained that this art of equitation entails "commanding without threatening." If executed correctly, when discipline or force is required the horse would seldom complain, for its will would become so wedded to that of its master that "it seemed, as he borrowed the horse's body, so he lent the horse his mind."[24] Dressage, as Lefebvre uses the term, can be understood accordingly, as both self-discipline and discipline forcefully imposed. The concept has clear parallels with Foucault's work, and his understanding of the micropolitics of power; of discipline and biopolitical regimes of governance.[25] Lefebvre focuses on the banal and seemingly innocuous ways in which discipline is imposed through the rhythms of everyday life and the repetitive and recurrent interactions that pattern themselves into and upon our bodies.

Capital's relationship with innovation (and therefore with entrepreneurs) can be understood as a form of dressage. JB's invective to *kill the inventor* may as well be rephrased as *break the entrepreneurs in,* bend them, teach them to be bent, to follow rules, to run at the pace and along the path of an investor-sanctioned commercialization model. This is not the outright destruction of creativity, so much as its disciplining and control, a setting of the terms and conditions of validated creative expression (even if that creativity will often exceed the bounds of this control). Landry explains that the horse's obedience was meant to "give off an aura of contained wildness, of massive physical power and independent spirit."[26] We can see a direct analogue for the entrepreneur, cast as a heroic and independent spirit rising up from the untamed wild of the "Schumpeterian waste," to be trained and disciplined into obedience by her investors, who will, as Sir Sidney suggests, borrow the entrepreneur's body, and lend her their mind.

Within the context of geopower, or the emergent form of geological governance mentioned at the beginning of this chapter, the result of this dressage translates into a narrowed focus on creating environmental transformation through commercially viable technologies that offer incremental improvements to the status quo. This might mean improving the components of hybrid and electric vehicles or developing fuels from new sources (that can be used to do the same things) or capturing wasted heat from industrial operations, all efforts to improve the efficiency of already established technologies and processes. Of course, it would be hard to deny that this is a pragmatic path for any innovator to take. Without a willing market, it would be impossible to create a viable business and see one's technology actually implemented and deployed. But we still need to see how this market pragmatism is far from natural, or perhaps we might better say, how it is an imposed and produced, trained and disciplined nature, a way of seeing and believing that market opportunities are the only opportunities, and then acting accordingly. Investors' spurs dig deep into the flanks of potentially tame, yet still somewhat independent entrepreneurs, training with the kick of their proverbial heel, steel to flesh, "Forward! Faster! On my terms! Hi-ho Silver, away!"

This argument is not meant as a categorical rejection of cleantech innovation, but to accept the need to critically assess its orientation, objectives, and perhaps most importantly, omissions. To take one example, consider the work being done by Ecovative Designs to create biodegradable, nontoxic materials. This company uses agricultural wastes—woody biomass—as a growing substrate for mycelium (essentially a dense web of mushrooms, or fungi). After inoculating the biomass with mushroom spores, it is put into a custom mold. After five days of growth the mycelium completely takes over, turning what began as a woody slurry into a sturdy form. The applications and implications of this technology, a biodegradable alternative to petroleum-derived materials, extend far and wide. And thinking towards the future, any significantly decarbonized world will have to have ways to create useful materials that don't depend on petroleum-derived feedstocks. Yet Ecovative's initial business model and main product narrowly focuses on one application only: using this material to replace custom polystyrene (Styrofoam) packaging. Images on the company's website and in presentations about the firm show consumer electronics packaged with mushroom blocks instead of polystyrene, and emphasize that these blocks, once they arrive in the hands of the final consumer, can simply be added to one's compost pile (assuming of course, one has a compost pile). This novel material is primarily being used to create disposable green packaging for consumer goods.

Ecovative's product is far more environmentally sound than polystyrene, both in terms of its production and disposal. And the company is actively researching and developing additional materials, such as a plywood substitute (its mycelium is able to replace the formaldehyde-based adhesives typically used in engineered wood products) as well as a flexible resin that could potentially replace all manner of synthetic foams and cushioning materials. According to its mission statement, the company is "committed to working with industry and consumers to rid the world of toxic, unsustainable materials … without having to sacrifice on cost or performance."

My point is not to question the environmentally transformative possibilities of Ecovative's cradle-to-cradle technology, but to highlight the ways in which its commercial success hinges on finding ways to incorporate this technology into an otherwise unchanged landscape of industrial production and consumption. Ecovative is doing exciting work, and the materials it is developing could potentially have far-ranging applications. These initial forays into high-end packaging materials may very well be a stepping-stone that allows the company to amass the capital and develop the infrastructure needed to push its innovative technology to new levels. In this regard, capital may indeed spur (encourage) innovation. But as we go on to explore below, it is important to recognize the relationship between inventiveness and funding, and the ways in which market considerations narrow the window of technological possibility to focus on a relatively small subset of possible applications and commercial opportunities. It is in this latter sense that capital spurs (disciplines, orients) innovation. Trajectories of sociotechnical innovation emerge through the dynamic and often unpredictable interplay of these distinct—sometimes compatible, sometimes contradictory—opportunities and imperatives.

The "A Round"

Throughout my research, I noticed that inventors cum entrepreneurial founders were seldom seen to be fit for the role of running a successful, venture capital–funded business. The problem with entrepreneurs being inventors at heart was twofold: First was their difficulty with giving up control over their invention and the business that formed around it. Second, when representing their companies, they could not conceal the first problem, and therefore did not convey the sort of leadership that investors were willing to fund. Simply put, they were either control freaks or bad performers; usually a bit of both. These critiques are not altogether ungrounded. I definitely saw my share of inchoate presentations made by inventors incapable of explaining their ideas clearly. Others were quite articulate and charismatic—like the chemist above—but their ideas ventured into areas where investors preferred not to go.

On many occasions Funders Forum attendees explained to me that it takes a different sort of mentality, and a different set of skills, to invent a product than it does to create a business.[27] This makes perfect sense— building a business is a much different project than building a new technology. But seldom did I hear them admit that one of these business-building skills—perhaps in some ways the most important one—is a willingness to cede control to investors, including to one's inner-investor; the entrepreneur-as-owner, whose fiduciary responsibilities are perfectly aligned with the interests of all other shareholders like them. Through this process, many-sided technologies (with multiple applications and directions for development) must become one-dimensional innovations with a discrete marketable application. The production and separation of these two elements, the business-focused innovator and the commercially viable innovation, is what creates a potentially fundable business (and a potentially fundable entrepreneur).

In other words, the inventiveness and extra-market creativity of the Schumpeterian entrepreneur must give way to the calculative profit-maximizing logic of the neoclassical entrepreneur. This comes through in the cleantech investment pitch, where it is essential that the entrepreneur's performance demonstrate an acceptance of this transition. One can, at most, briefly expand upon the broader sociotechnical implications of a new technology—but only so long as this tangent is quickly and assuredly contained within the overall pitch as an interesting aside, a gesture toward shared excitement about the disruptive potentials of technological innovation and a reminder of the shared project and transformed future that cleantech promises. To the extent that they are present at all, other possible applications and trajectories of development must be relegated to a single slide listing "future possibilities," which often capture the greenest and cleanest implications of the technology. These futures are carefully insulated from the short-term commercial objectives of the startup, which cannot appear to be seeking funds to make these futures; not-yet, not-now, not when it is first necessary to focus on getting a commercially viable product to market.

The subtle, unspoken, key to being a fundable entrepreneur has everything to do with presenting oneself as willing to be managed. And to this extent, the basic and overarching issue is control. Here's more from GF, the strategic consultant quoted above.

GF: The entrepreneur doesn't realize that we could make him or her more money than they thought ever possible—even if they don't own a majority interest—because we are going to bring resources to bear to make this a viable significant business. And the math is simple: What is 100% of 0? If I'm the mad entrepreneur and I own 100% control of my business it's going to be worth 0. That's one end of the scale, versus going with giving up control: 10% of a lot is a lot.

As GF suggests, an entrepreneur seeking investment can only have control or capital, seldom both. Accordingly, *kill the inventor* is a demand that one be willing to subject oneself to the market: to play along and be manageable, moldable, and containable. The entrepreneur's creativity and vision, the capacity for making new technologies, and perhaps beyond that, new worlds, is only valuable once harnessed. After one of the Funders Forum sessions a regularly attending investor showed me a draft prospectus for a new investment fund that he was beginning to circulate. The fund will only target early stage companies, and most importantly, the prospectus read, "Stable, controllable company management will be an absolute."

Despite the many popular tales of self-made, independent, and maverick entrepreneur-heroes, at the end of the day fundable entrepreneurs are the ones who are willing to be managed. In order to receive venture funding, they must relinquish much of their control, they must be willing to be employed, directed, and likely replaced. While some of the entrepreneurs I interviewed welcomed the discipline that venture investors would bring to their project, others were far more skeptical, and understood the risks that working with venture capitalists could entail. FP, for instance, an inventor I met at the Funders Forum, was working on a groundbreaking technology that transforms low-density hydrokinetic energy into electricity. Ideally, he sees this technology deployed as a distributed, low-maintenance power source for pumping water in under-resourced areas. The funding he has access to is more interested in seeing whether this technology can power underwater autonomous vehicles (drones). He has received grants both from the US Navy and the New York State Energy and Research Development Authority (NYSERDA) for this work. The latter gave him access to their entrepreneur-in-residence program. The entrepreneur that he was assigned suggested he take her class, titled "So you want to be an entrepreneur?"

"How presumptuous," he tells me. "No. No, I never wanted to be an entrepreneur. I have to become an entrepreneur because it is the only way I can continue to develop this technology."

FP thoroughly understood how inventors are treated as a disposable element in the commercialization process—a nuisance, hanging on to the intellectual property that they've created, getting in the way of this intellectual property's ability to function like an optimally profit-generating commodity. They are inefficient, a drag on commercialization, a fetter on the path towards commercialization. FP explained his experience as an inventor seeking funding via analogy.

FP: It doesn't matter to them. I mean what if you're a sex trafficker: you need the beauty of these young women but you don't give a damn about them. It's the same thing; it's a commodity and as soon as the inventors have served their purpose then you just get rid of them as fast as possible. And without recognizing that what they do, and what they have, is what gave you your success.

As we will see, there may be some truth to FP's sensational metaphor. In his own version of the *kill the inventor* trope, William Janeway discusses "cash and control" as the basis of success in the innovation economy. Each provides a level of autonomy from the market that allows a new business the space it needs to make decisions necessary to succeed. While entrepreneurs are expected to spend their cash, ultimately it is the investors for whom this principle most directly applies. He explains: "The venture capitalist's responsibility ... is to follow the cash with intense focus in order to observe in timely fashion when the entrepreneur's vision and the recalcitrant reality of the market deviate too far from each other."[28] Janeway regales his readers with tales of successful iterations of this process, where businesses were rescued from their errant entrepreneurs. At one point Janeway recalls his mentor, who helped him become a venture capitalist:

Fred's excellence lay in his ability to take a business apart analytically and dissect the interaction of its functional operations and its financial cash flows. He was a notoriously difficult human being, treating CEOs as subordinates and subordinates as trash.[29]

"Fred," of course, does not embody the same vision that venture investors offer to aspiring entrepreneurs. Venture capitalists present themselves—to the world and to the founders they consider investing in—as partners and mentors, big brothers who will guide their portfolio firms toward success, providing tutelage and ever-important connections with investors and other strategic partners. Though some of this is unarguably true, the underlying fact remains that at the core of this partnership lies an investment agreement that structures an unequal relationship in which venture investors serve as bosses and founders are positioned as at-will employees.

Let's look more closely at the details of this relationship. Typically, it is with an "A Round" of funding that entrepreneurs first formalize their relationship with a venture investor. Prior to this, a start-up likely has had to secure pre-seed and seed funding from non-institutional investors, which might include angel investors, grants, and most likely some initial amount of support from the "3 F's"—friends, family, and fools. In these earliest stages, founders almost invariably retain complete control over their companies. It is typically not until the A round when venture investors get involved and make initial efforts to structurally transform a fledgling startup into a full-fledged corporation.[30] Sophisticated shareholder agreements and organizational hierarchies have to be developed, so as to clarify the specific avenues of power and authority that the new partial owners—the venture investors—will be afforded. From this point on, the venture investors will get to impose their control upon portfolio companies, resulting in a stricter market discipline than the startup has yet experienced.[31]

Some entrepreneurs warmly receive this market discipline—at least those providing testimonials on venture capital websites. An entrepreneur's testimonial about Khosla Ventures, one of the first and most well-known firms to invest heavily in cleantech, explains: "What I love about Khosla and Keith is that it started as a friendship...a much more natural relationship, and I've learned so much."[32] At Chrysalix, another cleantech venture firm's website, an entrepreneur's testimony explains that, "the relationship between Chrysalix and the management team has been outstanding throughout, with a mutually supportive approach to fundraising and to building the team and the business at key points."[33] For entrepreneurs such as these, venture investors seem to provide a welcome dose of professionalism that helps provide structure for a new enterprise (bending, as opposed to being bent).

That said, it is hard to deny that the terms of this new structure come at a steep price. Incentive measures meant to encourage "optimum effort" and to avoid "opportunistic behavior," allow venture investors to assert substantial control over the startup and its founders.[34] In fact, venture investment deals are structured in such a way as to transform the actual experience of entrepreneurship and the rights afforded by entrepreneurial equity into that of an employment relationship with a stock-based compensation package, earned over time in exchange for good service.[35] There are three primary mechanisms for accomplishing this: the pacing of investment and equity accrual (staged financing), the differentiation in rights afforded to preferred versus common share holders (vesting schedules), and the establishment of an investor-friendly (if not outright investor-controlled) governing body (board of directors). We can briefly review each of these, in turn.

Staged Financing

Financing is very likely to take place in a sequence of investment rounds that begins with Series A. Investors assume that multiple additional rounds of financing will be necessary: a B Round, a C Round, and so on. Staged financing gives investors multiple chances to either pull, or threaten to pull, funding entirely. Doing so likely means the end of a startup, as such an event sends a strong negative signal to other potential investors, who have not themselves done any due diligence work on the firm, and therefore are more likely to rely on the negative assessment of the incumbent investors.[36] Each round of a staged investment is scaled to help the startup achieve an agreed-upon set of near-term goals, and it is explicitly acknowledged, by investor and investee alike, that should the startup successfully meet its benchmarks, it will almost definitely need further rounds of investment.

This allows the venture investors to keep a startup on a relatively tight leash; if the founders want to maintain a stake in their company, they have to meet aggressive benchmarks that will result in increasingly optimistic valuations at each funding round.[37] When these benchmarks are not met, the company risks being revalued at a lower level, resulting in what is called a down-round. When this happens, investors can invoke anti-dilution rights to adjust their share of equity, maintaining the total value of their investment by claiming a larger ownership percentage of what is now considered a less-valuable entity. This will dilute, or even at times completely. wipe out, the equity held by founders.[38]

Vesting Schedules

While venture investors receive all of their preferred shares immediately upon finalizing an agreement, founders are required to relinquish most of their equity stake, agreeing to repossess it according to a pre-established vesting schedule. Typically an entrepreneur will be granted one quarter of their equity up front, and then the remainder will accrue over the next three years. Should the entrepreneur leave the firm prior to being fully vested, they will have no claim on the remainder of their unvested equity, which remains the property of the firm, and will likely be used as an incentive to hire their replacement.[39] These conditions make a founder's ownership claims effectively contingent upon good performance. This is a far cry from the investor's ownership claims, which are not only insulated from bad performance (via the anti-dilution provisions mentioned above), but are fully secured from the outset.

Board of Directors

Ultimately it is the board of directors that assesses an entrepreneur's performance, and A Round agreements specify how this board is to be constituted. There will be a portion of seats that investors are able to select, another portion that founders are able to select, and then a third portion either selected by the board or mutually agreed upon by all. Although investors don't always end up controlling a majority of board seats, they are often able to effectively control the board, as the outside members are more likely to side with the investor-selected board members who represent more long-term and potentially valuable connections in their business community.[40]

The net result of these legal formalities is the creation of a corporation governed by a board of directors in which formerly self-employed owner-operators are transformed into a dual existence: owners of common stock and key employees. In a standard stock purchase agreement, published by the National Venture Capital Association, a key employee is defined as

any executive-level employee (including division director and vice president-level positions) as well as any employee or consultant who either alone or in concert with others develops, invents, programs, or designs any Company Intellectual Property.[41]

A section further on in the document addresses the dynamic regarding a key employee's termination:

To the Company's knowledge, no Key Employee intends to terminate employment with the Company or is otherwise likely to become unavailable to continue as a Key Employee, nor does the Company have a present intention to terminate the employment of any of the foregoing. The employment of each employee of the Company is terminable at the will of the Company.[42]

Entrepreneurs may remain owners and investors in their firm, for the time being at least. But they are now also employees who can be fired at the discretion of "the Company" or, in other words, at the discretion of the board of directors in which they most likely have minority representation. Once these papers are signed, the founders effectively lose control. Their role as owners is functionally separated from their work as creators. As a noncontrolling shareholder, the primary focus of the founder's relationship with investors is modeled upon an employer-employee relationship. As the legal scholar Manuel Utset writes:

The incentive mechanisms are of the types ordinarily used in an employer-employee relationship, where the goal is to get the employee (the agent), to exert maximum effort and not to take actions that would hurt the interests of the employer-principal. The venture capitalist reserves the power to fire the entrepreneur and end her employment with the firm.[43]

Here we see how FP's sense of impending disposability as an inventor-entrepreneur holds a fair bit of truth. Once an A Round has been completed, it is not uncommon for founders to be ousted from their startup, in favor of management that the new board of directors finds more suitable to the new tasks at hand. Such is the unpredictable fate of so-called key employees.

Venture capitalists explain this transition in a slightly more positive light. One of them described it to me this way.

PZ: Well, it kind of goes with the territory that people who start companies are not necessarily the ones who should lead them once they are bigger. I mean there are plenty of examples of people that do both, but it is a very different skill set. Someone who sets up something early may be bored by the time that it is discovered, or isn't a people person, or isn't a bureaucrat, and so as companies get bigger they need professionals; professional management that sometimes entrepreneurs can step up to but sometimes they can't or they don't want to.

PZ offered an even-handed explanation of why entrepreneurs may want to leave their firms once they are no longer startups, as their independent, risk-taking spirit may no longer be fulfilled. However, left unspoken is the unquestioned presumption that whether they stay or not, it is expected that the company needs "professional management" that will put the needs of shareholders—the imperative to maximize profits—above all else.[44] Further, it is presumed that these now-bored entrepreneurs were primarily motivated by creating a new business, and not creating (and continuing to create) new technologies. In other words, they are presumed to be neoclassical, as opposed to Schumpeterian entrepreneurs, so that their dismissal can be framed as generously respecting their core, risk-taking nature, by freeing them to pursue new opportunities.

Inventor Hazard

Here's the irony—or at least an unspoken contradiction—at the heart of this investor-entrepreneur relationship. On the one hand entrepreneurs are a source of economic dynamism, and as such the market exalts them as pinnacles of heroic economic activity. And yet on the other hand entrepreneurs are a threat: seen as egotistic figures and self-determining creators, they represent a force that must constantly be brought under control. This tension can easily be overlooked in accounts of entrepreneurship and innovation that presume entrepreneurs and investors are all part of the same capitalist class, the same innovation ecosystem—and are therefore ultimately working toward compatible ends.[45] What gets lost is a fundamental class conflict at the heart of this commercialization process: a struggle between entrepreneurs as creative workers and investors who hope to transform these workers into distinct roles of being an employee and an investor, in the process separating them from the product of their creative efforts.

In many ways, invoking the *kill the inventor* refrain gets at what less-colorfully expressive economists discuss as information asymmetry: entrepreneurs, to the extent that they are inventors or innovators of some new technology or service, represent a monopoly on specific innovative information, putting them in what these economists see as a potentially unfair position vis-à-vis their investors. This information affords the entrepreneurs power that is not fully under (investor) control. Economists call this an agency cost, which accrues when one actor is dependent on the actions of another over whom they do not have full control. The entrepreneurial founder represents an agent who is at risk of acting "opportunistically," privileging their own self-interest, which in this case manifests in putting innovative refinement before the financial interests of the firm and its owner-investors.[46]

The legal experts Jesse M. Fried and Mira Ganor explain that these agency costs lead to a risk of moral hazard, or a lack of incentive to guard against risk. The concept of moral hazard figured central to post-recession narratives of financial collapse in 2007 and 2008, with banks that knew they were too big to fail left with no incentive to curb their risky behaviors.[47] Here, however, a different sort of moral hazard is being presented—not the unchecked risk taking in profit seeking, but the unchecked risk taking of invention—and the possibility that such risk taking might impinge upon a safer and more predictable route to profitable commercialization. We might more accurately describe this as an inventor hazard: the risk that entrepreneurs' inventiveness and creativity might eclipse or obstruct, or perhaps even derail the generation of value.[48]

This is precisely the risk of investing in a "mad entrepreneur" whose creative spirit may not be easy to contain. One of the most interesting explanations of this risk came from just such a person—actually an inventor—who presented at the Funders Forum and subsequently attended numerous times. TC was an aerospace engineer with a passion for technology and innovation. For decades he had been working on a modular farm system—a self-contained unit built into a shipping container that was capable of producing a constant stream of barley grass. His first attempts failed, and he subsequently got caught up in a "pump and dump" scheme that resulted in his work being left to rust in a warehouse behind locked doors. He was hoping to give the project another shot, and pitched this updated idea to the room. After his presentation, TC lamented with me about how investors want their returns too quickly, how money is squeezing out any possibility for seeing another Nickola Tesla or Thomas Edison make it today. But a year later, after attending a number of Funders Forum events, becoming an investor in his own startup (thanks to a home equity loan), and enlisting another Funders Forum regular to serve as his CEO, his tune had changed noticeably. He was no longer convinced that investors are the ones limiting the innovation process. He now told me about a number of "game changers that have never happened," and not because they were thwarted by big business or investors. Instead, "a lot of them are shut down by inventor's egos, and just getting ahead of the curve or falling ahead of the curve." These inventors are guilty of being "ahead of their time" and not sufficiently focused on making immediately commercializable innovations. TC explained that inventors are too self-absorbed and have an overly inflated sense of their importance and of the value of their work. These irrational egos—and not the temporality of venture investment—were what presented an impediment to innovation; the problem was an unwillingness to submit to investors' guidance and control.

Doubly Free Entrepreneurs

The value of a promising entrepreneur is twofold: On the one hand there is a specific innovation or technology being developed—and if it is still in an early stage of development the initial creator is likely to be critical to its continued development. On the other hand, entrepreneurs represent relatively cheap and thoroughly committed managers—willing to work for very low wages and very loose promises of possible returns down the line. This connection between the entrepreneur-inventor and their innovation is at the heart of the venture and its potential value. As Utset explains, even if venture investors might be able to purchase innovative technology alone, it often makes more sense to keep the entrepreneur-inventor around "until she has properly transferred all rights to the innovation to the venture. After that, a venture capitalist can usually fire the entrepreneur with little financial loss."[49] Here is the reason:

Once the innovation has been transformed into a marketable product, the entrepreneur and the transformed innovation are no longer complementary. In other words, the value of the new product is independent from the entrepreneur's human capital.[50]

Although investors initially look to fund an entrepreneur and their inno-vation together—as a package deal—once in control their aim is to break up this assemblage and rearrange it according to more advantageous terms. They aim to separate innovators from their innovations: the former are to become employees and investors, the latter are to become investor-owned assets.[51]

This process of separation is reminiscent of the way Marx described the process of encouraging the development and acceptance of wage-labor. Whereas the political economists of his time understood the rise of capi-talism, and with it the proclivity for otherwise unemployed individuals to seek out waged employment as an unquestionable, natural flourishing of human industriousness, Marx suggests instead that for most people, this process was not at all so benign. In order to secure a population of individ-uals "freely" willing to subject themselves to waged work in the "satanic mills" of early industrial production, capital (and by this I mean investors, industrialists, and state actors, along with the more general system of social relations that they both wittingly and unwittingly reproduced) had to first separate the laboring population from their means of productive engage-ment with the world. The enclosure of common lands was central to this separation, a process endorsed by the few who stood to gain and vehe-mently opposed and resisted by the majority who stood to lose the entire basis of their livelihood. Marx facetiously referred to the result of these dispossessions as the production of the "doubly free laborer": freed from any means of production and reproduction, and freely willing to subject themselves to wage labor under capital's control.

This production of the doubly freed laborer remains ongoing, whereby the creative process of producing and reproducing one's lifeworld is ori-ented toward employment of one form or another, so as to pay for the con-sumption of goods and rents that would otherwise be unattainable.[52] It is in this vein that we can interpret the refrain *kill the inventor* and the process of separating innovators from their innovations. Dressage, as discussed earlier in this chapter, is an extension (although far less bloody) of this ongoing effort to make and maintain the presence of the doubly freed laborer, only here with a shift in focus from the repetitive drudgery and abject precar-ity of industrial wage labor to the flexibility and creativity of a relatively privileged sphere of entrepreneurship. Despite this privilege, and despite the glorification of entrepreneurs as capital's wellspring of innovation and growth, they are nonetheless still subjected to this tried and true process of becoming employees. Entrepreneurs are "freed" from their innovation, and "free" to work for investors as key employees. The result is a separation between the innovator and the innovation, a making-employee on the one hand, and a making-intellectual property on the other.[53]

These separations are not always experienced or perceived as violence and dispossession. Many entrepreneurs reaching the point where venture funding is available have already embraced the freedom to willingly enter into these agreements, and regard the process as a necessary and inevitable step in the maturation of their firm. Venture investors, along with a wider community of professionals in the entrepreneurial ecosystem, are likely to be received as mentors, readily willing to help entrepreneurs grow and mature as founders and businesspeople. There is no reason to question that this does in fact occur, at times to the benefit of all involved (unwelcomed terminations not withstanding). In this regard, dressage does not appear to be a form of violent coercion, imposed from without. Instead, it is an internalized and seemingly consensual process. The entrepreneurs accept their demotion to employee in exchange for admission into a community of money, as co-investors in a company whose orientation, as with all capitalist firms, must naturally be toward maximizing profitability and more specifically, the financial returns of its investors.

Creative investments in the process of innovation relegate the entrepreneur to the status of an employee, whereas financial investments in the innovation as commercially viable property elevate the entrepreneur to the status of an investor-owner. While a successful entrepreneur may be able to occupy both of these roles, it is only the latter of the two, the entrepreneur as investor, that affords the individual some semblance of control, and then only as an investor with—as we will see in the next chapter—a fiduciary responsibility to put profit maximization before all other concerns. Meanwhile, the entrepreneur as creator, at the point when control over the innovation has been successfully transferred to the firm, will only be able to stay employed so long as they continue to meet the investors' objectives.[54]

Rather than focusing on any specific injustices done to specific entrepreneurs, we instead need to scrutinize this orientation toward the needs of investors, including but not limited to entrepreneurs as investors. Beyond accepting the fact that entrepreneurs are able to grow and mature, we need to recognize just what they are growing and maturing into—agents of capital first and foremost, so committed to their investment that they would gladly fire themselves as an employee, were it best for their shareholder interests. Along precisely these lines, Wasserman quotes a venture capitalist who tells him: "Upfront, I ask founders to level with me. If they are interested in working with me on the basis of being a big shareholder, then I am interested. If they are interested in working with me because they have to run the company, then it's probably not going to make sense for us to work together."[55]

An Enclosure of Creativity

One of Schumpeter's most important observations, which mirrors a similar critique leveled by Marx, has to do with the limitations of capital and its inability to innovate.[56] Capital can control creative processes, but it cannot itself be creative; its singular focus on expanded self-reproduction leaves room for only the most pecuniary forms of experimentation and innovation. Marx and Schumpeter both seem to agree that people, not capital, are creative. For Schumpeter, it is specifically entrepreneurs who are able to provide capital with its extra-market creativity and systemic dynamism. Marx on the other hand, never singled out a class of entrepreneurial innovators to explain capital's dynamism, leading critics such as Mark Blaug to argue that Marx follows a path set out by David Ricardo, where the process of business innovation is considered as a near automatic effect of market pressures and opportunities.[57] Blaug argues that Marx had little interest in exploring the genesis of decisions made about what to produce when, where, and how, and even conflated the figures of capitalist and entrepreneur. As he concludes: "Marx, who claimed to be alone in truly analyzing the 'laws of motion' of capitalism, had simply nothing to give of the actual source of the acknowledged technical dynamism of capitalism."[58]

While it is true that Marx afforded little space to the investigation of innovative capitalists, he did have an explanation for the source of capital's technical dynamism. He refers to it as a process of "general industriousness" which entails the mobilization of an accumulated wealth of technological knowledge and skills, and its orientation toward meeting general, as opposed to local and particular, human needs.[59] The pursuit of this generalized wealth and the meeting of universal human needs requires the mobilization of a collectively laboring and thinking social body, not just individual workers put to work in individual productive capacities, but even more importantly, a collective intelligence channeling the multigenerational power of science and technology. He refers to this collectively creative capacity as the "general intellect" and sees it as a creative force undergirding the modernizing potential of capitalism, where production for profit has released social production from the parochial constraints of local and particular needs and stands instead as a proxy for production oriented toward general social need.[60] Instead of identifying a unique class of innovators, Marx identifies the general intellect as the source of innovation and economic dynamism. It is, he explains, a form of universal labor that accounts for "all scientific work, all discovery and invention. It is brought about partly by the cooperation of men now living, but partly also by building on earlier work."[61]

This does not contradict those placing entrepreneurs at the center of innovation and dynamism; it merely reframes their position in relation to the class dynamics of capitalism. While many understand entrepreneurs to be the most innovative branch of the capitalist class, for Marx (and I would argue for Schumpeter as well) those operating as entrepreneurs and those acts considered entrepreneurial are first and foremost instances of creative labor—and therefore part of a general intellectual capacity of society at large. Seen in this way, we arrive at a far less triumphant version of creative destruction—where capital is not only an essential engine of innovation, but also a parasitical nuisance. Marx writes of the entrepreneur's fate:

Pioneering entrepreneurs generally go bankrupt, and it is only their successors who flourish, thanks to their possession of cheaper buildings, machinery, etc. Thus it is generally the most worthless and wretched kind of money-capitalists that draw the greatest profit from all the new developments of the universal labor of the human spirit and their social application by combined labour.[62]

This is a fitting moment to return to Janeway, who earlier regaled us with tales of his mentor, Fred, "treating CEOs as subordinates and subordinates as trash." In trying to make sense of the innovation economy, Janeway uncovers a peculiar contradiction. On the one hand, entrepreneurs are meant to be controlled and treated as disposable employees, yet on the other hand, "the waste generated by experimentation is essential to progress and tolerance of that waste is a prime condition for leadership at the frontier."[63] Inventors, experimenters, and tinkerers all represent a vast sea of "Schumpeterian waste" that must be tolerated and eventually harnessed. Janeway's choice of terms is apt. Waste is, as Vinay Gidwani writes, capital's "incitement to value," a terrain of *not-capital* that is available to be recast as *not-yet capital*.[64] This is not the waste of a trash heap or toxic dump. Instead, think of this waste as creative potential, an unkempt, untapped, and uncontrolled wilderness, a fecund wasteland available to be brought under the yoke of investors—or to stick with the theme of this work—improvers.

Janeway's simultaneous embrace and dismissal of this Schumpeterian waste parallels the way that 18th- and 19th-century agricultural improvers engaged with the common wastelands that they aimed to enclose. These lands, central to the productive but not-capitalist functioning of local common-right economies, were simultaneously seen as a dangerous remainder that needed to be subdued and a source of untapped potential, available and ready to be transformed into capital.[65] In the innovation economy, investors, as well as all those who have internalized and embraced it's capitalist logic, play a similar role as these agricultural improvers, seeking to enclose the Schumpeterian waste, or perhaps even the general intellect, by transforming it into a source of commercially viable innovations; intellectual property (intellect-as-property) that can be profitably put to work.

We have to pay close attention to the transformative nature of this process. It is not as though there is some preexisting sea of creativity, entirely separate and distinct from the capitalist economy, to be mined and refined, as if creativity was a raw material like coal or oil. Many inventors and innovators live, work, and create in a world that is at least partially shaped by the same cultural and economic logics that animate the investors looking for promising opportunities. This is why Friedman's gardening metaphor is more apt; not only do investors look for commercially promising innovations that are suitable to be "plucked and harvested," but prior to this plucking, their active management of the "garden" of ideas—pest control, weeding, selective breeding—is what makes suitable innovations available in the first place. In other words, the investors' logic, which in the next chapter we will explore as the smarts of "smart money," permeates the broader Schumpeterian waste of creative production, which is, accordingly, a socially produced nature.

Enclosure has typically been envisioned as a process of closing off resources to those who had relied upon them, such as common lands being fenced off and parceled out into individual private holdings. But this process is also, and perhaps even more importantly, an opening up of these newly privatized resources to the flows of capital. We can say the same about the enclosure of green technological creativity. An immaterial landscape of intergenerational, intellectual capacities is both closed off (by being parceled out into intellectual property claims) and opened up to the flows of capital. In this process of opening up we see the production of a very specific type of creativity promoted and nurtured, one narrowly oriented toward the production of marketable, commercial technologies, worthy of investor support. This occurs at so many levels, from the reorientation of academic research centers around the dictates (and funding) of private capital all the way to the pitch competitions and venture capital offices that have become nearly synonymous with entrepreneurial innovation.[66] As a result, innovative ideas, the product of a general intellectual creativity, are being marshaled into the service of capital, while those who help midwife these ideas, these innovations, are asked to either step aside or play along. These are the only two options.

In no way do I mean to take anything away from the ambition and genius of individual creators or, for that matter, their ability to resist and rework these seemingly unavoidable pressures, and to remain creative dreamers through and despite the pressures of venture investment and the challenges of commercialization. Instead, I ask that we acknowledge the complex ways in which their individual creativity is embedded within a thick intergenerational mesh of knowledge and capacities, without which they could never invent or innovate in the first place. To the extent that cleantech entrepreneurship becomes accepted as the only or most viable path toward marshaling sociotechnical innovation to address the problems of environmental destabilization, the diverse potentials of this social, intergenerational creativity are being reduced, channeled, and narrowed into the potential to become (green) capital. That is the essence of this process of enclosure, the abstract and abstracting violence it enacts upon our "Schumpeterian waste."

As we will continue to explore in the chapters to follow, planetary improvement envisions a world of "dirty" or not-yet green technologies and infrastructures that are available to be cleaned through incremental improvements—increased material and energetic efficiencies—and that can be integrated into already established markets and already established ways of life. What results are non-disruptive disruptions focused only on what is commercially viable and rapidly scalable, and accepting only of technologies that fit into the everyday status quo of society, extended perpetually into a future incrementally improved, but never fundamentally transformed. Ultimately, this will lead us to questions about where we locate innovation, science, and experimentation, and which social practices are seen as legitimate productions of sociotechnical-environmental knowledge. Who do we understand to be our innovators, and what worlds are they given license to create?

4 Smart Money: The Cultural Logic of Cleantech Venture Investing

In this chapter I largely set aside one aspect of "green" (a commitment to transforming the environment or, going further, to "saving the planet") and focus on that other "green" (financial wealth or money) and the venture investors operating in its name. The political ecologist Scott Prudham explores the ways in which high-profile green entrepreneurs help to legitimize green capitalism through their active commitment to environmental goals, effectively helping to produce and promote what I've called a green spirit of capitalism. It is not just their outspoken environmental commitments that matter, but also an underlying, "virulent, muscular neoliberal, masculinist subjectivity" defining them as entrepreneurs in the first place.[1] I extend Prudham's observations by turning from the performance of green entrepreneurship to the performative nature of cleantech venture investing. Venture-investing scripts exert a strong influence upon the present and future of green sociotechnical advance, helping to establish an understanding of what is and is not possible (based on what is and is not fundable).

Just as entrepreneurialism can function as a more general subjectivity and orientation that extends beyond the specific individuals at the helm of new businesses, the same is true of venture capital.[2] While there are of course specific networks of interpersonal connections grounding this investment process,[3] we must also consider something more than these networks, a more abstract, relational space of venture investing, establishing its general and diffuse precepts, norms and patterns. We might call this its cultural field, a pervasive common sense, or an everyday rhythm: that which makes this, or any market for that matter, more than the sum of its parts.[4]

During my fieldwork, I found that venture investors were referred to as "smart money" because of their ability to select the most promising, commercially viable startups, as well as for all of the extra-market support, connections, and mentorship that they gave their portfolio companies. In chapter 3 we explored the ways in which this support is structured by a disciplinary relationship, or dressage, in which entrepreneurs are expected to become malleable, flexible, employable, and ultimately expendable. Here we add another layer to this process, to see how these trainers are themselves trained. In this case, the fiduciary responsibilities that venture investors owe to the professional money managers who contribute to their investment funds result in both an unquestioned orientation toward maximizing returns and a deference to the laws of the market. These laws appear to function as a natural, gravitational force, pulling all creativity—and notably for us, all of cleantech—into its orbit.

This gravitational pull extends beyond specific investors with specific fiduciary responsibilities, into a more generalized and pervasive common-sense understanding of what projects, what futures, and ultimately what natures are possible in the first place. A wide array of strategic consultants—from brokers and financial advisers to boutique investment bankers and accountants—take on, experiment with, and rehearse the very distinct "intelligence" that it takes to be a venture investor. And so, while venture investors are exalted as "smart money," this is in the context of strategic consultants proving to entrepreneurs, investors, each other, and themselves that they can exhibit these same sorts of smarts; that they are smart-without-money.

The result of these rehearsals is a naturalization of capital's imperatives—or what the political economist Moishe Postone calls the process of abstract domination—underlying the green spirit of capitalism.[5] The scripts of smart money portray capital's abstract and abstracting logic as an unquestionable intelligence, ultimately demanding that all cleantech innovations, all attempts to make an impact-beyond-capital, accept the market's gravitational force. This is the force, we might say, that tethers the green spirit to capital.

Environmental Crusaders

There are a number of very public, very wealthy individuals who have embraced the project of green capitalism, and who perform this commitment on the world stage. John Doerr's talk at the TED2007 conference was one of the more notable examples. Doerr began his tech career as a salesperson for Intel, but has since made his fortune and name as a venture capitalist, funding internet technology companies such as Google and Amazon. He was one of the leading figures in venture capital's shift into cleantech, and began his TED talk on the subject with a confession: "I'm really scared. I don't think we're going to make it."[6]

This moment of truth came at the behest of his daughter, who told him one night, "I'm scared and I'm angry. Dad, your generation created this problem. You better fix it." Fix it he will. Doerr goes on to explain a number of cleantech-related topics: the significance of Walmart going green; the importance of compact fluorescents and the stupidity of bottled water shipped across the globe; the necessity of good policy—such as a market in carbon and national fuel mandates; and the potential for cleantech companies such as Amyris to create better biofuels. He announced that his venture capital firm, Kleiner Perkins, was investing $200 million in new disruptive clean technologies. He admitted that even this is not enough to meaningfully address the climate challenges that we face, cautioning that no single investor, or firm, could invest enough money on their own to save the planet. What we need is an entire, systemic transformation, he declared as his talk continued:

We have to make this economic so that all people and all nations make the right outcome the profitable outcome and therefore the likely outcome. Energy is a six trillion dollar business worldwide - it is the mother of all markets. You remember that internet? Well I'll tell you what, green technologies, going green is bigger than the internet. It could be the biggest economic opportunity of the 21st century. Moreover, if we succeed it is going to be the most important transformation of life on this planet.

Doerr choked up at the end of his presentation—barely getting his last lines out. He exhorted the audience of his peers and fellow "TEDsters" to "multiply all of our energy, all of our talent, and all of our influence to solve this problem." Only then, he explained, will he be able to look his daughter in the face, and honestly say that he's done what he could to fix the world's climate problems.

Prudham argues that the performance of the elite entrepreneur as an environmental crusader plays an essential role in the legitimization of green capitalism.[7] In both political and cultural terms, green entrepreneurs constitute a "terrain of consent" by presenting themselves as innovators and architects of better futures, as opposed to those whose primary goals are to perpetuate (and profit from) an environmentally destabilizing, growth-oriented economy.[8] As Doerr's TED performance suggests, the same can be said of venture investors, for whom the lines between entrepreneur and investor are often (quite deliberately) blurred.

Venture capitalists present themselves as adventuresome, risk-taking pioneers, operating at the cutting edge of technological innovation and driving the motor of progress.[9] In the field of cleantech, this self-image becomes closely linked to technological salvation—by investing in the most innovative, most "disruptive" clean technologies, venture capitalists are working to reshape our world, to commercialize the technosocial foundations of a better, cleaner economy. Venture capitalists like Doerr, Vinod Khosla, and of course former vice president Al Gore, have all justified their commitment to cleantech as a moral and environmental imperative, one that has them set out to capture a multitrillion dollar energy market that is not-yet, but potentially green, as they search for innovative technologies that can transform life on this planet. These investors present themselves as world-makers first and foremost, entrepreneurial spirits who want to make an impact-beyond-capital. We will see, though, that this sort of creativity— for these investors, for this smart money—is all too often subsumed by the very real and unrelenting pressures of their fiduciary responsibilities, which demand that priority be placed first and foremost on maximizing profits.

Picking Winners

Evidence of these performative ambitions were peppered throughout my fieldwork, embodied in the clear sense that making an impact-beyond-capital can and must proceed by making an impact-as-capital. For example, during a brief keynote address at a networking and pitch event one evening, the presenter, a venture capitalist invested in cleantech, told the audience about his firm, its four funds, its belief in renewable energy, and the possibilities for renewable energy to make "massive efficiency gains." Only then, in an oddly expected about-face, did he switch gears from cleantech champion to stoic investor and bring home the point he was there to make: "In the end it's all about profit. For us, it's all about profit." With a staged grimace and furled brow, he added, "I don't like short-term thinking, but it's the way the market works." As a cleantech champion he could be excited about renewable energy, but as an investor he had to adhere to the temporalities of capital and be smart about tending to *its* needs. The exciting and "disruptive" clean technologies on display at this and every similar pitch event were very much for sale as investments. He understood this well, and made sure that the audience knew that he knew that in the end, the market had the final say.

After all of the presentations were complete, it was time to network. In the lobby of the law firm hosting the event I saw the presenter standing in the corner. A small gaggle of entrepreneurs and consultants vied for his attention, waiting their turn for a moment to sell him on whatever projects they were connected to. Precious minutes would pass before he would say, "let's be in touch." Business cards would then change hands—a ceremonial signal to the acolyte that it was time to move on.

Venture capitalists will tell you that they receive a veritable avalanche of proposals from startup companies: an inbox filled, every day, with the hopes, aspirations, and financial projections of new companies looking—sometimes desperately—for their A Round of funding. At networking events like the one I just described, it is always possible to spot the venture capitalists among the swarms of entrepreneurs, boutique investment bankers, and strategic consultants. They exude a very particular form of confidence that accompanies wealth, or at least the temporary control thereof. It's like watching empowered consumers browsing their options, nonplussed by the cacophony of sales pitches, special offers, limited deals, new and improved upgrades, certain that in time, and on their terms, a purchase will eventually be made.

The television show *Shark Tank* runs in a similar vein. Based on a Japanese program called *Dragon's Den*, *Shark Tank* debuted in the US in 2009. Each episode features a panel of "shark" investors vetting fundraising pitches from a series of entrepreneurs who will presumably invest their own money in the contestants' businesses if deemed worthy. This is not a typical game show—the prize is not a bundle of money or dream vacation awarded to winners on *Jeopardy* or *Wheel of Fortune*. Instead, *Shark Tank* offers the possibility of forming specific investment relationships with specific investors who will expect, as all investors do, a healthy return. The show's drama centers upon the excitement of seeing whether an entrepreneur is "investable." The sharks challenge each of the contestants: *show me why I should spend my money on you.* When a contestant wins, the investment market has spoken.

What does it mean when the market speaks? In fact, there are multiple markets at play here. Ultimately, for any business, the end-market matters most—consumers who will be willing to pay for a product or service. Without them, there is nothing. For this reason, neoliberal discourse hails the market as the ultimate arbiter, a computational assemblage able to identify the preferences of society better than any centralized or "command and control" state apparatus ever could.[10] Hence the common refrain, often recited in relation to cleantech innovation, is that the government should never be in the business of championing specific technologies, "picking winners" that could otherwise be far more efficiently vetted by the market.

Venture investors are ultimately trying to assess whether a startup will attract a customer base and capture a share of the market, but at the same time these investors are potential customers in a somewhat different market—one in which companies, as opposed to products and services, are bought and sold.[11] In this market, the sharks, or a very particular set of venture investors, are the consumers that matter, determining which startups get a chance to test the product market in the first place. In this investment market, the abstract and general intelligence attributed to markets more generally (via consumer demand) gives way to the more concrete and pointed intelligence of a small set of investors vetting specific companies, picking winners, and then actively helping those companies to succeed. This more concrete intelligence—not one of markets in general but of individual venture investors—is what many of the people I spoke with referred to as "smart money.".

The smarts of smart money boil down to two main capacities: the ability to make the right choices—as consumers in a marketplace of investments—and the ability to help companies succeed. Elsewhere, smart money typically refers to placing a good bet, perhaps based on superior (or inside) knowledge. In the startup world, however, the term *smart money* is specifically reserved for venture capitalists and other high-profile, experienced, and well-connected investors, investors with a range of skills and capacities to offer a startup something beyond just a pile of cash. *Smart money* characterizes the investment relationship one might have with a venture firm in contrast to the relationship one could expect from other, less helpful investors, such as the typical angel investor who may be a well-intentioned wealthy individual with little relevant experience or, even worse, the derided "3 F's": friends, family, and fools. It is all of the extra support, beyond "just" money, that sets venture capital apart as smart money. Understood in this way, smart money is somewhat different than the pure, abstract, and undifferentiated wealth most often associated with capital. It is instead a very specific, concrete wealth associated with specific concrete relationships with other investors, other business leaders, and other professionals who may or may not help a startup succeed.[12] The actors in this market are not only trying to pick winners, but are actively working to produce winners out of the companies that they've chosen to invest in.

The social scientists Michel Ferrary and Mark Granovetter outline five specific ways that venture capital firms contribute to the health—or in systems terms, the robustness—of an innovation ecosystem: selection, collective learning, embedding, signaling, and financing.[13] To summarize: in making their funding decisions, venture capitalists play a central role in selecting which companies will have a chance to succeed. They embed these companies within established business networks, provide guidance grounded in collective learning born of previous efforts, and signal to this network that the chosen startup has promise. Beyond their direct capacity to choose whether or not to fund a given company, venture capitalists are involved in a wide range of roles focused on their prowess navigating the startup world. They are well represented on panels presiding over pitch competitions, on deciding admission to startup accelerators and incubators, and even administering federal and state grant competitions. They also serve, as I've noted above, as celebrity investor-judges on shows like *Shark Tank*.

But venture capital is not the only "smart" investing community. In Karen Ho's ethnography of Wall Street investment banking, she details this other investment world's obsession with pedigree and intelligence.[14] Banks sell themselves to potential recruits as well as to potential clients as the repository of the smartest and brightest thinkers, as evidenced by the elite, Ivy League credentials that their employees boast. As I discussed in chapter 2, the cleantech entrepreneurial space defines itself in opposition to Wall Street and its narrow focus on maximizing profits. Yet the cult of intelligence still pervades this early-stage investment space. Here, it is centered upon venture capitalists as opposed to investment bankers, and pedigree has less to do with Ivy League diplomas than entrepreneurial experience. In fact, one of the greatest compliments in this early stage cleantech space is to call someone a *serial entrepreneur*. It is a way to describe someone as *entrepreneurial* in a strong, active sense—not just exuding the qualities of an entrepreneur, but having directly and regularly lived the experience.

Venture capitalists are, almost by definition, entrepreneurial. The classic narratives of successful venture capitalists portray heroic figures proving themselves as founders of their own startups before transitioning into their new roles as investors and advisers.[15] While access to money is important, hands-on experience with starting new companies (or the appearance thereof) is the credential that really matters, the one that qualifies venture capitalists to determine which startups are worth investing in. They are seen as hands-on investors, or as PZ explained, venture investing is "a more roll-up-your-sleeves kind of thing." They actively work with their portfolio companies, guiding them (and as we saw in chapter 3, training and disciplining them) through the commercialization process. This type of active management is lauded by economic sociologists and business scholars as an integral piece of what makes an innovation network function and succeed.[16] Their entrepreneurial experience, not only as founders of startups but as experienced advisors to other startups, affords venture capitalists a wealth of knowledge and connections that they can offer to the companies that they fund.

Venture Capital and Fiduciary Responsibility

As we saw in chapter 3, the autonomy, creativity, and risk taking of entrepreneurs only tells one half of the story. Just as a good, investable entrepreneur is one who is willing to be brought under control, trained, and disciplined by the mentorship of investors, something similar can be said of the investors themselves, who have their own set of obligations, or fiduciary responsibilities. A brief overview of how venture capital is structured helps clarify these obligations.

Venture capital is a special breed of institutionalized private equity investment capital, focused on high-risk investments in early-stage companies. Its 19th- and early 20th-century predecessor was a highly unorganized market for high-risk capital primarily comprising wealthy families and individuals, such as John D. Rockefeller, who invested in new industries as they saw fit. Only in the 1930s and 1940s did some of these investors begin hiring professional managers to seek out investments.[17] In 1946, the first two modern venture capital firms were founded: American Research and Development Corporation (ARDC) and J. H. Whitney & Company. Unlike professionally managed family wealth funds (which still operate today, and are referred to as *family offices*) the new venture firms raised money from a number of unrelated investors, organizing these pools of capital into separate legal entities defined by an agreement between limited partners (who provide money but have little say in the management and investment of that money) and general partners (who manage the investments on behalf of the limited partners, and receive both a management fee as well as a percentage of any profits generated).[18] Nearly all venture capital firms today use this partnership model, with the venture capital firms acting as general partners, managing the wealth of any number of limited partner investors. The general partners—the venture capitalists, or smart money—have a legal obligation (a fiduciary responsibility) to do everything they can to maximize the return on investment for their investors.[19]

The all-important concept of fiduciary responsibility stems from trust law. It names the legal obligations that a trustee owes to the beneficiaries of a trust. Prior to the 1970s, this responsibility was interpreted as a conservative requirement to shield a trust and its beneficiaries from financial risk, so as to preserve their wealth over the long term. Individual states would create a "legal list" of appropriately safe investments (such as treasury bills), and all trusts in that state would have to invest in some combination of these assets. The "legal list rule" eventually gave way to the "prudent man rule," which widened the gamut of potential investments that a trust could make to anything that could, individually and on its own merits, be considered a safe, wealth-preserving asset.[20]

It was not until 1979 that changes to the Employee Retirement Security Act (ERISA) began to reinterpret this rule in light of modern portfolio theory (and its analogue modern investment theory), which called for risk to be evaluated at the level of an entire portfolio, as opposed to each individual investment.[21] Far from protecting beneficiaries, the prudent man rule came to be seen as an encrusted legal prescription that limited investment opportunities for huge pools of capital—and even forced fiduciaries into imprudent, nondiversified money management strategies. As a historian of trust law and the prudent man rule, Bevis Longstreth writes, "Widely accepted lessons of modern economics push hard against these constraining notions of prudence. Indeed, it would not be an exaggeration to observe that today the prudent man rule…would virtually compel a fiduciary to act imprudently in terms of economic reality."[22]

The new interpretation of the prudent man rule, which would subsequently be codified as the prudent investor rule, allowed institutional investors managing large pools of money to allocate a percentage of their total portfolio to risky investments, so long as these investments were balanced with other more secure assets.[23] With the shift to the prudent investor rule, a legal prescription that was formerly defined as *wealth preservation* in opposition to speculation was reinterpreted as *wealth maximization* through diversified speculation. In the breakdown of this division between speculation and fiduciary responsibility, vast amounts of new capital—held in large public trusts—were made available to speculative markets such as venture capital. As a result, from the late 1970s on, venture capitalists increasingly answered primarily to institutional money managers with an unrelenting focus on short-term performance.[24]

These developments have shaped how today's institutionally funded venture capital typically works: Venture capital firms need to raise money to invest, so they look to high net-worth individuals and institutional investors (such as pension funds) to pledge money, which the venture firm can eventually count on receiving when they make a "capital call" to fund a specific investment. Typically the venture capitalists will earn "2 and 20," which means they receive a 2% management fee on the money raised, as well as a 20% performance bonus when and if investments realize a return.

The year that funding for a new fund closes and the partnership agreements are all signed determines a fund's "vintage." From an investor's standpoint the money committed to a VC fund is going to be spent over the course of the next two to five years, possibly longer for investments that need many rounds of follow-up financing. Then, as the fund matures, the limited partners will hope to see returns on their investment, over the next 6 to 10 years, and increasingly even longer. As with fine wine, one must be patient to enjoy the fruits of a good vintage, but not too patient; the longer limited partners must wait for a return, the lower the annualized rate of return will be, leaving investors less satisfied with their investment.[25] Venture investing is, in many ways, a race against time. As TW, the director of an entrepreneurial incubator describes, for a startup receiving venture capital funds, "it's like strapping a time bomb on your back." Entrepreneurs feel this pressure from the venture investors breathing down their necks, and the venture investors feel this pressure from the impatience of their limited partners.

The influence of these limited partners, or more abstractly the influence of the fiduciary responsibility that venture investors owe to their limited partners, trickles down throughout the cleantech innovation ecosystem. As we will see, it is accepted and rehearsed by investors and consultants alike as the way things are, an unquestionable force pulling all into its gravitational field.

Smart without Money

If Doerr's TED talk represents a front stage proclamation of the green spirit of capitalism, then the Funders Forum and other entrepreneurial pitch events where I conducted the bulk of my fieldwork might best be considered a backstage venue, where ideas are rehearsed and refined. Many of the Funders Forum attendees I spoke with explicitly described the event in this way, as a dress rehearsal space, a place for entrepreneurs to practice the art of the pitch. This was the stated focus of the event, with cleantech founders headlining each month's event with a practice investor pitch. However, these pitches were not the only form of rehearsing going on, or for that matter the most interesting. In a space like the Funders Forum, there were not a lot of investors and not a lot of money available to be invested. And yet, there was no shortage of money's "smarts." In other words, those who were present, despite their fiscal limitations, nonetheless embraced and rehearsed a venture capital script, attempting to display the specific sorts of smarts that make smart money so enticing.

In this context I prefer the term *rehearsal* to *performance*, as it focuses attention on the scripts that are being memorized, interpreted, reworked, and reproduced. Although "green and clean" scripts are important, and provide a legitimizing sense that cleantech as a project is about more than just making money, the scripts of smart money are equally important to this green spirit, as they insure that environmental efforts will be pursued through the overarching legitimacy of the market.

In this regard, it's worth asking why a television program like *Shark Tank* has been so popular. What is the allure? Each episode profiles three entrepreneurs who pitch their businesses to a panel of celebrity investors. When the show first aired, the panel comprised actual venture investors who were subsequently ousted in favor of celebrity-investors, such as the outspoken owner of the NBA's Dallas Mavericks, Mark Cuban, who could portray the smarts of smart money with more televisual flare. The show encourages its audience to play along with this performative version of venture investing, to become imaginary investors-by-proxy: "I'd invest in that one." "No chance I'd give that one money." The audience is put in a position to internalize, deploy, and even rework the logic of a shark. On *Shark Tank*, venture investing is rehearsed and repeated in a living room near you.

As a process, venture investing entails a diverse network of actors, from accountants and engineers helping to perform due diligence reviews, to lawyers structuring the specifics of shareholder agreements, to consultants helping broker deals. The specter of smart money permeates this entire field, extending beyond discrete nodes of this network to a complex entanglement of actors, including both formally important institutional actors (VC firms, law firms, etc.) as well as the harder-to-characterize remainder: all of the numerous individuals participating in less formal ways as self employed consultants, brokers, and agents, who must ultimately prove that that they are smart-without-money.

If we relate this idea of the "remainder" to a network model, these are the men and women who fill out all of the spaces between nodes, operating as independent agents of one sort of another. Instead of constituting their own nodes in any cohesive sense, they are more like a general medium, or connective tissue, permeating the complex system they are a part of.

In this cleantech space, the generic title of strategic consultant accounts for this very active remainder. Some actually refer to themselves that way. Others are broker-dealers, boutique investment bankers, entrepreneur coaches, former entrepreneurs, serial entrepreneurs, independent researchers or event planners, and likely they identify as more than one of these things. In one guise or another, these are (mostly) men looking for employment or consulting fees from startup companies, and/or finder's fees for connecting a startup with funding. These strategic consultants are the least formally connected and therefore the least formally powerful actors within the cleantech innovation ecosystem, operating in and through the margins of deal flows that they desperately want to be included in. And yet, despite this relative marginality, these strategic consultants exert a subtle, albeit diffuse, influence over the cleantech space, as they enact, perform and rehearse the culture of their market.

Events such as the Funders Forum are some of their most familiar terrain. They participate keenly, circulating among anxious entrepreneurs and disinterested investors, and hinting at their access not only to other inventors, entrepreneurs and investors but also to opportunities they could provide beyond the confines of the room. The strategic consultants very literally occupy the cleantech space. They are its commoners, its denizens: the rank-and-file white-collar workers of this green economy. They do not have the security or luxury of large amounts of investable venture capital at their disposal, which would make whatever they say or do, by extension, smart. Instead, they have to enact the intelligence of the cleantech market— of smart money—through their everyday rehearsals of and in the market they call home.

When I first arrived at the Funders Forum, it was an intimidating space filled with (mostly) men in suits; the majority of them seemed to already know one another. At one early session I attended, after serving myself fruit salad and a mini-bagel, I took a seat at the large conference table next to MF, a strategic consultant who introduced himself as a boutique investment banker. At the time, I didn't know what made an investment bank "boutique." The whole industry conjured images of Wall Street investors who acted as if they were masters of the universe, and MF did not disappoint. He seamlessly shifted our conversation—which happened to be about resource extraction in Africa—into tales of the large-scale deals that he regularly handled; deals in the hundreds of millions. As he explained, project finance rarely went smaller.

Coming from an academic context where finances are significantly more austere, it was hard not to be impressed, and as I realize now, that was the intent: wow the uninitiated with large numbers, and the ease with which they are discussed. Over the years I attended the forum, I saw this same performance enacted numerous times, each with a unique twist, but always with the same intended effect.

As I would eventually find out, the "boutique" qualifying MF's investment banking credentials meant (in this particular case) that he was a self-employed consultant, scouring events such as the Funders Forum for potential deals and leads on future work.[26] When you first meet strategic consultants like MF, it is easy to get taken in by their boasts—the ease with which they talk about those small $5 million raises and $200 million equity financing rounds—astronomical figures in an average person's day-to-day realities—making it all the more impressive when they seem so at home with these sums. But the more you see consultants like MF, hear them, watch them operate, watch them tell the same stories, make the same quips, offer the same pithy (albeit boilerplate) advice, the more you realize how much of an act the whole thing is—and how just under the surface, events such as the Funders Forum are filled with precariously financed people vying for access to other people's money, other people's projects, and other people's inventions. The last time I saw MF, I watched as he introduced himself to a first-time Funders Forum attendee as a partner in an impressive sounding cleantech hedge fund. Having already interviewed the fund's creator, I knew that this fund had been gutted by the 2008 financial crisis, held a worthless portfolio of struggling cleantech firms, and had no investable capital to speak of at all.

Strategic consultants like MF go to great lengths to prove to investors, entrepreneurs, and each other that despite their limited funds, they are nonetheless just as smart as smart money (and therefore worth employing). Strategic consultants want to turn their excitement and their self-assessed ability to navigate the tumultuous waters of funding, bankers, investments, raises, convertible debt, bond issues, and so on, into a legitimate, value-added contribution to early stage cleantech projects—and to be rightfully compensated for their efforts.

Without the backing of actual capital available to be invested, strategic consultants would often compensate by presenting an appearance that such capital is well within their grasp, just as it has been in the past. Boasting of large deals and past success, like MF did, is a common modus operandi. So is promising to make connections and insisting that they are just "between projects" at the moment. For some, this is certainly the case. But for many this in-between moment can be quite long, and it can become a project in and of itself. Unfortunately, it may not be a project they are well compensated for. Almost all of the strategic consultants I spoke with either had other means to support themselves—such as a spouse with a regular income or savings from a past profession—or were in a relatively precarious economic position. The range is staggering. One consultant offered to meet me over expensive tapas (his treat, he insisted). Another asked if I could pay for his pasta lunch; he was so broke, he explained, that he had to ride a bicycle around the city instead of using the subway ("I suppose at least that's green," he told me, sheepishly). All told, there are few regularly paying gigs for these consultants in the cleantech space. They will occasionally receive a finder's fee for helping connect an investor with a startup (serving in the role of a broker-dealer), and on some occasions will receive an upfront retainer for helping a startup seek out investors. A few have been able to make money writing research reports, and one was paid to provide translation services for French startups. But the challenge they all face is structured into their chosen project: it is difficult to extract money from a startup that is still scraping by as it tries to raise money. Strategic consultants, who felt that their expertise was being unduly devalued, regularly voiced this frustration. "You have to spend money to raise money," I was told, repeatedly.

So what exactly should one spend money on? What exactly are these skills, these services that are being devalued? Strategic consultants boast of having important connections to important people—just like venture capitalists—only for the strategic consultants, many of their important connections are to investors, including venture capitalists. The consultants are confident that they can get clients exclusive audiences with investors who are ready to cut a check, so long as they like what they see and hear. This leads then to the second set of skills that the consultants claim to offer— the ability to help improve a startup's pitch; to make a startup look and sound like an attractive investment opportunity, a smart investment for smart money.

If we see this market as a speaking community,[27] a set of individuals with a shared language that both forms and is formed by those using this language to communicate with one another, then the strategic consultants often act as the community's elocution specialists, coaching the uninitiated—which could include almost anyone: academics like myself, journalists, fellow consultants, entrepreneurs, and even at times investors—on how to speak with smart money (for entrepreneurs) and how to speak as smart money (for everyone else).

A number of the consultants who attended the Funders Forum breakfasts were entrepreneurial mentors and coaches, participating in programs affiliated with either a cleantech business plan competition (such as the Cleantech Open), with one of the regional cleantech incubators, or with NYSERDA. NYSERDA, in partnership with a number of local tech incubators, runs an entrepreneur in residence (EIR) program to pair startups with consultants who can help them develop their business. (This was the same program that the inventor-entrepreneur FP was enrolled in, in which his EIR mentor advised him to take her class called "How to be an entrepreneur.")

In this specific instance, NYSERDA pays for a predetermined amount of the consultant's time. After these hours are exhausted, the consultant and startup are free to negotiate a new arrangement, which in the best of circumstances might result in the consultant being offered a position on the company's board of advisers, or even on their board of directors (assuming they've made it that far in their development).

The Cleantech Open, another common broker of free consulting services, matches multiple mentors with competing startups. Unlike the NYSERDA program, mentors must donate their labor to participate. This is in exchange—as someone involved in the process explains to me—for "exposure" and "a great chance to meet new people." The coaches agree to work without pay for the duration of the contest, after which they may try to become a paid consultant with the startup they've advised, or even try to get involved in some more formal capacity, as a service provider, an employee, director, or adviser.

Entrepreneurial coaching is not limited to these formal arrangements, and at the Funders Forum, most sessions entailed a fair dose of this service, provided free of charge. PC, a strategic consultant who had previously been involved in the grease hauling industry, was one of the most unabashed purveyors of such pro bono services. He spent most of his career as a salesman in one capacity or another, and now, as a strategic consultant, he quickly settled in to the idea of selling himself. When in attendance, PC would regularly interrupt an entrepreneur's pitch with questions meant to demonstrate his excitement for the project and the potential services he could provide to help the startup realize its vision. At times, it felt like PC was presenting to the presenting entrepreneurs, more than they were presenting to him, as he interrupted their pitch with "questions" that simply provided an opening for him to explain how they should market their product or build their business.

At one session I attended with PC, there was a particularly unpolished pitch presentation made by an utterly unprepared presenter from rural Pennsylvania who was somewhat frozen by stage fright and the pressure of his first time presenting in "the big city." PC, along with a few other attendees, attempted to salvage the session by turning it into a more interactive workshop. They quizzed the presenter about what he wanted to sell, where and to whom, how his project might be structured as a business, and what sorts of funding this might entail. At one point, PC decided to offer the presenter—and by extension the entire room—some general advice. "Before you come to these things you should watch *Shark Tank* for a week." The whole room responded with an approving chuckle, prompting him to reiterate the point three more times over the remainder of the session. Without any vocal shark investors in the room, PC took it upon himself to insure that this room, and this presenter, understood what smart money expects.

One of the most poignant rehearsals of this smart-without-money intelligence came during an interview with KL, a retired company man looking at cleantech for one last go at the business world before retirement. He had been laid off from his position as an insurance claims manager in 2006, and after his outplacement counseling he decided to try out solar financing. At each breakfast, during the round of introductions, he would provide the same well-rehearsed introduction, "KL, solar financial analyst." He attended Funders Forum breakfasts as a way to secure a deal in his new profession. During our conversation told me:

KL: I've talked the walk a lot of times and educated a lot of people but I haven't made a lot of money from it.
JG: Is there a time limit for you?
KL: I think I've passed it.

So far, it had not been going well for him. He'd come to the breakfast for exposure, to meet some of the players who are actively making things happen. He'd come to the Funders Forum to get a taste and a view of the inside, where deals are happening, where money flows and where people are employed. (This was the same space critiqued for its lack of deal flow by others who are more plugged in—but perceptions still matter.)

After one of the breakfasts we walked over to Grand Central Station and found a place at a table in the downstairs seating area—no meal, no drinks— just KL's empty disposable Poland Spring water bottle between the two of us. As I tried to understand KL's involvement with cleantech, he rehearsed his commitment to the market. He demanded speedy returns for his non-existent clients: "Show me the money now—I want 30% now, not bonds or feed in tariffs or money five years out—I want the sure thing tomorrow!" He pounded his fist on the table, proclaiming his business logic, the logic of this market that he so desperately wanted to be part of.

KL spoke the truth of his market and of his deals without having either. He spoke the language, personality, and perspective of money—even though he had none of his own to invest. He told me that he would buy an electric car (Nissan Leaf) if he could afford it. He was looking to get some fire-sale solar panels for his farm—where he doesn't really grow much of anything for the market, but he could. It is a gentlemen's farm, his fallback. If all else fails, he can invest in his farm—he'll finance his own deals if he can't finance someone else's—even if, as he disparagingly acknowledged, he'd ultimately be doing it out of heart.

KL's rehearsal was not uncommon. Many strategic consultants would recite for me their sense of how things should work—what entrepreneurs should and shouldn't do, how investors should and shouldn't make investments. This was simply the general medium through which they interacted, with me and with each other. It was the common currency that connected them to one another and to the cleantech startups pitching each month, something you could break the ice with, strike up a new conversation with, and make small talk about—as if you were simply commenting on the weather.

Animating and structuring this well-rehearsed script was the seemingly natural and unavoidable laws of the market, those fiduciary responsibilities to maximize returns that ultimately determine just how "smart" smart money actually is.

Black Hole Capital

With all of this work to be smart-like-money at the Funders Forum, it became clear that venture capital, or smart money, has an active presence in its absence. This absence takes a number of forms. It is the market—that mystical and all-knowing collective intellect—whose reaction to newly proposed commodities must be anticipated but never supplanted. It is the investors who strategic consultants, brokers, and boutique investment bankers promise to know, networks and rolodex's that will lead to private meetings, subsequent pitches and those all-too-elusive checks, signed and delivered. And to extend this one step further, it is the investors' investors, the actual repositories of capital that venture capitalists speak for, the "other people" whose money they bear, and to whom they are bound by a legal responsibility to deliver adequate returns.

KD, a Funders Forum attendee and the director of climate change–related operations in the New York office of a major global financial institution, helped me make sense of these absences via analogy. "Capital," he explained, "essentially functions like a black hole." At the center of a black hole lies a singularity, an infinitely small, infinitely massive point generating a gravitational force powerful enough to keep just about everything—including light—from escaping its grasp. KD described the gravitational field surrounding the singularity as a black hole's "basin of attraction." Anything that falls into this basin of attraction will inevitably collapse into the singularity. "Capital also has a basin of attraction," he told me, "and its pull is profitability." Once something becomes profitable, it is automatically pulled into capital's basin of attraction. Therefore, he continued, if we want something like cleantech to succeed, all we have to do is make it profitable, and capital will take care of the rest. According to KD then, the capital being invested in cleantech—other people's money managed by venture investors looking for their "2 and 20" returns—is part of the singularity at the heart of capital's universe; an absent center pulling all that reaches the event horizon into its undifferentiated mass, forcing all to succumb to its seemingly irresistible gravitational pull.

Naturalized conceptions of the profit motive harken back to the classics of political economy, from John Locke to Jeremy Bentham.[28] Through the narratives they weave, capital and the markets operating in its name cease to be understood as discrete historical entities, and instead take on the aura of a universal, abstract law of nature, or in KD's case, a gravitational force.[29] While it can be enticing to envision heroic entrepreneurs and (entrepreneurial) investors forging ahead in the creation of a new, green economy, free to take risks and to radically transform the world as we know it, there remain less visible and less triumphant forms of discipline, training entrepreneurial creativity into specific paths or, we might now say, pulling it into capital's basin of attraction.

Moishe Postone refers to this seemingly unquestionable, apparently natural force of market imperatives as *abstract domination*. Not the domination of particular individuals or institutions, but a more general and pervasive field of force. He writes: "Social domination in capitalism does not, on its most fundamental level, consist in the domination of people by other people, but in the domination of people by abstract social structures that people themselves constitute."[30] Naturalized concepts of capital, greed, and profit, seen as little more than expressions of ingrained human nature, provide justification and legitimization for those who wish to accept these social relations as given. Instead of abstract domination, they are more likely to offer accounts of social Darwinism and an implicit conception of a Hobbesian world of competitive struggle.[31]

Conversely, popular attempts to address this domination can easily fall back upon simple narratives pitting evil capitalists against an innocent, virtuous working class. As the argument goes, it is the bosses and the financiers, the wealthy 1%, who dominate the rest of us, hence returning to a conception of concrete and direct domination of some people over other people, and allowing for "bad apple" narratives that hold out faith for technocratic adjustments to rid capitalism of its worst inequalities and injustices.[32]

This is where a Keynesian critique of liberal capitalism often surfaces, understood as an effort to mitigate the worst and most destabilizing effects of capitalism through state-led, technocratic adjustments focused on ameliorating short-term challenges to political and economic stability.[33] As the political economist Geoff Mann explains, this results in an effort to enact revolution without revolutionaries: to temper the worst of capital's effects by insuring that people's basic necessities of life (materially and socially) are adequately provided. With respect to environmental concerns, "green Keynesianism" has focused on myriad state-led efforts across the globe to support the development of cleantech and most centrally, renewable energy generation. From Germany's path-breaking subsidies for distributed renewable energy generation, to international efforts to forge binding targets for CO_2 emissions, much of what we might consider green Keynesianism has been centered upon a wide range of technocratic, state-led strategies to manage and mitigate the worst effects that global capitalism now seems to incontrovertibly have upon the biosphere. The goal is not to eradicate these effects (just as, Mann describes, Keynes and Keynesianism more broadly never considered ending poverty to be a realistic goal), but to keep them within acceptable limits, such as the aim to stay within a 1.5-degree Celsius temperature rise as established in the Paris Accords.[34]

Planetary improvement offers another variant of a revolution without revolutionaries. Cleantech's non-disruptive disruptions target individual aspects of an environmentally unsustainable system (the bad apples) that can be singled out for improvement, without calling into question the more pervasive patterns, or underlying social relationships that have given rise to the system in need of improvement in the first place. The only problems worth solving become those that someone is willing to pay for—whether Richard Branson offering a reward for more efficient jet fuels or Bill Gates attempting to fund a clean and abundant source of nuclear energy. And the only clean technologies that appear worthy of investment—not just financially but emotionally and culturally as well—are those voiced by the imaginaries of smart money. These will inevitably be technologies that provide cleaner (so long as they are cheaper) alternatives without disrupting the throughput of commodities—the flow of capital and the cheap natures supporting that capital—upon which profitable business depends.

Along these lines, it is telling that self-driving vehicles are being couched as a successful dimension of cleantech innovation. The Cleantech Group lists "transportation services" as a growing dimension of cleantech, and in Paul Hawken's edited collection of essays, *Drawdown*, autonomous vehicles are listed as a future technology with potentially positive environmental effects.[35] Some in the automobile industry fear that autonomous vehicles will shift consumers away from purchasing individually owned vehicles, as they will enable a dramatic expansion of ride-sharing services like Uber, one of the companies heavily invested in developing these technologies. $7 billion out of the $8.7 billion that Uber earns in fares is paid out to its drivers, making it easy to see the company's incentive to develop driverless technology.[36] Perhaps this is just speculation, but the idea that autonomous driving technology is going to somehow reverse the deeply engrained culture of privatized automobility that has been developing for over a century seems hard to accept. Car sales are more likely to be affected by stagnant wages, mounting debt and the massive unemployment inevitably precipitated by replacing drivers with machines. Furthermore, the idea that autonomous vehicles represent an environmental improvement over their human-piloted counterparts seems incredibly suspect, especially when the material and energetic costs of producing and maintaining these sophisticated computer systems are taken into account. But there is money in autonomous vehicles, so they must therefore be good and (potentially) green.

Along these lines, let's consider the social power that the "smarts" of smart money conveys. At a basic level, money affords its possessor access to any and all things that money can buy. It imbues respect upon those in its possession, and makes their opinions seem that much more significant and worthy of note. Successful businesspersons, the thinking goes, must be intelligent, ingenious, and deserving of their success. In his 1844 man-uscripts, Marx offered a somewhat humorous reflection on "the basis of money's omnipotence."[37] Speaking as a hypothetical capitalist (and it is hard not to read a certain real estate tycoon turned president into these lines) he explained:

I am a wicked, dishonest, unscrupulous and stupid individual, but money is respect-ed, and so also is its owner. Money is the highest good, and consequently its owner is also good. ... I am mindless, but if money is the true mind of all things, how can its owner be mindless? What is more, he can buy clever people for himself, and is not he who has power over clever people more clever than them?[38]

As Marx explains, money has the power to turn wishes and desires conjured by the imaginations of those in its possession into real, material effects, making it *appear* to be a "truly creative power." But the true test of money's intelligence is whether those without money repeat money's message, confirming that it is not just the inchoate musings of rich fools, but also the sensible intelligence of well-established thinkers. This is what shifts our account of planetary improvement away from an isolated focus on specific wealthy individuals (the 1%)—who purchase their power and prestige like Richard Branson or, like John Doerr, advocate for a cleantech revolution—to an account of a more general and diffuse intelligence, a common sense, shared and rehearsed.

To the extent that these figures and this smart money shape a collective sense of what can and should be possible, then our social creativity is, as KD anticipates, captured by capital's gravitational pull, spiraling toward a singularity that flattens all natures—including all ideas—into potential cap-ital. This black hole is not just a metaphor for market competition operat-ing in some abstract economic sphere—it is itself an active nature-making phenomenon whose exaltation masks the production of a very destabilized and increasingly undesirable nature. This is the nature that many are now naming as the anthropocene or as Jason Moore and others would have it, the capitalocene, a nature produced by capital, by this abstract domination, and by unflinching recourse to "the way markets work."[39]

Acidifying oceans, mass extinctions, and melting arctic ice are cast as problems *out there*, aspects of an external nature that must be fixed, secured, repaired, or saved, in part through the adoption of cleaner technologies. At the same time *in here*, in the flows of commodities and natures into which these clean technologies will ultimately be incorporated, there is only market society—cultures taken for granted and ways of life meant (by whatever means necessary) to be sustained. Climate destabilization and environmental destruction is becoming increasingly difficult to deny or ignore, and yet, as we will continue to explore in chapter 5, capital's nature-making is precisely what cannot, must not be acknowledged—at least not without risk of jeopardizing the coherence or "ontological security" provided by cleantech and the green spirit of capitalism.

And so, as we will see in the next chapter, planetary improvement depends upon managing a separation between the laws of the market discussed herein—making an impact-as-capital—and aspirations of saving the planet or making an impact-beyond-capital. By keeping these two imperatives connected and at the same time, functionally insulated from one another, one "green" (environmental benefit) is able to serve as a legitimization of capitalism while another "green" (capital, money, profit) is able to legitimize cleantech and business environmentalism, without the contradictions between the two ever serving to delegitimize the whole affair.

5 Green Capital Denial: Insulating the Green Spirit from Capital

As part of my research, I went to visit OG, a young venture capitalist working in the cleantech space. When I arrived at his building, the elevator deposited me in a reception area shared by a number of separate firms, but there was no receptionist in sight. I was unclear what to do—the room was cluttered with disorganized furniture, almost like an office supply warehouse. So I sat in what most closely resembled a waiting area, and waited. I overheard conversation coming from the adjacent conference room; a group of young men engaged in passionate discussion were detailing the mechanics of something I imagined to be an innovative new technology. I strained my ears to listen, to get a sense of what they were talking about. As it turned out, one of them was explaining to the others a complicated drinking game he had played the night before.

Before long, a well-dressed man in his 30s got off the elevator, noticed me sitting there, and introduced himself. It was OG. He apologized for being late and took me back to his office. A mix of artwork and ephemera hung on his walls: prints, photographs, and old maps—one depicting the geographic area of Hindustan and another of Greece. As OG would explain—and he was not the only person to tell me such a tale—he first solidified his commitment to social entrepreneurship during the time he traveled as an entrepreneur on projects in the developing world. It's why he finds himself now working "at the intersection of impact and business."

While speaking about his investments in cleantech, I noticed a row of wooden cubbyholes above his desk. Most held binders and loose papers, but in two of them were books, piled about eight high. To the far right was a compilation of the same green capitalism texts stacked on my own desk—titles such as *Plan B, Earth: The Sequel,* and *Strategies for a Green Economy.*[1] At a pause in our conversation, I tried to ask about them. "Tell me about the books you have up there."

OG turned for a moment toward the shelf and then energetically complied, lifting out of his chair to pull down the books he assumed I was referring to—only he chose the other pile, which included management texts such as Eric Ries's *The Lean Startup* and Steve Blank's *The Startup Owner's Manual.*[2] He set them on the desk between us and began leafing through a few as he looked for specific pages and charts to show me, excitedly reciting his favorite pearls of wisdom from each. He explained that he tells all the founders he meets with to read these books.

After indulging him for a while, I asked about the other pile of books, the one at the far end of the shelf. He turned to see what I was talking about. "Oh, those. Those are the big-picture books, the inspiration, the books about opportunity."

They never made it out of their cubby.

The "Big Picture" in Perspective

Those books that OG set aside, the ones about "opportunity" and the "big picture" really are just that. They present visions of a radically transformed world, one that leaves behind the toxic legacies of the present, along with the irrationalities of industrial capitalism, paving the way for a new world in which social and environmental problems have largely been solved. Had OG opened up Fred Krupp and Miriam Horn's *Earth: The Sequel*, we would have found on the first page a triumphant statement of systemic transformation. Its first line reads: "A revolution is on the horizon: a wholesale transformation of the world economy and the way people live."[3] This revolution is sure to "create the great fortunes of the twenty-first century," but even more importantly, the authors say, it depends on confronting climate change. Along these lines, their book surveys promising clean technologies, profiling "inventors who will stabilize our climate, generate enormous economic growth, and save the planet."[4]

Inspiring, big-picture ideas like these play an important role in planetary improvement. They provide an affective force animating cleantech and grounding a largely unspoken, largely unsubstantiated promise of the wide-scale social and environmental transformations that make cleantech—as a project—worth pursuing. Moreover, it is important to again recognize that they do so with reference to an undifferentiated "planet" in need of "salvation". This entrepreneurial savior complex, in which it is taken for granted that one's chosen forms of salvation, or improvement, are universally desired and unquestionably good, supports the feeling that this work is truly "making an impact".[5]

But as we saw in chapter 2, it can be dangerous to overly embrace these sort of world-making ambitions, out of fear of being labeled an idealistic (and therefore ineffective) environmentalist. The prophets of Silicon Valley may have license to cry for their daughter's future and extol a wholesale crusade to save the planet, but down in the trenches, where early stage startups are fighting for survival, in order to attract funding from venture capitalists like OG, any such planetary aspirations must be carefully managed. Managed, but not categorically dismissed: without these aspirational visions there would be nothing separating cleantech from all of the boring industries that make up the wasteful economy in need of improvement. And so, the promise that cleantech can and will deliver more than "mere" profits has to be kept at a distance, simultaneously gestured at and kept at bay.

Accomplishing this requires work, developing and internalizing a number of strategies for reconciling and redirecting the inherent and often contradictory tensions between "saving the planet" and creating the great fortunes of the 21st century. In this chapter I explore some of the ways that these contradictions are managed through the construction and maintenance of four conceptual—and practical—separations. The first is a separation between the personal and the professional; this provides space for people to express environmental concerns without getting in the way of the business of commercializing new technologies. The second pits doing against thinking, offering a way to acknowledge the need to think about environmental problems, while insulating these thoughts from any more immediate pressure to get things done. The third separation involves the creation of a division between the abstract and the concrete; climate change and other such holistic or systemic concerns are considered too abstract and therefore less operational than more concrete assessments of specific problems that can be directly targeted and incrementally improved. The final separation is between now and later; the present is a time for getting concrete things done, while larger-scale or more ambitious transformations can be set off into the future, as possibilities for some other time that is unlikely to ever arrive. These four separations allow one to gesture vaguely toward world-making ambitions, while at the same time insulating these visions from the day-to-day business activities and short term financial projections that ultimately govern the economics of the cleantech space. Or, to return to KD's black hole metaphor from chapter 4, as capital pulls everything into its gravitational hold, into its "basin of attraction," not everything can collapse into the singularity; there must be some trace of an animating spirit that is allowed to remain, some sense that what is at stake is more than "just" profits, more than "just" capital.

After reviewing these overlapping separations, each of which attempt to normalize a distinction between political and economic spheres of activity, we will see how they provide the conceptual armature that grounds planetary improvement, offering a way of seeing the world as not-yet clean, and of seeing the future as a forever receding horizon of possibility whose radical transformation remains safely insulated from the status quo, which can therefore persist in perpetuity. Planetary improvement provides a temporality of progress that defers wholesale transformations to a not-yet, a never-yet that is too abstract and too cerebral to directly impact the here and now, where incremental improvements are pursued as the only pragmatic alternative.

But improving what exactly? The planet? Nature? The environment? While these are the implied goals of the cleantech project, and of making an impact-beyond-capital, the relationship between these goals and the smaller, more proximate steps meant to achieve them are reduced to a narrative of technological progress, where cleaner and greener technologies will gradually improve the functioning of discrete aspects of industrial society until somehow we've arrived at a still industrial (and still capitalist) future that is no longer environmentally destabilizing. Here the true, unspoken answer comes to the fore—what is being improved (or sustained, or greened, or cleaned) is not so much "the planet" as it is a very distinct mode of inhabiting this planet, of making natures and organizing lives (human and nonhuman alike). In other words, the persistence of the very sociotechnical processes that are actually known to be causing our environmental problems—an expanding, global system of resource-intensive production and consumption, animated by an insatiable thirst for economic growth—is accepted as a natural, unquestionable condition of working in the cleantech space.

Along these lines, we could ask: Is cleantech really clean? As I found throughout my research, this question was difficult to broach, as it cut too deeply against the grain of everything that cleantech promised, against the visions that made cleantech a project worthy of emotional investment. The unwillingness to engage with this question revealed a deliberate and socially constructed process of not-knowing—knowing what we don't want to know—that parallels what the environmental sociologist Kari Norgaard calls everyday climate change denial.[6]

Throughout this chapter, I will use Norgaard's work, *Living in Denial*, to make sense of the specific forms of everyday denial that ground planetary improvement as a way of seeing, and therefore also as a way of not-seeing. In this work, Norgaard explains how people in a Norwegian ski town came to manage their contradictory relationship with climate change.[7] People Norgaard met during her research were largely aware of the problems that climate change posed to the world as well as to their immediate culture and livelihood. They were also aware of the ways in which their national wealth (largely derived from fossil fuel extraction) was implicated in these transformations, and therefore needed to find ways to insulate their everyday lives from this uncomfortable reality. Norgaard calls this a "double reality," one clearly expressed by a young teacher she interviewed who explained: "We live in one way, and we think in another. We learn to think in parallel. It's a skill, an art of living."[8] Norgaard sees this as a form of denial—not an absence or lack of knowledge, but an absence of deeming it necessary or possible to act upon this knowledge. Climate change denial, understood in this way, is less about knowledge deficiencies than it is about the management of painful and uncomfortable ideas—knowing that one would prefer not to know. Or, as the case may be, that it's in one's best interest (individually at least) not to know.

Many of the subtle cultural norms and strategies of denial that Norgaard identifies in her ethnographic work can be seen in the cleantech space. These strategies amount to what I will call *green capital denial*; a denial of the vast gulf between cleantech, as it has been defined and pursued, and any aspirations of saving the planet or creating an ecologically viable, socio-ecological metabolism. This version of "double reality" might be framed accordingly: we make business (profitable) in one way, we think about environmental problems in another.

Separating the Personal from the Professional

Let's begin with this most basic question: Is cleantech clean? During interviews I would ask my participants whether, at a macro scale, cleantech represented a positive environmental benefit. This question, in the numerous iterations it took, turned out to be a very productive failure. Initial responses were often confused at the seeming tautology of my query—as if I had just asked whether blue was blue. The question suggested that we might share a deeply uncomfortable sense of systemic instability, holistic problems, and the related shortcomings of the cleanteh project; knowledge that those with whom I spoke knew that they did not want to know. On a few occasions the responses ranged from somewhat patronizing to dismissive to downright hostile. I was told that I made no sense asking such questions, and that in fact doing so threatened my credibility. One person accused me of sounding like a communist. Most however, took a less aggressive tack, simply reinterpreting the question to a scale that made sense to them—individual consumer choice. After discussing some of the limitations of cleantech and its ability to tackle the formidable global environmental problems that we face, I would ask. "Is cleantech clean?" And from those who were willing to entertain the question, the most common response was, "I recycle!"

Many of the people I spoke with readily found ways to be environmentally conscientious in their everyday lives outside of the workplace, and saw this as a first, unquestionable step toward meaningful environmental and cultural transformation. We all do what we can. FG offers a paradigmatic example.

FG: I'm certainly worried about [climate change]—I am certainly worried about it for my kid's future, my kid's kids' future.... I don't know at the end of the day who I believe or what I believe, all I know is that it seems to me that a lot of the things we're doing are not helpful or good for the environment. Moving forward, would I like to change that? Absolutely! And if I have an opportunity to do something even myself to change that—absolutely I would. Recycling is a good example.... I was one of the first ones in my neighborhood to say this is a great idea. Absolutely, I'm going to recycle anything and everything I possibly can.

FG turned focus away from his professional life in the cleantech space and toward his private life, where he takes personal responsibility to recycle his waste. Regardless of whether cleantech is clean, he assured me that *he* is clean, at least as evidenced by this one specific consumer behavior.

It is not surprising that recycling was commonly offered as a mark of responsible environmental stewardship. Environmental sociologist Samantha MacBride argues that since the 1970s recycling (as opposed to reduction and reuse) has been promoted by the manufacturers of disposable goods as a means of deflecting attention away from more costly—and effective—waste management strategies.[9] Heather Rogers, in her book *Gone Tomorrow*, explains that after World War II the beverage industry rapidly moved away from refillable glass bottles toward disposable aluminum (and eventually plastic) containers.[10] This resulted in a very visible litter problem, and disposable beverage containers became a prime target for environmentalists, who pushed for a return to refillable containers. In response, a beverage industry front group, Keep America Beautiful, launched a national lobbying campaign to defend disposable containers. Their messaging diverted attention away from any issues of inefficient production and focused instead on improper consumption, introducing the now infamous "litterbug" to the American public.[11] The problem was not with disposable containers, they explained, but with irresponsible consumers not doing their part to dispose of these containers properly. As recycling became an increasingly viable alternative, it became the proper means of disposal—and remains to this day an appropriately progressive environmental response to the excesses of consumer waste.[12]

Without disparaging all recycling efforts and those committed to them, it is worth considering some of the ways in which a focus on consumer recycling programs systematically avoids broader questions: about an economy structured around single-use goods, for instance, or about scrutiny of the producer-generated waste streams that dwarf the consumer wastes being mitigated. Or what about a history of alternative approaches to commodity provisioning rendered unfeasible, irrational, or simply anathema to the American way of life?[13]

And so I should not have been surprised when interviewees responded to my question about the cleanliness of cleantech by explaining their own personal commitments to environmental stewardship: I recycle. Two respondents even asked me if I remembered the memorable Keep America Beautiful commercial, in which a Native American (played by the actor, Oscar Cody, who is actually the son of Sicilian immigrants) cried for his homeland, distraught at the litter that had not been properly thrown away.

Throughout my fieldwork there was a clear sense that personal environmental commitments had to remain separate from the realities of professional responsibilities. After speaking at length with RG, an energy storage specialist working as a research analyst, about the need for a carbon tax, the unsustainability of corporate industrialism, and other related themes, he told me:

RG: Oh yeah, I love that stuff. I'm like very...I have my ideals. But when I'm working, I try to be very conservative and skeptical. But I have my own ideals.

Business is not a place for environmental ideals, and cleantech is ultimately a business. Accordingly, saving the planet may be a virtuous goal, but as we saw earlier, telling people that that's what you're doing isn't always the best strategy. Let's revisit a response from the exchange I had with EN, in which I asked him if he considered his startup to be cleantech:

EN: Saving the world is a noble cause; no one would argue with that. When speaking with my team I can tell them, "Hey, let's make a difference." However, when I go to speak with potential clients, I have to put on a different hat.

As EN makes clear, audience matters. Employees can be rallied with visions of environmental change and making a difference, but clients and investors can be repelled by these same visions. In other words, it's smart not to mix economics and politics. The latter is to be reserved for personal efforts, either private opinions expressed with friends or motivational discussions with one's team. But when it comes to economic relationships, whether with bosses, clients, or investors, environmental concerns cannot be allowed to intercede.

Separating Doing from Thinking

For the people I spoke with, one of the most satisfying aspects of working in the cleantech space was the sense that it was a world comprised of doers and makers. Thinking about big-picture ideas of social transformation may have a place, but not if it ends up distracting from the immediate goal of getting things done, which usually means seeing technologies commercialized and sold. In other words, thinking about making an impact-beyond-capital can easily become an impediment to doing something now, to being a successful entrepreneur and making an impact-as-capital.

When I first met PC, he'd come to the Funders Forum as a sector expert, slated to comment on a waste-to-energy project being pitched that month.

At the time, he worked for a large waste management firm, in its environmental division. PC attended four Funders Forum sessions in early 2012 and then disappeared for a year. He reemerged in 2013. Reintroducing himself to familiar faces after his hiatus, he would say, "You might remember me as the waste guy." Now, he explained, he was in business for himself as a strategic consultant, ready and willing to help cleantech startups succeed.

PC cut his teeth in the portable toilet business before moving into grease hauling; then, as a strategic consultant, he began to look into cleantech for new opportunities. (When we met for an interview, he was still in the grease disposal business.) During our conversation, he offered me a variation on the Haudenosaunee Nation's seventh-generation principle, the idea that decisions should be made with respect to the well-being of future generations. While most interpret this as a precautionary call to think carefully about the long-term consequences of an action, PC flipped it into a justification for incremental technological advance: gains may appear slow, but perhaps in seven generations we will have really gotten somewhere.[14] "If you ever step back and look at things in time," he explained, we will have to accept the fact that "we're not there yet, we might not be there in my lifetime, we might be there in your kids' lifetime."

PC continued on to explain that there was no reason to push recklessly toward big-picture visions of transformation. Achieving long-term goals of large-scale environmental transformation required patience, and a willingness to make progress one step at a time. I asked PC where these long-term goals should come from, and he answered: "I think on this topic we need to create a think-tank—maybe it's already out there—but something like that."

As he elaborated, I came to realize that PC was not all that interested in pursuing the concept of the "think tank." (If you remember from chapter 4, he prefers to operate in the "shark tank" of venture investing.) When I tried to push him to explain his environmental perspective, as well as his understanding of the relationship between capitalism and the environment, he told me:

PC: I have not spent any time at all thinking about these things, sitting back and thinking what is the meaning of the environment—I believe it is meaningful, and I'm trying to work on bringing some of that meaning to life in what I do every day. I probably don't have the talent or the patience to actually worry about it. It's very wonderful for an educational thing, but for business guys doing a thousand things, they don't ever resonate with that stuff, that's for the think-tank people.

For PC the think tank was somewhat akin to the large grease tanks his fleet hauled around the metro region, a receptacle for unwanted waste-thought, a sanitary disposal system for long-term thinking. The think tank was the "away" to which we are to send ideas that won't facilitate getting things done here and now. I don't mean to imply that he was entirely dismissive of environmental thought or the need to work toward broader environmental transformation. In fact, the following month, PC would put his arm around me at a Funders Forum session and proclaim to the room how important our work was, how essential it was for us to show the world that sustainability was profitable, by actually *doing* the work of commercializing cleantech. *Doing* was not meant as an alternative to or antithesis of thinking about environmental sustainability, but was, for PC, its most pragmatic expression.

JQ is an entrepreneur whose one-man energy-savings company (ESCO) does energy-efficiency retrofits for small institutions. His own frustration with environmental activists' lack of "doing" was similar to PC's "boots on the ground" response. For JQ it was all about having the right tools to do the job. He worked his way toward that point as we spoke.

JQ: People are absolutely correct when they say let's cut carbon with the use of renewable energy.... They say that a lot, they go to a lot of meetings. Okay good—but no one's doing it!

To make his point, JQ suggests that we think about a hypothetical conference focused on "being green." What would happen if we checked the trunk of each participant's car as they arrived, to see what sorts of tools they were working with. In JQ's trunk you would find a lot of useful tools, he explained, referring to himself in the third person: "He's got a ladder in there, cables, a couple of motors that he is investigating, fractional horsepower VFD's, pulleys, wrenches ... he gets to go in." But on the other hand,

JQ: If I open your trunk and I see a bunch of flyers saying "get green!" we're going to turn you around and tell you to go back and do something. The word is *do*. D-O.

There was no questioning JQ's commitment to making a positive environmental impact. He was one of the people who explained his entry into the field as a need to follow his heart, and to escape a professional life that centered on marketing "boring" consumer goods. For him though, as with PC and his disparaged think tanks, he was deeply frustrated with people who would talk about the need for environmental changes without "doing" anything about it.

JQ's selective definition of productive activity raises a pertinent point. Why try to change people's minds with flyers when you can actually make the institutions they occupy more energy efficient? He cast political work (symbolized by making flyers) as an immaterial effort to change the way people think, but not as an alternative way to transform the same sorts of institutions that he strives to improve through physical (albeit incremental) energy-efficiency gains. For JQ, political efforts like making flyers, in which thinking displaces doing, are completely ineffectual. He explained, "I think that the people preaching just preach louder and louder, hoping that if you preach louder it will happen." JQ labeled these sorts of people "do-gooders," and saw them as often causing more harm than good.

For JQ, those preaching environmental concerns are disconnected from the "doing" of the green economy, which he saw as the only space where change can happen. He explained that do-gooders focus on "prayer and motivation" and at best accomplished a cathartic clearing out of any discomfort that might actually encourage people to challenge the status quo. In fact, Andrew Szasz, in his book *Shopping Our Way to Safety*, offers a similar critique of eco-consumerism as primarily a guilt-assuaging activity; making some people feel better, greener, and cleaner in their personal consumption practices, but doing little to address systemic transformation.[15] However, it remains somewhat unclear as to whether JQ's alternative, of actively making small incremental changes, is actually any different. Are these energy retrofits any less of a guilt-assuaging activity, meant to make all those involved feel a modicum of personal satisfaction for the attempts they are making to help "save the planet"?

PC and JQ both spent hours speaking to me for this research—by far the two longest interviews I conducted. Their generosity and passion was unquestionable—and their subtle critique of my work, as thinking as opposed to doing, was hard to miss. With our pie long finished, our coffee mugs empty, and the bill already paid, PC asked me a frank question about my research: Why was I operating in his proverbial think tank as opposed to joining in the fight more directly, with my boots on the ground?

PC: Look, we all know that once you get done with your research you'll come to the same conclusion: we have to do something tomorrow. So what's the purpose?"

This question has stayed with me ever since. I may be critical of PC's approach to environmental change, but can I justifiably see my own work as somehow more efficacious? "What's the purpose?" Initially his question caught me off guard, but were I to answer now, I would say: The purpose is not to deny the need to get things done, as soon as possible, but to call into question what things we prioritize getting done, and what sorts of futures these things will help create. What if, for instance, the most immediate tasks at hand are about building a different sort of power, not the sort generated by solar panels and wind turbines, but political power, the kind of power that can eventually challenge the social relations underlying this energetically and materially intensive status quo?

Separating the Abstract from the Concrete

While for some the big picture was relegated to a space of personal ideals or professional pontificators, for others it was dismissed as too abstract. This relates directly to the boots-on-the-ground ethos I described above; PC's critique of think tanks and JQ's critique of do-gooders were both very much critiques of what they perceived to be abstract thought displacing concrete action. As we will see, it is important to acknowledge just how fluid these categories can be. What makes something abstract can often be less about some inner nature of the idea in question that the way people choose to make sense of it.

For instance, I found that climate change—broadly understood—was a regularly disparaged abstraction. Climate change, I was told, was too big and too all encompassing to be understood in any meaningfully concrete terms. Understanding climate change this way allowed for a clever form of climate pragmatism to take hold, in which the effects of climate change could be acknowledged while the process itself remained under question. In most of the cleantech spaces I spent time in, directly addressing climate change science in anything more than a cursory way was considered socially unacceptable. An example of this separation between abstract and concrete interpretations of climate change came during an interview with KD, the director of climate change advising at a major financial institution. Considering his job title and institutional affiliation, I asked KD how climate change was affecting the investment strategies at his institution. His response was both dismissive and evasive, as if he had to keep the conversation from heading somewhere he wasn't willing to go.

KD: First, take climate change off the table, because there is no such thing as climate change. Whether such a thing as climate change does or doesn't exist, maybe, but there is no such thing as climate change.

Seeing that I was a bit confused, he continued to explain that the problem with an idea like climate change is that it is too vague and too abstract—it does not map to any specific measurable variables that can be integrated into quantitative calculations of investment risk.[16] Precipitation patterns, severe storms, and other discrete weather events are worth discussing, as well as the status of specific resources such as soil and phosphorous, but not climate change. Climate change was just an umbrella category, too general to be meaningful to the investors that he advised. Its effects are real, concrete, and measurable, but climate change itself is abstract, general, and unpredictable. For KD, the concept of climate change only became legible by first being broken down into specific variables with direct economic implications. If his team can't operationalize a climatological effect by inserting it into their risk-assessment algorithms, then it is too vague to be meaningful.

Jessica Dempsey, in her book *Enterprising Nature*, explores a similar dynamic in the realm of biodiversity conservation. Dempsey observes ecologists working with economists to make their concerns legible to those with power, a process that entails grossly simplifying their ecological understanding of biodiversity threats so as to accommodate assessment tools grounded by quantifiable models. While these conservation scientists pragmatically accept these "translations," as a means of "amplifying" their concerns, what actually ends up being measured (and therefore potentially managed) is something qualitatively different than their initial and primary concern. Dempsey shows how holistic (and therefore abstract) understandings of the socioecological complexities of protecting biodiversity writ large are displaced by concrete measures focusing on the cost–benefit analysis of protecting specific lands and specific species from discrete threats.[17]

This process, whether in the case of cleantech or biodiversity loss, is not born out of any ignorance of more holistic analyses of systemic complexity. It arises from a tactical decision to put this knowledge aside, to know that for the time being, and in order to keep one's seat at the table, it is best not to know. In this way, these translations can be understood as a form of what Norgaard calls everyday denial. In Norgaard's work, silence regarding climate change was in part attributed to a process of scalar distancing.[18] Her interviewees explain to her that climate change is a planetary and national issue, as opposed to something that can be proactively engaged on a local level. By contrast, in the cleantech space there is no aversion to engaging with large, even planetary scale problems; as we saw previously, making an impact requires one to eschew small-scale, lifestyle entrepreneurialism and to think—or act—big. And yet climate change was, just as in Norgaard's experience, a conversation nonstarter, not because it represented an issue that was too big, but because it represented an issue that was too abstract. A number of important studies have shown how many people cease to focus on climate change once they realize that no easy solutions are available, and that they have difficulty discussing climate change because it appears to them as a problem without any real or tangible solutions.[19] Accordingly, general or systemic environmental concerns were considered too abstract to be meaningful for everyday cleantech business practices or for the immediate commercial needs, goals, and strategies of whatever entrepreneurial project might be under discussion.

As a result, climate change or other large-scale environmental issues rarely emerged during my interactions in the cleantech space. Even the most liberal and progressive participants adhered to this unwritten rule. For those who might otherwise be willing to talk about such things—in their personal life of course—silence around these issues was justified as a pragmatic means of inclusion; it is always possible that one of the people involved in a deal is a climate skeptic; best avoid the subject altogether. PL explained his working relationship with a conservative Texas investor, one who also happened to be a climate skeptic.

PL: We agree on energy security, we agree on energy efficiency, and we don't agree on anything else—but at least we can talk.

The success of cleantech was often attributed to the way in which it could appeal to arguments for both energy security and environmental security. Nothing bad can come of reducing our nation's ecological footprint: if you don't believe that anthropogenic climate change is a threat, you likely do believe that reliance upon Middle Eastern oil is a threat. So, as one of the venture capitalists I spoke with explained, either way cleantech is "a good thing for the Earth or a good thing for America depending on how you view that prior conversation." By conflating these two—America (by which he clearly meant the US specifically) and the Earth—the interests of this one globally dominant nation are subtly presented as universal interests. From this imperial vantage point, saving the planet and saving America (along with the American way of life) may as well be the same project.[20]

To demonstrate the arbitrary and socially constructed nature of what is considered concrete, and what is considered abstract, consider the implications of focusing on energy security as opposed to climate change: potential terrorists are real, and lurking everywhere. Yet all these other potentialities—glacial melt, blown-out offshore oil rigs, droughts, desertification, methane off-gassing of Siberian permafrost, ocean acidification—somehow all of these only cohere into a sense of climate change that is too abstract to act upon and against. Why might this be? The scholar Rob Nixon discusses these environmental concerns as slow violence, "calamities that patiently dispense their devastation while remaining outside…the purview of a spectacle-driven corporate media." Of course, the threats of slow violence are only "abstract" to those people fortunate enough not to already be concretely experiencing their effects.[21] In this regard, abstraction represents a socially constructed ability to not see something as a concrete reality. Perhaps then, climate change is seen as too abstract because there are no singular and spectacular characters—like the Islamic terrorist—to vilify and no general populations (of potential terrorists) to rally against?

But what if there actually are a wide range of characters that could be singled out as a threat to the global environment, and these villains are, in fact, the imperial "us," a population determined to maintain patterns of industrialization, consumption, waste, and privilege that enable life in centers of relative wealth and privilege, and whose existence depends upon a global network of production and extraction kept largely out of sight and out of mind?[22] In other words, is it possible that the one process which can never be questioned—the one enemy that will always be too abstract—may be inextricably wedded to the one process that we should actually be saving the planet from? Instead of questioning this imperial subject position and its material and energetic footprint in aggregate, as a complex systemic assemblage or socionatural force, planetary improvement allows it to be reduced to individual actors, making individual consumption and disposal decisions—billions of people from of all walks of life who can potentially say, "I recycle."[23]

This is not to suggest that all human productive activity is inherently or equally problematic in so far as it exhausts energetic and material resources, but that some forms of activity, and some ways of living, exhaust far more resources than others—and it is not hard to discern which ones they are. An Oxfam report published in the lead up to the 2015 United Nations Climate Change Conference (COP21) found that the richest tenth of the world's population accounts for half of global carbon dioxide equivalent (CO_2e)

emissions.[24] And in another study, Lucas Chancel and Thomas Picketty found that in terms of a consumption-based estimate of per capita CO_2e emissions, the richest 1% globally generate 14% of annual emissions (while the poorest 50% account for 13% of the total).[25] North Americans generate 3.6 times the world average of CO_2e per year, which is over 17 times greater than a sustainable average (calculated as the amount of emissions that might have a chance to keep the world below the 2-degree Celsius threshold). Further, they estimate that the top 1% of individuals in the US alone generate 318 tons of CO_2e per year, which is over 240 times greater than this sustainable level.

Auden Schendler, the director of sustainability at Aspen Resorts, provides a good example of how the careful management and production of abstractions can help to avoid dealing with the seemingly straightforward implications of these sorts of studies. In his text, *Getting Green Done,* he addresses the seeming hypocrisy of trying to make a green ski resort and is well aware that skiing, by its very nature, is an incredibly energy-intensive activity, far more so than snowshoeing or bird watching. And yet, he defends his resort, arguing that we cannot simply demand that Aspen should not exist, because the next logical step would be to outlaw the Marriot, then the Motel 6, and then all forms of Western vacation accommodations, which are, when measured against the "slums outside of Mexico City and Bangladesh," still relatively wasteful.[26]

The fact is that when you spend a dollar in this planetary economy, a portion of that dollar creates more climate-changing carbon emissions. So *we're* not going to solve this problem by picking and choosing what businesses are acceptable.[27]

Since "we" are all guilty to one extent or another, the very possibility of choosing between different products and forms of service provisioning is untenable. Instead, Schendler argues, all businesses need to be improved and therefore maintained, including Aspen:

Certainly Aspen's lifestyle is lavish. But then, so is the entire US lifestyle. . . . So what do we do? Close down Aspen, then close down the United States? . . . In the absence of God-like qualities of judgment over the world, we have to fix the whole system, not pick and choose.[28]

This is a fascinating moment in Schendler's text, where he comes face to face with a tremendously uncomfortable idea, one that he absolutely knows he does not want to know: Aspen is a resource-intensive luxury, at the apogee of a US economy that is filled with a wide range of incredibly resource-intensive luxuries. Any political judgments—such as those, for instance, substantiated by Chancel and Piketty's research—must therefore be too abstract, too "god-like," to be taken seriously when it comes to determining "what *we* should do." Here, the forceful and unspoken privilege of this imperial "we" should ring clear. For Schendler, only decisions made within a market framework, where consumers are allowed to follow their individual desires and preferences, should be allowed to pick and choose between lifestyles and their socionatural effects. This is the "whole system" that Schendler asks us to fix—not a complex world-system that is coming undone by the global networks of production and extraction supporting the excesses of fossil-fueled lives, but instead a world comprised of millions of interlocking businesses, each of which—including Aspen—can and should be individually targeted for improvement. Schendler instructs us to resign ourselves to the pragmatism of getting things done here and now, to concrete, market-based solutions that incrementally improve each business, no matter how extravagant or wasteful it may be, while avoiding any "god-like" assessments of systemic unsustainability.

The naturalized worldview of planetary improvement provides a very carefully constructed context within which problems can be identified and solutions proposed. It creates a cognitive space in which conversation—and therefore imagination—is bound, a concrete ground of actually possible discussions about actually possible efforts to make an impact, insulated from the abstract ether of planetary-scale concerns such as climate change or the global flows of capital and wealth. As we've seen, the latter are best left to the think tanks and technocratic experts—so long as they stay out of way. Planetary improvement does not require one to categorically dismiss abstract, big-picture environmental concerns. Instead they are set aside, or as we will now come to see, set into the future, a future that cleantech can appear to be working toward, while remaining largely unencumbered by its implications.

Separating Now from Later

MX, a cleantech investor-turned-academic, tried to explain to me the difference between the big-picture ideas promoted in green capitalism texts and the cleantech market. The former gazes into an idealized future, he tells me, whereas the latter focuses more narrowly on present market possibilities.

As far as MX was concerned, this did not make the two incompatible, it merely represented a "shift in focal length." Both, he argued, aim in the same direction, and share the same goals and the same vision, only they approach these things from very different perspectives. One focuses on present-day market opportunities, immediate and rapid returns on investment (ROI), and generous and expedited internal rates of return (IRR), while the other looks further out, at the possible implications of all this enterprise, as it somehow aggregates into a greener, cleaner economy.

Norgaard argues that the characterization of climate change as too-abstract of an issue "reflects a disjuncture between the local sense of time and place…and the sense of time and place that would be needed to conceptualize climate change for it to seem 'real.'"[32] Accordingly, she finds a decided focus on the local as a means of spatially and conceptually distancing everyday public discourses from issues such as climate change. In the cleantech space, however, it is time more so than space that serves as the primary axis of distancing. Instead of a space of local action, we have a time of short-term decision-making, immediate market opportunities, and quick returns on investments. It is a temporal parochialism of sorts, which sets apart long-term planning and the problems that such thinking might address. Concerns of this sort are either left to the think tanks, or at best, to the inspirational imaginary of visionary entrepreneurs, cast in no less triumphant terms then as the makers of our future. Here I heard a common refrain. When a "good" technology fails it is "ahead of its time," or as MX would say, "we're just not there yet." MX would follow up by explaining that we are getting there, that we are working toward these future realities, and that was what was so exciting about the accelerating pace of cleantech innovation.

Occasionally, these contrasting focal lengths made their way directly into an entrepreneur's pitch. For instance, at one of the Funders Forum meetings an entrepreneur representing an energy storage technology presented a slide that began with the headline "The World Needs Better Batteries" and illustrated three reasons why: "To be truly mobile, to transform transportation, to improve the environment." In this case, the battery technology being presented targeted the consumer durables market—cell phones and other high-tech gadgets. Their aim was not to make these batteries smaller or more environmentally responsible, but to provide small hand-held devices with greater capacity per charge. They were essentially aiming to supercharge a device that has only recently become a staple of mass consumer economy. How would their technology eventually, ideally, "improve the environment"? I tried to find out after the presentation. The entrepreneur explained to me that initially, these batteries would target cell phones, but beyond this, it was possible that their technology could support electric vehicles and other large-scale energy storage needs. If and when that occurred, he explained to me, then the technology would be able to make a difference environmentally.

There is an unspoken function that aspirational environmental visions like these play in socially and ecologically legitimizing clean technologies, distinguishing them from just another extension of "boring" industries and the wasteful economy that they support. This longest focal length, which essentially promises to "improve the planet," has little bearing on the actual business case being made about the actual product being developed. It simply provides a vague moral and environmental promise that the technology is ultimately oriented toward a larger, shared vision of planetary improvement. So goes the idealistic promise that makes cleantech clean, and therefore worth pursuing. I might be making cell phone batteries today, but tomorrow I'll be making electric vehicles, and after that, a totally transformed world.

Only very late in my research did I begin to realize that cleantech is not just legitimized by promises of a cleaner future, but that in a broader context, cleantech itself serves as a promise, offering a sense that all technologies, all industries, all technosocial processes can and should "go green." Cleantech not only represents a set of technological fixes to environmental problems, but it also serves as a promise that technological fixes are possible, and that they can begin to chip away at a solution to ecological problems at a planetary scale.

This became clear to me when I met PH at a cocktail party. PH had worked his whole life on Wall Street, until being made redundant a few years prior, in the wake of the 2008 financial collapse. Since then he had been taking care of his young children, and was only recently starting to get back to work, by founding a boutique investment fund focused on the energy sector. This was his first foray into the energy sector, he told me. It was a shift motivated by his environmentalism, he explained, even though, he sheepishly continued, he was currently investing primarily in dirty energy. "It's just the reality of how things work." I asked him if this included any fracking companies. He told me, "I'm embarrassed to say that I am—I'm not proud of it—but I'm invested in fossil fuels."

We kept talking. I told him about my research, a topic he latched onto—fascinated, and also clearly excited to change the subject. He asked me whether I'd come across anything promising in the cleantech space. Sure, there are some great projects, I told him, summarizing a few of my favorite presentations from the Funders Forum. I asked him whether he sees a path back into his environmentalism with what he's currently doing. He shrugged, clearly chagrined, and said, "I hope so."

I want to understand how it is that someone can become a self-proclaimed "dirty energy" investor, and still tell me that he got into the field because of his environmentalism. As we kept talking, PH explained to me that he was excited about the promise of clean technologies, and specifically the possibility of producing meaningful quantities of clean energy, which will translate, he continued, into the possibility, if not the inevitability, that one day soon, companies like Exxon Mobil—the "dirty" companies that he invests in—will be renewable energy companies. It may not be enough to allay all of his ethical concerns, but you can start to see the connections that PH was making. Cleantech was not merely a subsector of the broader energy economy—it also operated more generally as a field of force, a sanitizing agent for the entirety of the energy sector. All energy producers could potentially become clean energy producers. Even the most "dirty" of energy investments were, according to this logic, not-yet clean. In fact, a number of clean technologies that I came across actually aimed to clean up fossil fuel production—capturing wasted (flared) natural gas on drilling rigs for instance, or fuel additives that enabled oil furnaces to burn cleaner and more efficiently. As Joseph Lacob, a partner in the venture capital firm Kleiner Perkins, explained in a 2007 *New York Times* article, "'If we can improve the efficiencies of the oil and gas exploration, in some ways that's a green message as well."[33]

Low-Hanging Fruit and the Persistence of Waste

Taken all together, these separations begin to delineate a coherent way of seeing the world that is not-yet, but potentially improved through incremental improvements in technologically mediated efficiencies. Major environmental transformations, along with political views that might assert their necessity and potential trajectory, are both acknowledged and neutered—named, and then set off into an abstract future that is all thought, no action. Meanwhile very specific types of thought and the people empowered to do this thinking—in the here and now of making an impact—are taken for granted, insofar as they exhibit the pragmatic expediency of working within (and for) the market.

As a result of needing to remain "realistic," radical ambitions for systemic transformation are deferred in favor of incremental changes to the status quo, which are expected to accumulate piecemeal until we arrive at a truly transformational end point, sometime in an unspecified future. The best way to achieve these possible green futures, as I was regularly told, is by getting concrete things done, here and now. PC explained this as a need to capture the "low-hanging fruit," as opposed to pushing toward the more ambitious, harder to reach prizes to be saved for sometime later (read: never). This fruit metaphor is important. Think about a fruit tree—there is not much qualitative difference between the fruit growing near the top or the bottom of a tree—it is all relatively the same. Likewise, planetary improvers presume that all changes are ultimately incremental changes, and all incremental changes are relatively exchangeable, like a basket of fruit that one can gradually fill. This speaks to a general way in which environmental problems are broken up into consumable, interchangeable parts, so that individual clean technologies can be proposed as viable—even preferred—solutions.

For instance, one entrepreneur presenting at the Funders Forum pitched a technology that captured low temperature waste heat from industrial production sites, converting it into electricity. In this presentation, the company's founder showed a slide with a huge plume of white steam coming out of an industrial facility's exhaust pipe—representing the wasted heat that their technology would turn into energy. With a press of the clicker, the white plume was overlaid with an image of money. It was now a cloud of gold coins and $100 bills, cueing the presenter to explain that their technology is "100% green." Capturing industrial waste-heat and transforming it into energy can only be seen as "100% green" if we take this waste-stream as a discrete problem with no relation to the broader process causing the heat in the first place. In order for an industrial process to be "cleaned"—in this case their target was large paper mills—it must first be segmented into individual parts, each of which can serve as a potential target for cleantech innovation. With the source of this exhaust taken for granted, all that is left to be done is cleaning and greening specific parts of an otherwise unchanged (still "dirty") system.

Maneuvers such as this allow planetary improvers to avoid questioning the broader industrial flows of energy, materials, goods and wealth that their technological solutions augment. Instead they fall back upon a mechanistic worldview in which socioecological complexity is reduced to a system of discrete, interchangeable parts. As Leo Marx, a historian of technology, has explained, missing is any sense that technologies are part of complex sociotechnical systems—and, we might add, sociotechnical-*environmental* systems.[34] This can easily tend toward the reification of technology: the car, the computer, the battery, energy. Leo Marx calls this a "phantom objectivity" that masks the discrete relations of power and property which determine how these technologies are produced, used, distributed, and further developed.[35] Technologies take on a "seemingly magical power of historical agency" and appear as the most practical, and certainly the most economically viable, means of achieving social and political goals. As a result, this technological fetish "relieves the citizenry of onerous decision-making obligations and intensifies their gathering sense of political impotence."[36]

Accordingly, the cleantech imaginary suggests that we need not bother attempting to have political conversations about which technologies and which innovations or social practices are best to pursue, but only economic conversations about which are most likely to succeed in the market. To attempt the former would be to risk imposing an abstract, "god-like" capacity upon the otherwise rational and calculating world of measurable effects and consumer preferences. What results then, is a sense that politics happens somewhere else, sometime else, so long as it doesn't mess with the project at hand: incrementally cleaning an utterly and persistently dirty world.

As we saw with PH, clean technologies can become visible symbols of promise for the future—repositories of an abstract ideal of green progress, or ecological modernity. In this worldview, where parts have replaced the whole, the arrow of time pushes a perpetual present into the marginally improved future. There is a uni-directionality to this relationship: dirty or wasteful processes can potentially be cleaned, but clean technologies can never be potentially dirtied, or rendered wasteful by their deployment within otherwise unsustainable industrial processes. To take a very basic example, household electricity consumption can be cleansed or greened with the introduction of solar panels (or even with an agreement to use an energy provider who has an agreement to purchase some energy from renewable sources somewhere else), but solar panels or renewable energy more broadly can never be "dirtied" by its deployment within a suburban landscape of intensive resource use and consumer excesses. No one ever says "I dirtied my solar panels by using them to power my 98-inch plasma TV so my cat can watch YouTube videos of birds," and no corporate PR office ever worries that they've "dirtied" their firm's solar panels by placing them on the roof of the corporate headquarters for a business committed to some form of energy intensive-production or consumption. These narratives only work in the other direction: the whole world is not-yet, but potentially clean.

What follows from this conception of a world that is not-yet clean is an unfortunate and unacknowledged dependency that runs to the core of the cleantech project. In order to make clean technologies profitable, there must be a dirty world, forever in need of cleansing. Cleantech actually depends upon the persistence of a waste-producing, environmentally devastating, industrial economy that provides so many pieces of "low-hanging fruit" to incrementally tackle. As environmental sociologist David Pellow and his colleagues show, urban recycling provides a good example of how technologies that reproduce the waste stream (such as recycling) are privileged over technologies that challenge its very existence.[37] Here we run up against the limits of cleantech as an approach to environmental politics. If the only problems worth addressing are the low-hanging fruit of actionable, incremental change, it is not as if the high-hanging fruit will ever get any lower—it will remain qualitatively distinct, unactionable, and too abstract, too ahead of our time, now and forever.

In this way, planetary improvement refracts its visions of possible futures through a perpetual present that is endlessly improved but never superseded; a world that is potentially, but not-yet green. It can offer endless improvements in automobile efficiency—hybrids, electrics, and even self-driving capabilities—but very little discussion of transitioning beyond car culture (along with the mass consumerism it supports) into a system that relies upon public transportation or even a spatial reconfiguration of how we live on this urbanized planet. While scholars such as Erik Swyngedouw discuss the apocalyptic character of climate change politics as a sense that ultimate devastation is always a future possibility that will somehow never arrive, cleantech and its market solutions have a similarly apocalyptic character—their visions of large-scale transformation are forever receding into a future that while inevitable, can never actually be upon us.[38] Hence, as mentioned above, we are faced with a pressing need—politically—to think what it means to assert an alternative temporality, one in which the future is not contained and neutralized by an impenetrable horizon of deferred possibility and incremental gains, and where pragmatic efforts to get our boots on the ground don't unwittingly leave us marching lockstep to defend the status quo.

Denial

What if—as the overwhelming climatological evidence increasingly suggests—we are truly running out of time? Does this mean planetary improvement's incrementalism must be sped up? Infused with more resources and more state support? Or, does it mean that we need to reconsider how this cleantech "project" can and should be conceived in the first place? Or that we should be asking, *is cleantech clean?* To conclude this chapter I return once more to a discussion of denial. As we've already established, climate change is not being denied in the cleantech space—far from it—but there is another form of denial taking place. In other words, denial is inherent in the inability to ask, directly, if it may be the case that capitalism just can't provide adequate solutions for its own dirty practices. At a microeconomic level, one in which parts replace the whole and incrementalism reigns, cleantech innovations provide real, meaningful solutions to the very discrete, isolated problems that each individual technology or service intends to address. Meanwhile, planetary improvement appears impervious to any macroeconomic reflections on the system-level effects of such technologies and their commercialization in and through existing (and expanding) circuits of capital accumulation. What I found in the cleantech space then was not climate change denial (though there is some of that) but first and foremost green capital denial.

As Norgaard suggests, this need not be a question of greed, inhumanity, or stupidity, but might also be seen as a compassionate and morally thought-out commitment to bettering the world.[39] The fact that we can talk about climate change denial is predicated upon a shared sense that there "really" is a problem called climate change, and that it needs to be immediately addressed. What would it look like then, if we also agreed that there "really" is another problem called capitalism—planetary in scale, equally abstract, all-encompassing, and seemingly unstoppable—that also must be immediately addressed? This is a challenging proposition. Questioning capital is a threat to the "ontological security"[40] that undergirds our culture, and is difficult to broach without red-baiting aspersions meant to silence the inquiry.

The scholar John Immerwahr argues that people feel apathetic toward climate change when they do not believe that anything can be done.[41] The same can be said about capitalism; to the extent that first-world consumption patterns and the industries supporting them are unquestionably an environmental problem, those for whom everyday life is defined by these sociotechnical-environmental systems will be hard-pressed to validate any "solutions" that question the material and energetic throughputs underwriting their privilege. Meanwhile, cleantech promises readily available, attainable, (and fundable) solutions to planetary problems. In this regard, it offers an opportune outlet for those with environmental concerns (and environmental privileges), those unsatisfied with apathetic resignation and who want to do something, but maybe not anything, to make an impact. The problem—as Eliasoph, Norgaard, and Swyngedouw all suggest—is that social transformation, and with it *political* action, is off the table. This leads both to the cultures of everyday climate denial and apathy that Norgaard recounts, as well as the green capital denial of cleantech and its new green spirit of capitalism.

Individualism may, as Norgaard and others argue, disempower people politically in the face of climate change, giving them a sense that there is nowhere to turn. In a culture where business is far and away the most socially valorized form of collective action, and where civic activity is denigrated or imagined to be all but extinct,[42] it is not hard to see why these market-based strategies offer such an enticing way to make one's impact upon the world. As we've seen, it is not that visions of significant environmental transformations are entirely absent from cleantech entrepreneurship, but that they are disciplined to stay in their place, so that planetary improvers can exert a moral righteousness and aspirational orientation toward "saving the planet" without ever having these environmental commitments impede the everyday flows of capital that they depend upon. The *green* of this green spirit of capitalism must always be contained, set off in a spatiotemporal register where it can serve as an ever-receding future possibility, an abstract promise, a directionality, and an orientation toward a future that has not yet arrived, set off from a world that will forever be not-yet green.

Even the most revolutionary future-scenarios can be safely regarded as possible outcomes of present activities and relationships that we are simply "not ready for" or that are "ahead of their time." There is no sense, as Norgaard suggests, that what we may actually need is a qualitatively different time, one that is no longer beholden to the short-term market logic that envisions all actionable problems to be local and all possible solutions to be incremental;[43] a time that allows, as Walter Benjamin wrote almost a century ago, for us to take "a tiger's leap into the future."[44]

6 Whose Planet? Whose Technology? Green Keynesianism and the Privileges of Petromodernity

In 2015 I attended a small climate-justice rally protesting plans to build the Atlantic Coast Pipeline. The event was coordinated by student activists in collaboration with one of Virginia's largest environmental organizations. The march weaved its way to the plaza in front of the corporate headquarters of the regional power company, Dominion Energy, where student leaders shared a bullhorn and led the crowd in call-and-response chants. At one point, a young woman began:

"What do we want?"
"Clean energy!"
"When do we want it?"
"Now!"

I've attended numerous climate rallies where "clean energy" has been promoted as a core, largely unqualified demand. Throughout the mainstream environmental movement, the fight *against* dirty energy extends seamlessly into a fight *for* its presumed opposite. In this fight, technologies like solar power and wind turbines serve as ubiquitous markers of an alternative to the fossil fuel economy. As symbols of present and future possibility, these technologies are presented as unassailably good, clean, and desirable—proof that a more benign modernity can and should be possible.

Along these lines, there may be some reason to be optimistic. Advances in solar and wind power have dropped the cost of electricity produced by these technologies to record lows, and renewable energy is being installed relatively rapidly across the globe: so much so that in the spring of 2016, reports circulated that Portugal went four full days powered entirely by renewable energy.[1] In 2017, Pilita Clark of the *Financial Times* offered an optimistic survey of the state of global cleantech development, noting the "disruptive impact of green energy on companies—and entire industries—around the world." Focusing on technologies such as wind and solar power, as well as the turn toward electric vehicle development, Clark reports that the global transition toward clean power has finally begun to accelerate at a pace that no experts could have predicted. Leaders from the fossil fuel industry, she writes, are finally on notice that a new "industrial revolution" is underway.[2]

Though the first round of venture capital investments in cleantech largely fell flat, losing over half of the $25 billion invested between 2006 and 2011, this does not seem to deter a new round of optimists.[3] As the investor Bruce Huber admits, "I have been early twice in financing the low-carbon energy transition ... but we feel it's third time lucky."[4] Many renewable energy technologies no longer need government subsidies to boost their competitiveness or help them access markets, but can finally stand on their own solid economic fundamentals, offering the same basic commodity—energy—at lower prices than incumbent fossil fuels.

However, as Clark points out, "None of this means the problem of climate change has been solved, or that fossil fuels will vanish in the near future." For the past 25 years, oil, coal, and gas have accounted for around 86% of global energy capacity, and coal and gas-fired power plants are still being built worldwide. Wind and solar only accounted for 4.4% of total electricity generation in 2015 and electric vehicles sales represented 0.9% of the global total.[5] As of 2013 renewables still only accounted for 19.1% of global final energy consumption, and while this share continues to increase (new additions to global energy generation are 58.5% renewables), so too does the total amount of energy generated and used.[6]

The challenge then is not just to get new clean energy production online, but also to address the more daunting challenge of getting fossil fuel infrastructure offline. Adding renewable energy sources into an ever growing energy mix doesn't actually do much to change the core aspects of what makes the underlying economy so unsustainable in the first place. Clark cites the energy scholar Vaclav Smil, who reminds us that even if electricity generation can transition to renewables, there remains "a dearth of green alternatives to the fossil fuels used to make steel, cement or plastics."[7] In other words, even with the massive amounts of renewable energy infrastructure coming online, the centrality of fossil fuels to the production and reproduction of global capitalism is not really under any imminent threat.

In his *Utopia of Rules,* David Graeber reflects on the stultifying effects that neoliberal bureaucracy has on imaginative life. He argues that whereas early Soviet science pursued "poetic technologies" that creatively pushed towards fantastic visions of possible futures, Western capitalism and the US in particular has largely responded with "bureaucratic technologies" that tinker around the edges of the status quo, "telling its citizens that we simply can no longer contemplate grandiose enterprises, even if—as the current environmental crisis suggests—the fate of the earth depends on it."[7] If neoliberal thought is buttressed by the belief that there is no alternative to the capitalist economy, the same holds for a similarly stubborn belief in the inevitability of the technologies that have come to define this capitalist system.

Graeber contrasts a conservative impetus to "be realistic," which entails a tacit acceptance of prevailing structures of power (along with the coercive force backing them), with a "political ontology of the imagination," which foregrounds the human capacity to first imagine what one then sets out to create. Capitalism stifles this latter, imaginative orientation towards the world, provoking Graeber to end his essay with an exortation: "Break free of the dead hand of the hedge fund managers and the CEOs.... Free our fantasies from the screens in which such men have imprisoned them, to let our imaginations once again become a material force in human history."[9]

As we have seen, cleantech exists in the contradictory space between these two impulses, on the one hand trapped by the gravitational pull of market realism and its relentless pursuit of profitability, and on the other hand compelled by a deep sense that we are capable of saving the planet through technological innovation. But who is this "we" and what is this "planet" that is being targeted for salvation? These questions are regularly asked with regard to forms of green urbanism and nature conservation politics, where efforts to green a city or preserve a tract of land can impose the values and objectives of a global elite upon those with other visions of how and by whom these spaces might be used and maintained.[10] Just as Cindi Katz, in her essay "Whose Nature, Whose Culture?,"[11] critiques corporate approaches to environmental stewardship for treating nature as an accumulation strategy, here we see how planetary improvement and specifically the cleantech project invites a similar critique: Whose planet? Whose technology? Whose lives will be enabled by the promotion of a cleaner and greener version of the status quo? And conversely, whose lives will continue to be disabled, subjected to the slow violence of extraction and seepage, toxicity and disposability, under resourced recovery efforts and uncompensated labors?[12]

One way to make sense of planetary improvement's implicit answers to these questions is to read them as a form of green Keynesianism. Geoff Mann argues that the roots of Keynesianism actually precede John Maynard Keynes himself, going back to Robespierre, Hegel, and the French Revolution. He argues that at the core of this more broadly understood Keynesian project is a desire to save civilization from the dual threats of, on the one hand, capitalism and the ravages of unfettered profiteers, and on the other, a revolutionary multitude and the ravages of their unfettered pursuit of justice, equality, and liberty.[13] To read planetary improvement as a form of green Keynesianism, we would identify its objective focus as an effort to save civilization, only now voiced instead as an effort to save the planet. Keynesians envision a sphere of experts, technocrats, and intellectuals actively deliberating and experimenting to solve society's most pressing problems, even if these solutions at times require illiberal means. This deliberative body is not meant to be a broadly constituted public, but instead a more narrow community of "respectable" people deeply invested in maintaining the status quo. As Mann explains, the "essential problem that obsesses all Keynesians at all times [is] the political sustainability of modern ('bourgeois') privilege."[14]

It is important then, to push back against the implicit biases of planetary improvement's green Keynesianism by asking directly: Whose visions matter? Whose visions are empowered to matter? Whose visions do we invest in, not just financially, but emotionally, culturally, and politically as well? As I argue throughout this book, when trajectories of technological innovation are left to be shaped by investment logics that look first and foremost for commercially viable products, by smart money looking for smart investments and entrepreneurs looking to be those smart investments, then any broader publics are excluded from political, ethical, and moral debates about the future trajectories of sociotechnical advance. The *we* enlisted to solve environmental problems ends up deferring to a bourgeois public sphere of entrepreneurial innovators, the investors who fund them, and their visions of planetary improvement.

What might we do about this? Without becoming overly prescriptive—or holding up specific projects as models to emulate—I want to push the conversation beyond the confines of my admittedly narrow focus on one small community of cleantech entrepreneurs and investors and move toward a more prospective reflection on ways to envision a radically reconstructive politics of technology and innovation.

Just as the investors and consultants that I met boasted of *killing the inventor*, it may be necessary to respond with an opposing maxim: *kill the investor*. In other words, let's put into the foreground the possibility of untethering innovation from the fiduciary responsibility of venture investors who firmly orbit within capital's gravitational pull. How might we produce while beholden to different responsibilities altogether? The answer is not simply to unfetter cleantech entrepreneurs from the disciplinary bonds of money and its "smarts," so as to let these heroic figures spread their wings. It is important to interrogate the extent to which these entrepreneurs, any entrepreneurs, along with their visions and innovations, are shaped by the desire to sustain existing patterns of socionatural life (along with the climate disruptions that they entail); non-disruptive disruptions for a "revolution without revolutionaries."[15]

Where Are the Visionaries … with Money?

Let me recount one last story from the Funders Forum. The event's 107th session featured a company called Lawrenceville Plasma Physics (LPP). At eight o'clock on a Friday morning, 38 people crammed into a small conference room to attend a presentation by the company's founder and chief scientist, Eric Lerner, about his work developing an aneutronic fusion reactor. LPP is one of a handful of firms attempting to develop a viable means of generating energy from controlled nuclear fusion reactions in small-scale reactors. Their technology relies on knotting filaments of plasma upon themselves in a reactor filled with a non-radioactive boron-based fuel. The plasma knot creates the astronomically high temperature (over a billion degrees Celsius) required to create a fusion reaction, producing excess energy that can then be harnessed. As Lerner explained, his reactor is currently able to create extremely short pulses of fusion, and therefore relatively small amounts of excess energy. If the pulses can be cycled fast enough he believes that the reactor will be able to produce a useful amount of energy with minimal negative side effects.

In the 1980s, NASA's Jet Propulsion Lab funded the bulk of Lerner's work. As he explained to me, only somewhat facetiously, all he would have to do to get money those days was convince NASA's program officers that if they weren't allowed to continue their work, it was likely the Soviets would develop the same technology first. This funding stream dried up with the end of the Cold War, and Lerner has since had to find other ways to support his work. His current project, LPP, has been hobbling along with precarious, bare-bones funding. Some of his nuclear energy competitors have been able to find wealthy tech benefactors: Paul Thiel funds Helion Energy, Paul Allen funds Tri-Alpha Energy, and Jeff Bezos has backed General Fusion.[16] But Lerner has not been as fortunate, and it is not hard to see why: he is adamant on maintaining power over his company and his technology. He has structured the ownership of his business in a way that precludes any potential investors from ever exerting a controlling influence. As we saw in chapter 3, this firmly establishes him as a "mad entrepreneur," unwilling to cede authority to more business-savvy investors and the managers they might choose to put in his place.

Truth be told, if there is anyone who fits the mold of a modern day mad scientist, Lerner is a prime candidate. His thinning gray hair is long and disheveled, his attire is similarly mismatched and clearly an afterthought. His most prominent public presence is due to a book he wrote in the 1980s challenging the growing consensus for the Big Bang as a theory of the universe's origins.[17] Yet there is nothing "mad" or even irrational about Lerner's politically calculated refusal to sign away control in exchange for cash. He believes in the world-shaping potential of his technology and the possibility of a distributed power source that could fundamentally transform the distribution and access to sustainable energy across the globe. He does not want to see this technology developed for military purposes, and therefore refuses to even consider taking money from the defense department or the US Navy.[18] Ultimately Lerner wants to be part of deciding who uses his technology and how they use it. But this is precisely what makes him a "mad entrepreneur," since it entails taking these sorts of decisions away from the one entity that is supposed to make them: the market.

Lerner has scraped by with an assortment of foundation and private support—including a crowd-funding campaign that netted him $180,279 from 2,211 donors.[19] He described in one of our interviews the experience of speaking with dozens of people with hundreds of millions of dollars or more to invest:

The feedback is almost always the same: either, "come back when you have more results," or even more ridiculously, "come back when you have a working generator," to which I always respond, "why would we need money if we had a working generator?"

Lerner was brought to the Funders Forum by DD, who was working at the time as a consultant, trying to help LPP raise the capital they needed to continue their work. DD is a lifelong salesman—from carnival prizes as a young man, to windows, to cleantech companies. On that Friday morning, during the half hour or so before presentations began, he assured me, as well as anyone else that would listen, that "this focus fusion thing has biblical implications!" Both he and Lerner agreed that the reactor would likely be much further along if LPP had a steadier stream of funding, but DD was beginning to lose faith in a world that seemed intent on withholding its capital from the project. He told me, "There is no vision in this world. There are no visionaries... [who] have money."

In fact, the matter is a bit more complicated. Perhaps the problem is not the lack of visionaries with money, but that these visionaries see the world with (and as) capital. Lerner may want to see his technology disrupt prevailing patterns of social and ecological life, but investors are looking for proven technologies that disrupt markets, not worlds.

When speaking with investors and consultants, LPP was seen as one example in a tragic category of good technologies that were never likely to get funding because they didn't translate into good businesses. Not that they couldn't eventually and ideally become a good business, but that the path to any realistic commercialization was so long and expensive that private venture capital investment made little sense. In fact, resource- and time-intensive technologies like LPP's focused fusion are considered to be one of the prime reasons that venture capital's first round of investments in cleantech failed to deliver adequate returns.[20]

Throughout the cleantech space, there is widespread frustration with the limitations of venture capital funding models and their incompatibility with the riskiest and most ambitious technological projects that cleantech's advocates consider to be "urgently required to address climate change."[21] Bill Gates, as we've seen, is mobilizing billionaire investors to help close this gap in funding. The day before the Paris climate talks in 2015 he announced his Breakthrough Energy Coalition—a network of billionaires who were willing to forego maximizing short-term, or even medium-term profits, in the development of carbon-free energy technologies, or "tools to power the world." Gates's project is a direct response to the acknowledged failures of the venture capital model to support the sort of transformational project that cleantech innovation would have to become if it is truly going to "save the planet."

As the explanation on Breakthrough's website reads: "That innovation will result from a dramatically scaled up public research pipeline linked to truly patient, flexible investments."[22] Gates proposes to replace the impatience of venture investors with a model of patient capital or, in other words, capital that is willing to wait much longer for any potential return. But despite this talk of patient capital as an alternative model of investment, Gates still remains committed to a venture-investing paradigm that is primarily focused on developing commercially viable technologies that can capture the multitrillion dollar "mother of all markets" that energy generation represents. While the clean energy market will be risky, Gates explains that even in the tech sector, "90 percent of the companies that got started went under, and yet the Apples, Googles, Microsofts more than made it worthwhile for those private investors."[23] Ultimately, Gates's patient capital model is little more than a grander scale of venture investing—more (smart) money (hundreds as opposed to tens of millions of dollars) invested patiently, over a longer period of time. As he explains, "The market's big enough and the barriers tend to be daunting enough that the rewards of the few who make it through that minefield [are] gigantic. So I still see it as on-balance, a smart investment."[24] Gates remains committed to the general idea that smart money should provide a guiding force in the cleantech innovation ecosystem, because at the end of the day, "when there is profit to be made, which in the long run, there really is here, its great for capitalism to fund dozens of different ideas."[25]

Gates makes it clear that cleantech's patient capital should not be solely private, but developed in collaboration with "visionary countries" that are willing to devote significant funding to cleantech research. These visionary countries should be free to take risks on novel and potentially transformative technologies, and to become what Mariana Mazzucato has termed the "entrepreneurial state."[26]

Mazzucato's vision of the entrepreneurial state focuses on the active role that states can (and sometimes do) play in the development of new commercial technologies. She focuses specifically on the US state, and its successes in funding and directing basic research and early stage, high-risk innovations that have been instrumental to information technology, biotechnology, and clean technology—the three fields that venture capital typically takes credit for as the fruits of their risk-taking activities. Mazzucato argues that venture capital is actually quite risk-averse, and more likely to fund incremental gains to already established technologies (and therefore already established markets) then to fund truly cutting-edge, high-risk early stage technologies with the potential to actually transform society in meaningful ways. What is missing, she argues, is precisely the sort of "patient finance" being proposed by Gates—investors who are willing to take a long-term perspective and invest in the very earliest stages of development of new technologies without needing to be immediately rewarded with short-term gains. This is where the entrepreneurial state comes into play, as a source of patient capital, oriented around visions of desirable sociotechnical futures (And of course we ask: Whose desires? Whose futures?).

In many ways Mazzucato is simply rebranding the idea of state planning as entrepreneurial vision—an important distinction that allows fellow travelers, such as the fellows and affiliates of the Breakthrough Institute (cofounded by Ted Nordhaus and Michael Shellenberger, not to be confused with Gates' project), to "reject the planning fallacy of the 1950s"[27] while still supporting a resurgence of active state involvement in shaping the innovation economy. This is particularly important with respect to the neoliberal context that these thinkers operate in, which as Phillip Mirowski argues, has been from its emergence in the early 20th century a "concerted effort to counteract the rise of planning and other market-skeptical movements that grew out of the great depression and the experience of World War II."[28]

It is worth noting how, at the moment when venture capital's foray into cleantech had largely fallen flat and investors have largely retreated from the earliest stages of funding, figures such as Gates, Nordhaus, and Shellenberger all look to the state to come to the rescue, and bail out the cleantech innovation ecosystem with early stage, patient capital that venture investors are unwilling to provide. Far from being a counterweight to neoliberalism, as might be implied by a turn back toward state planning, proposals for an entrepreneurial state are far more likely to further entrench corporate interests and the "marketplace of ideas" into the fabric of governance. Just as we learned that a good entrepreneur is a manageable entrepreneur, we can see the same unspoken truth in these visions of an entrepreneurial state, and in figures such as Gates asking for the state to de-risk and support the development of a patient-but-still-venture-investing pipeline of innovations.

This results in an unspoken tension. On the one hand there is a desire for the state to have stronger authority over and in the market—but then visions of how this authority might actually operate can easily become simple extensions of market logic transferred to the state, positioned here as an investor instead of a regulator. Those calling for this active, entrepreneurial state are not necessarily looking for an autonomous state that will control, regulate, and direct the market, but instead for a source of capital that is not obligated to reproduce itself, and can thus rely on the manna of state budgets (whether tax base, debt base, bailouts, or perhaps all three) to endlessly fund cleantech's market expansion.

Part of the allure of these ideas—whether patient capital, the entrepreneurial state, or beyond this, the varied calls for a "Green New Deal"—all fall back upon a sense that some form of nonmarket coordination and control, whether exercised by national or even supranational governing bodies, can reassert control over the economy.[29] During my fieldwork, I found this expressed in two distinct ways. First, as an idealized reference to China's industrial policy and its five-year plans, which represented the possibility of a state actively engaged in industrial planning, something my participants felt to be painfully absent in the US.[30] And second, via hypothetical statements. For instance, when confronting good technologies that make for bad businesses, or other limitations of the venture capital funding model, consultants, investors, and entrepreneurs would tell me what they would do if they had the sort of money that someone like Bill Gates or Mark Zuckerberg had. They would support the technologies that are otherwise being left behind; they would take risks on technologies that were less likely to be immediately profitable but had the potential to radically transform the world. As GF, the boutique investment banker and consultant explained: "I mean, if I was investing, if I had my own money, it would be a different thing. I would have a much different criteria." The presumption was clear: *I would not make the same decisions that capital seems to make. I would be smarter than smart money.*

In one way or another, these visions are enticed by the world-making potential of accumulating and directing social wealth toward the production of green and clean technologies, products, and ultimately worlds, which capital, in its current form, seems hesitant and unwilling to fund.

Capital may be powerful and smart and magnetizing, but it is also uncreative, self-preserving, and somewhat stifling. Perhaps then, underlying these visions, there is an emerging sense that money may be too smart for its own good, too committed to its own reproduction, and therefore incapable of taking the necessary risks or supporting the necessary forms of experimental excess that can lead to the transformative innovations that the present environmental predicament demands.

In this regard, the imagined autonomy of an entrepreneurial state (or of figures such as Gates, Zuckerberg and in particular for cleantech, Elon Musk) represents the possibility of a form of social wealth that is unbound from its responsibility to privilege its own expanded reproduction above all else. Here it is also worth mentioning the potential in alternative investment projects such as Regenerative Finance, an impact-investing network being developed by young wealthy individuals who aim to "work alongside our movement comrades who are building the new, radically different, caring economy." Their model is based upon making 0% interest loans, and in showing "investors how to participate in the next economy—humbly, holistically, and for the long term."[31] However, while accumulating alternative pools of money (money that is willing to forego its function as self-reproducing capital) may appear to be one positive step, this still leaves open the question of who controls these alternative investment resources and therefore who controls the decisions as to what social, political, and technological alternatives are and are not viable. As Lerner and DD suggest, we need to put money in the hands of visionaries, without presuming that those individuals who have already accumulated money are the visionaries we necessarily want to follow.

The Persistence of Petromodernity

In 2009 Mark Jacobson and Mark Delucchi published what has since become a widely circulated report mapping out the technical viability of a world powered completely by clean technologies.[32] Their work details how installing a combination of wind, solar, hydrokinetic, and geothermal power—"wind, water, and solar" or WWS—could supply all of the world's energy needs with already proven technologies, "eliminating all fossil fuels" in the process.[33] Such a transformation would require trillions of dollars rapidly invested in new infrastructural development across the planet. As proof that this is feasible, Jacobson and Delucchi site the massive mobilization during World War II—the environmental movement's prime example of nonmarket state coordination and control—which resulted in the rapid retooling of automobile-to-warplane production, as well as the subsequent construction of an interstate highway system, which in 35 short years entirely transformed American society. If the nation could mobilize its industrial base against enemy nations, why can't we imagine a similar mobilization against climate change?[34] In 2013, Jacobson founded a non-profit organization, the Solutions Project, to continue working on detailed plans for the implementation of a WWS renewable energy system.[35]

This WWS plan is not the only cleantech vision of how to create a viable post-petroleum energy system. Breakthrough Institute directors and fellows, for instance, see advanced nuclear systems—such as the work being done by Lerner and LPP—as a more viable alternative.[36] They argue that a wholesale transformation of our energy system will require significant technological breakthroughs in energy generation, distancing themselves from the relatively slow pace of progress that cleantech has so far been able to deliver. They advocate instead for the development of 'breakthrough' energy technologies that promise larger increments of change.

While nomenclature may shift, the underlying logic remains the same: new, clean energy technologies are essential in the face of accelerating climate change, so as to avoid disastrous and undesirable transformations of modern civilization. Whether advanced nuclear or wind, water, and solar, at the core of each of these proposals lies strikingly similar visions of a sustained abundance of cheap energy, unburdened by CO_2 emissions or any of the other pernicious externalities that seem to destabilize the biosphere.

Let me state outright that I too would like to see a radical transformation of the global energy system, and I am earnestly excited about the prospect of technologists helping to make other-energy infrastructures viable on any number of scales. It is very possible that some combination of clean technologies, either developed or under development, can and will provide some of the necessary infrastructure for a future worth inhabiting, and through my research I met many inspiring and inventive individuals who are working to do just this. That said, and as I have attempted to show throughout this work, it remains important to acknowledge the limitations of the cleantech project, along with its carefully constructed future-scenarios highlighting technological change as a beacon of hope and salvation.

I don't intend this acknowledgment to lead into a knee-jerk jeremiad against modern technology per se, but as a sober recognition of the material and energetic costs (not to mention the human costs) of producing and disposing of such a vast quantity of conveniences. Petroleum byproducts saturate lives in the developed world so much so that we might borrow a rhetorical device from Jean Baudrillard to suggest that the scandal of an oil spill such as the ones occurring on the *Exxon Valdez* or the *Deepwater Horizon*, popularly demonized with images of wildlife coated in petrol, is to distract from the larger scandal of everyday, modern lives, thoroughly drenched in that same black gold.[37]

Modern life, in other words, has over the course of the 20th century, come to be inextricably tied to a seemingly endless supply of cheap petroleum, breeding a petroculture or what Stephanie LeMenager has termed a petromodernity, where "desire is coordinated by and in relation to the use of fossil fuels."[38] As scholars and activists fighting against environmental racism and justice make abundantly clear, this is an uneven landscape. The fossil-fueled economy differentially enables and disables very specific communities, places, and lives, creating zones of inclusion as well as exclusion, and leaving a discernable and continually renewed wake of slow—and decidedly racialized—violence across the globe. In the face of overwhelming evidence of environmental racism and injustice, from the Niger Delta to Louisiana's Cancer Alley, environmental racism scholars such as Laura Pulido foreground the broader systemic flows of capital that ultimately depend upon these violently cancerous sites of extraction, processing, and refinement.[39]

Despite an increasing recognition of environmental injustices, questioning the American way of life and the petrocultures that it represents remains something like the third-rail of environmental politics—triggering memories (whether directly experienced or subsequently rehearsed) of former president Jimmy Carter's infamous fireside chat, in which he asked Americans to consider doing with less. Many credit that speech with precipitating his eventual defeat by Reagan, who countered with an upbeat promise of cheap oil and perpetual abundance.[40] As Matt Huber shows, the American way of life has been seamlessly woven into the fabric of automobility, and the gasoline infrastructure supporting it was (and still is), as George W. Bush infamously pronounced at the first Earth Summit in Rio de Janeiro, "not up for negotiation."[41]

As the Petrocultures Research Group writes, the outright taboo on suggesting that some lifestyles, some commodities, and some (most) affordances of consumer privilege may in fact be collectively damaging, narrows the scope of possible "solutions" to technological fixes that "make the world made by oil possible after oil."[42] Though waged as an effort to "save the planet," what results is an environmental politics committed to saving the very forms and patterns of life that have heightened environmental problems in the first place.

The Petrocultures Research Group characterizes this techno-fetishistic approach to solving environmental problems, what I have named *planetary improvement*, as a form of "cruel optimism," where attachment to unachievable fantasies of the good life actually serve as obstacles to meaningful development.[43] This leads to some rather large, and fundamentally important questions: Instead of thinking about the innovation of new technologies, is it instead possible to envision the transformation of sociotechnical-environmental systems, complex assemblages of lives, materials, technologies, and knowledge that can be situated politically, ethically, and morally? Who will build the infrastructure (social, technological, cultural, material) of these futures? Who will invest (financially, materially, spiritually, ethically) in these ventures, and who's futures will they even be?

An unflagging celebration of entrepreneurial innovation and technological development is incapable of acknowledging that cleantech represents only one possible path out of many. This is, as I've shown, how planetary improvement represents an enclosure of our collectively creative capacities: it narrows the conditions of possibility for technological advance and normalizes the commercial orientation and financial expectations of smart money into an overly simplified logic of incremental gains meant to capture markets and extend profitable consumption patterns indefinitely into the future.

When it comes to energy generation (or energy efficiency) it matters first and foremost what sociotechnical-environmental processes that energy is being used to power. The design theorist Tony Fry makes this point in regard to architecture and design. No building can be truly sustainable, he argues, no matter its technical specifications and material composition, so long as it remains embedded within unsustainable uses or practices.[44] We can say the same for clean technology. Unless we ask what underlying sociotechnical processes these technologies are being created to improve, we ultimately sidestep the fundamental question of what worlds (and whose worlds) we are aiming to sustain. The same solar panel can be on top of a Walmart, on top of a corporation's headquarters, on top of an oversized suburban house, on top of a rural health clinic, on top of a public school. In each case, its "clean" energy means something totally different, insofar as it sustains very distinct sociotechnical processes with very distinct social and environmental implications. Planetary improvement evades these sorts of questions by focusing instead on discrete technologies whose discrete effects—cleaning, greening, making more energetically or materially efficient in one specific way or another—can be cast as unassailably good, green, and desirable.

As we've seen, planetary improvement holds out the promise of a perpetual present, extended indefinitely into the future through the simple replacement of "dirty" technologies with their cleaner counterparts. As an orientation toward environmental politics, it is ultimately intent upon holding on to, or sustaining, what (a very specific, rather privileged) *we* have, a fossil-fueled way of life presented as unquestionably desirable, unquestionably good, and unquestionably worth maintaining at any cost. The assumption— and promise—is that with the steady and potentially accelerating growth in smart, green, or clean technologies, people and places enabled by petrocapitalism can gradually move away from the most environmentally damaging aspects of their lives, by replacing—or improving—their industrial infrastructure with more benign alternatives.[45]

Understood in this vein, cleantech can serve as a lightning rod for environmental hopes and dreams. You want cleaner skies? We've got a tech for that. Cleaner energy? No problem. The abstract and overarching problem of climate change is disaggregated into a series of discrete challenges, each of which can and should be met with a commercially scalable technology. In this way, cleantech helps legitimize a profit-based approach to social transformation, a green spirit of capitalism in which disruptive technologies and visionary entrepreneurs are tasked with building a future worth investing in. Whether it will ever become a future worth living in is an open and yet easily elided question, pushed off into a distant, abstract sense of a future that is not ever likely to arrive.

Lightning rods are meant to deflect energy away from the underlying structures that they protect. In this case, it is the infrastructures of a fossil-fueled industrial economy along with the ways of life, or petrocultures, that is being protected. For those whose lives are enabled by these sociotechnical systems, these infrastructures are seen as an unquestionable bedrock of modernity and civilization, and therefore the very thing that environmental efforts must be oriented around sustaining. Cleantech purports to offer disruptive technologies, so we can ask: What aspects of our lives are meant to be disrupted, and what aspects are meant to persist, or even intensify? Renewable energy is certainly not meant to be disrupting mass consumer lifestyles dependent on intercontinental travel and trade, global agribusiness, and the saturation of that lifestyle with new media forms and new technological platforms to support those media—flat screens everywhere, a tablet on every table and a cell phone in every pocket.

This leads us to the core problem of planetary improvement: clean technologies won't save the planet if they are simply incremental improvements of an otherwise-unchanged industrial economy. No amount of solar power, wind, or geothermal energy will, in and of itself, reduce the consumption of already proven fossil fuel resources, and in fact achieving the latter will likely require a fundamentally different sociotechnical imaginary. This imaginary will need to ask questions, for instance, about energy generation and use that do not already presume the necessity of unceasing flows of electricity and combustable fuels, or what Larry Lohmann calls the fetishization of "Big-E energy."[46] While there is no need to categorically reject clean technologies just because they only deliver incremental change, we may need to question whether we can afford—collectively, socially, environmentally—to proceed with this faith in planetary improvement, and with what amounts to an unspoken acceptance of the fossil-fueled economy, perpetually improved but never actually undone. Planetary improvement, and with it the promise of a future made clean by cleantech, can only ever offer a Faustian bargain: destroy the world in order to save it.

Coda: Learning to Let Go and Love Other Worlds

While it is important to challenge the ways in which planetary improvement naturalizes capitalist social relations and sees them as an inevitable core of any future world, it is also important to understand the ways in which these social relationships have irrevocably transformed the biophysical world. Even if we were to find ourselves in a future beyond capitalism, the residues of capital's past (and present) will necessarily persist, a toxic remainder shaping any new natures (and new societies) left to defend, accommodate, and embrace. This toxic inheritance is, of late, being discussed as the anthropocene, a world—an entire planet—that has been so thoroughly transformed by the effects of human civilization as to create the conditions for a new geological and climatological epoch.[1]

Evidence mounts that this transformation is well underway and likely irreversible; that the ruins are already upon us. And so while planetary improvement promises brighter, greener futures—more advanced, more prosperous times that await—it is becoming increasingly clear that some less savory aspects of this future, of any future, have already arrived, and they don't glisten as promised: a future of smart thermostats for some, perhaps, but also one of record heat waves for most; a future of global data networks and the devices to access them, again for some, and acidified oceans, bleached coral, unavoidable sea level rise and unpredictable megastorms for most. There is no longer time to plan for avoiding climate change, no longer time to save what "we" have from the implications of what "we" have already created: new natures, irrevocably transformed, perilously destabilized, and increasingly unable to be controlled.

Throughout this book, I have remained critically aware of the plural subject, "we." I have tried to avoid using it as an unqualified universal that might provide some reassuring sense that we are all in it together. Far from it. Some of us have and will continue to be differentially enabled by the material and energetic flows of fossil-fueled capitalism, while others have and will continue to be stifled, sickened, displaced, and dispossessed. As I will continue to explore below, it matters tremendously who we mean by *we*. It matters who we experiment and create with, who we listen and learn from, who we think and plan for. As the title of this coda suggests, learning to let go may very well require a fundamental reconsideration of who we think we are, and who we want to become.

Still, there is a we—perhaps one that is never fully constituted or forever in a state of becoming—that must come to terms with just how messy, violent, inhospitable, and undesirable any new natures are likely to be (and, in many cases, already are). It is unfortunate that capital has been able to progress as far as it has, to have enabled so much incredible technological social and cultural production while at the same time threatening the very conditions of life for humans and beyond. The "cruel optimism" of planetary improvement promises technological salvation and the hope that there is one more technological revolution out there, somewhere, waiting to save the day.[2] While this may seem increasingly unlikely, it still may be possible to find outlets to develop and explore a collective hope in future possibilities. As the geographer Rory Rowan writes, "Just as blind optimism risks lubricating existing forms of power, an equally blind pessimism risks stunting the collective capacities required to oppose them."[3] Even while rejecting the faith in capitalist trajectories and its unflagging techno-optimism, we must still remain open to the possibility that capitalism also has produced (or in other cases, not fully destroyed) conditions and capacities "from which other worlds and new collectives might be born, even within the wreckage of all that has been lost."[4]

As a means of grappling with these profound transformations, Roy Scranton suggests in an op-ed written for the *New York Times* that we must "learn how to die" in the anthropocene.[5] He draws a parallel based on his experience as a US soldier deployed in Iraq, where he witnessed the aftermath of a civilization utterly undone by a military intervention that he actively participated in, and the more general experience of living amid the anthropocene, an environment being utterly undone by the everyday rhythms of industrial and consumer life that again, he actively participated in. He writes:

Across the world today, our actions testify to our belief that we can go on like this forever, burning oil, poisoning the seas, killing off other species, pumping carbon into the air, ignoring the ominous silence of our coal mine canaries in favor of the unending robotic tweets of our new digital imaginarium. Yet the reality of global climate change is going to keep intruding on our fantasies of perpetual growth, permanent innovation and endless energy, just as the reality of mortality shocks our casual faith in permanence.[6]

Scranton offers a reprieve of the rugged frontier individualism of early US environmentalism, exploring the frontiers of imperialism only to find, unlike Teddy Roosevelt or John Muir, a distinctly toxic sublime.[7] He draws inspiration in an 18th-century samurai manual that instructs warriors to meditate daily on their inevitable death. By doing so, one is able to gain a sense of freedom and a release from their mortality, "to live as though his body is already dead."[8] For Scranton, embracing death becomes a means of reconciling with the truth of global climate change, with the reality that the anthropocene has already arrived, and that it will not be likely to support civilization as he has come to know and appreciate it. Scranton speaks for and as a very specific, rather privileged (and explicitly settler colonial) "we" that can ruminate abstractly on the inevitable climate-induced death of civilization (or collective ways of living and being) precisely because his "we" is not yet facing any of the climate-induced violence—along with premature deaths of people and of cultures—that has already begun to mount.

Thinking both with and against Scranton then, what if "learning how to die" instead meant learning how to let go of his very specific "we," so as to defer to other people with other ideas about how to constitute other ways of living in and upon this world? In other words, instead of only considering the individual warrior's sanity in the face of potentially species-level social death (or extinction), could we consider the possibility that what is actually at risk, or "already dead," is just one historically specific way of living, a late capitalist petromodernity that is irrevocably and irreversibly destroying its own conditions of possibility?

What does it actually mean for a way of living to die? Extinction may sadly continue to haunt our present as a dire and far too imminent possibility, but this question can also free us to envision other possible ways of living that are capable of emerging from the decaying remains of this present state of affairs. In this regard, we may have to learn how to be open to the possibility that we—and our techno-entrepreneur-investor proxies like Bill Gates and Elon Musk—may not have all the answers, or even know how to ask the right questions in the first place.[9] Along these lines, think about the invective to *kill the investor* as a means of freeing our conception of entrepreneurial creativity—or more broadly of world making and the ability to invent, shape, make, and maintain—from the logic of planetary improvement. Learning how to die, in this regard, might be differentially expressed as learning how to let go of a narrowed conception of cleantech entrepreneurship and innovation as keys to *improving the planet,* as well as to learning how to let go of the unspoken privileges of petromodernity that clean technologies are meant to sustain.

If investors, entrepreneurs, business people, and anyone for that matter who has internalized the smarts of smart money, act as representatives of this collective subject, then new technologies, perhaps even new policies and forms of governance, will be oriented around greening what this very specific "we" can claim as its fossil-fueled world; improving *our* lives and *our* planet, without ever questioning whether it is precisely *these* lives in possession of *this* planet that need to be challenged and ultimately transformed.

In the final pages of this book, I want to ask whether the sociotechnical capacities of entrepreneurs and innovators that are typically associated with or even collapsed into a green capitalist, techno-fix machine could potentially supersede their currently restricted form. The sociotechnical capacity is out there to transform the world in any number of ways. But realizing some of the more emancipatory (socially and environmentally) visions may require, as suggested in chapter 6, that we "kill the investor" and liberate our imaginations, our sciences, our technologies and innovations, from the narrowing, pecuniary logic of capital.

My own research put me into direct contact with only a tiny fraction of the creative minds working to create greener, cleaner, sociotechnical futures. Cleantech entrepreneurship is just one, albeit relatively well-supported, approach out of many, and admittedly it is more focused on appealing to smart money and the needs of the market than other approaches to environmental politics. Alternative sociotechnical perspectives are readily available, even if somewhat incomplete. In the industrialized world, particularly in Europe, the degrowth movement continues to offer a space for people to explore alternative ways to pattern social and environmental life.[10] Other concepts, such as *buen vivir,* conviviality, and plentitude similarly offer paradigms for a reorientation of social and environmental life away from the global fixation on economic growth as the ultimate measure of development and progress.[11]

The sociotechnical ideas coming out of these movements involve learning to live and thrive with less energetic and material consumption, and therefore with less formal economic activity. As a result, they are largely anathema to planetary improvement, whose proponents reject them as one form or another of technological Luddism or even neo-romantic naiveté: a pining for a return to simpler, purer, times, before technology ruined everything.[12] In this way, rejecting the development of specific technologies, deployed for specific purposes, can be dismissed as an irrational rejection of technology in general. Here, Geoff Mann's understanding of Keynesianism is again relevant in understanding planetary improvement. Mann argues that Keynesianism has to be understood as a post-revolutionary way of seeing the world, predicated upon a foundational distrust of a broadly constituted public (what Hegel called the "rabble") whose response to conditions of poverty and gross inequality feed into a violently destabilizing, revolutionary impulse.[13] The green Keynesianism of planetary improvement exhibits a similar fear of any popular sociotechnical visions that might threaten to decenter the cleantech imaginary and with it, the unspoken commitment to maintaining petromodern privileges before all else.

There is no point in dismissing all of the advances, conveniences, and affordances that have come to be associated with the ways of life enabled by fossil-fueled capitalism. Indoor plumbing, electricity, elaborate communication networks, life-saving medical advances—there are so many aspects of the modern world worth celebrating and holding on to. Yet, as discussed from the outset, this world casts a dark shadow over many other ways of life, and many other worlds, whose very existences are threatened by its colonial demands (extractions, debts, displacements) and excremental surpluses (emissions, toxicities, wastes). The promise of clean technology emerges out of this world-ecological reality, and out of a production system that still primarily relies upon the conventional extraction and processing of raw materials (as well as the conscription of cheap labor), whose social and environmental traces are decidedly not green or clean at all.[14]

Toward a Pluriversal Intellect

In the end, a politics of environmental technology and innovation must be able to think beyond simplistic binaries that peg all technology, all innovation, or even for that matter all entrepreneurship, as inherently good or bad, while finding ways to assess sociotechnical systems within what the decolonial scholar Walter Mignolo might call a pluriversal context, one in which (any specific) technological knowledge is considered to be one out of many legitimate ways of knowing and engaging.[15] This means developing an orientation toward creativity, innovation, and future-making where other(ed) ways of knowing are not simply asked to step aside, so as to let what is technologically possible in one dominant context overwrite sociotechnical strategies that may ultimately be more socially and environmentally desirable.[16] (Desirable for whom? That will always be the question.)

As the commitment to fossil-fueled capitalism and the petromodernity that it makes possible threatens the viability of life on this planet, perhaps it is possible to reassess the experimental significance of alternative sociotechnical arrangements, other sciences capable of envisioning and producing other worlds. And yet, these other(ed) ways of knowing have been easily dismissed, even by Karl Marx himself, as "traditional, confined, complacent, encrusted satisfactions of present needs, and reproductions of old ways of life."[17] Having the humility to understand alternative approaches to thinking and making as coherent and thoughtful knowledge-systems in their own right, is the first step in being able to genuinely ask whether and how radically different orientations, lives and constellations of thought, wisdom and capacities, can and should actively shape our creative engagements with the sociotechnical trajectories that we nurture and explore.

I do not mean to suggest that some mythic indigenous individual or society has figured it all out, or that such a society could simplistically offer a universal blueprint for a viable planetary future, or even that some discrete combination of traditional lifeways and technologies presents a necessary and sufficient ground upon which to build universal solutions to planetary crisis. Instead, I want to far more humbly make clear that there are other(ed) ways of living and knowing that are no less capable of producing and transforming sociotechnical-environmental systems, and that therefore represent modes of maintenance, innovation, experimentation, and intergenerational inquiry that cannot simply be dismissed as idealistic musings or anti-technological naiveté.

Taking inspiration from feminist, post-humanist, and decolonial scholarship in a paper we coauthored, my colleague Elizabeth Johnson and I ask what it would take to replace the "general" in Marx's conception of the general intellect with the more open and diverse concept of *pluripotency*—a term initially borrowed from the biological sciences that describes the generative capacities of living and nonliving processes.[18] As a repository of intergenerational knowledge and capacities, a pluripotent intellect recognizes the somewhat more diverse, diffuse, and differentiated forms that this knowledge and ability takes, as opposed to any narrower band of scientific and technological thought.

The problem is not that the *general* intellect necessarily and unilaterally supports capital's advance, but that it tends to support a generalized and universalizing worldview that delegitimizes any forms of knowing that are not immediately and directly related to advancing modern scientific and technological thought. Embracing and exploring a more diverse (or pluripotent) landscape of technology and innovation can, by contrast, become an essential step toward radically transforming our sense of what futures are possible and perhaps even more importantly, what avenues we have available to reach them. This is where *buen vivir*, plentitude, degrowth, and other approaches to living well (or for some, just living) without and despite capitalism matter—not as spaces where technology is eschewed and summarily rejected, but as spaces from which new technologies can be envisioned, old technologies can be reappropriated and repaired, and where the question of what technology even is in the first place can be thought anew.

Here it may be instructive to draw on a lesson from Lewis Mumford. In *Technics and Civilization*, he calls for a many-sided orientation toward technology that expands beyond economists and industrialists.[19] Instead of a world run by experts, Mumford envisions a world created by amateurs: people with the freedom, time and resources, to produce along untested lines. He argues that industrial production has made possible a more democratized form of experimentation. Whereas prior the skills involved with learning any particular craft were such that it would take a huge part of one's life just to learn a single trade, modern machinery allows for much more technical capacity to be available with far less of a learning curve or barrier to entry. In other words, industrial advances have made it possible for more people to potentially have direct access to more of the accumulated creative and productive capacity of modern society. This could result, Mumford argues, in a form of socialized creation, one in which a diversity of experience, knowledge, and experimental practice can all factor into the further shaping, augmenting, and perhaps most importantly, redirecting of society's productive capacities.[20]

Mumford's vision is of a radically democratic and open approach to scientific experimentation, but it remains fundamentally situated within a world enabled by petromodernity, both conceptually and geographically. By contrast, in 2016 the Zapatistas held an interdisciplinary and intercommunity conference exploring the relationship between science and social justice. One of the hosts, Subcomandante Galeano, explained in his opening remarks that his community very intentionally invited their international scientist guests to join them in San Cristobal, as opposed to traveling to meet them in the Global North:

We don't want to go away to the university, we want to build a university in our communities, for you to teach and learn alongside our peoples. We don't want to go to the big laboratories and scientific research centers of the metropolis; we want them to be built here…under our leadership and collective operation.[21]

Galeano explains that the Zapatistas are not interested in passively consuming knowledge created (and managed) elsewhere. By building the infrastructure of scientific inquiry where they are and under their control, they want to decolonize the practice of scientific inquiry, and hold a space for scientific practice to be situated within their community and their struggle. Frantz Fanon made a very similar argument in his 1961 book *Wretched of the Earth*. He writes:

If the building of a bridge does not enrich the consciousness of those working on it, then don't build the bridge, and let the citizens continue to swim across the river or use a ferry. The bridge must not be pitchforked or foisted upon the social landscape by a *deus ex machina*, but, on the contrary, must be the product of the citizens' brains and muscles. And there is no doubt that architects and engineers, foreigners for the most part, will probably be needed, but the local party leaders must see to it that the techniques seep into the desert of the citizen's brain so that the bridge in its entirety and in every detail can be integrated, redesigned, and reappropriated. The citizen must appropriate the bridge. Then, and only then, is everything possible.[22]

Like Fanon did 50 years prior, Galeano asserts the central importance of assessing where the control of scientific inquiry rests, and with whom. Just as solar panels mean something very different when deployed by the military rather than by a subsistence community, the science that makes clean technologies possible also means something very different when cloistered in institutions—whether corporations, universities, or state research centers—that are tacitly focused on maintaining the petromodern privileges of *their* modern lives, as opposed to being opened up to experimentation and reappropriation by communities living under their colonial shadow, who more directly experience the disabling effects of this rapidly changing world-ecology. When becoming scientists, Galeano explains, "We do not want to cease to be what we are. ... What makes us what we are is our land, our people, our history, our culture, and as Zapatistas, our struggle."[23]

To reiterate then, it matters where, with whom, and as part of what struggles, we pursue collective desires to invent, explore, and create a habitable future for the lives and liveliness of this planet. Where might radical scientists, whether Zapatista or from another community, locate the most important sociotechnical frontiers? In the commercial viability of clean technologies—whether solar and wind power or advanced nuclear—or perhaps as well in the ability for such technologies to support forms of expanded kinship, alternative orientations to the nonhuman, and alternative ways of sharing, making, and holding onto life?

Full Care

I want to approach my conclusion by way of a foil. Nick Srnicek and Alex Williams's book *Inventing the Future* attempts to reclaim a politics of technological advance for a radically anti-capitalist project with calls for "full automation."[24] They argue that the labor-saving capacities of advanced technologies promise to support a true "realm of freedom" in which scarcity and toilsome work have both been abolished, leaving space and time for creative experimentation and leisure. Srnicek and Williams distinguish their accelerationist politics from increasingly prevalent forms of "folk politics" exemplified by movements such as Occupy (and one would assume, the Zapatistas), which they regard as overly committed to small-scale, localist approaches. Folk politics, they argue, tend to offer a romantic vision of simpler times, which can then be simulated on a small, prefigurative scale. By contrast, they want to see the radical left embrace world-making aspirations and to see in modern technology the possibility of a radically reorientated world of technologically enabled abundance. For them, "full automation" is a utopian call to explore ways in which technology can enable the necessities of human life to be produced without human drudgery; robots and computers doing the repetitive and stultifyingly Taylorized work that would otherwise be left to low-paid laborers working in unhealthy conditions.

But at no point do Srnicek and Williams seriously consider the environmental implications of such an automated world, whether capitalist or otherwise.[25] Instead, their vision of a luxurious post-capitalism implies a foundational faith that clean technologies will make the world of full automation environmentally sustainable, resulting in an advanced industrial society that is somehow no longer environmentally destructive. As I discussed in chapter 6, this is ultimately a desire, even if never explicitly acknowledged, to "make the world made by oil possible after oil."[26]

Concerning issues of emotional and caring labor, Srnicek and Williams still regard full automation as the most radical possibility. They argue that the feminized realm of caring labor is just as likely to benefit from a technologically mediated reprieve from toil. But is that necessarily so? Here is where we can begin to push back. Perhaps not all care giving can or should be seen as "toil" to be automated out of our lives. In fact, what if we turned toward the long tradition of materialist ecofeminism, from Val Plumwood, Ariel Salleh, and Maria Mies through to Donna Harraway's recent work exploring webs of multispecies life, to counterpose something like *full care* to their accelerationist desire for full automation?[27] Instead of reducing all work to toil, full care might instead assert that there is an art of everything, and everything can become an art. Instead of envisioning a future world built upon the freedom *from* necessity, we would instead be following the subsistence perspective outlined by Vandana Shiva and Maria Mies and asking what freedom *within* necessity could become.[28] Instead of only looking for technological solutions to maintain abundance without the need for human labor, we would look for ways to reorient abundance around an ethic and practice of care-full attention to the more-than-human world—to objects made and used, to ancestors, descendants, and co-inhabitants, to natures, cultures and economies made and unmade—and thus craft a practice of living and making, holding and caring in which abundance is not just an accumulation of resources, but also an intensity and reciprocity of experience.

I don't mean to pit these two options, full automation and full care, against one another as if we must definitively choose sides. The real point is that any actually possible, sustainable, and desirable post-capitalist futures will likely have to negotiate both of these utopian impulses and their sometimes contradictory implications. To take one example: should we have full automation of our food system (as the Breakthrough Institute essentially suggests in their ecomodernist manifesto), or should we instead have full care, perhaps as envisioned by some of the land-tenure practices of indigenous peoples prior to and despite their to colonization and genocidal destruction? Between these two sociotechnical forms there are a million possibilities of distributed and diverse agricultural practices, partially assisted by any number of industrial and pre-industrial technologies, by logistical systems at any number of spatial scales, and by diverse socio-economic and cultural forms.[29]

To this extent, synthetic biology research looks much different when it is oriented around genetically modifying seeds to be Roundup Ready as opposed to work being done, for instance, at the Land Institute, where attempts are being made to develop viable, grain-yielding perennial plants that can offer an alternative to resource-intensive and soil-depleting annual grains.[30] The Land Institute's approach, which they call Natural Systems Agriculture, "matches the principles and insights of evolutionary and ecological science with the applied skills and knowledge of agronomy to partner with and intensify the beneficial relationships within living species, communities, and ecosystems."[31] Wes Jackson, the founder of the Land Institute, was actively part of the appropriate technologies movement of the 1960s and 1970s. Not only does he fundamentally believe that another, less acquisitive science is possible, but that the institute's work is "capable of generating conditions that are useless, unproductive and inefficient for capital, yet still valuable for more-than-human 'communities.'"[32] He writes: "The fundamental question is not, 'what can we do?' but rather, 'what kind of world do we want and what will nature require of us?'"[33]

Ultimately, we need to develop an orientation towards the future that allows for the reevaluation of diverse human practices at every scale, a discussion of where craft can and should be celebrated and developed, and where toil can and should be automated and eliminated. These will be complex sociotechnical-environmental discussions. Who participates in them, and what sciences and capacities they bring to bear upon these questions, matters tremendously. Or as Donna Harraway writes, "It matters which stories tell stories, which concepts think concepts. Mathematically, visually, and narratively, it matters which figures figure figures, which systems systematize systems."[34] I end then, with a call to expand the bounds of what is considered to be legitimate sociotechnical-environmental creativity beyond entrepreneurial (and technological) pragmatism; following the path set out by feminist and decolonial science studies, to always question the situatedness of science and technology and to think about world-making beyond market-making and the petrocultures of first world privilege.[35]

Here we can return to one of the cleantech visions detailed in chapter 6: Jacobson and Delucchi's proposal for an entirely renewable future based on wind, water and solar power. In some ways the most exciting aspects of their proposal—understood specifically as a call for an entirely renewable energy system—are the fundamental cultural, political, and economic transformations that such a technological feat would necessarily entail. Consider for instance, the transformations in food production that would have to occur once petroleum-based fertilizers were no longer available. In order to avoid starvation, new (and old) innovations in diverse agro-ecology practices would need to be explored and implemented on a global scale. Food systems predicated upon massive and predictable streams of soy and corn would need to be undone and replaced with innovative regionally specific approaches that incorporate a diverse set of crops into our food system (perhaps integrating the sorts of perennial polycultures being developed by the Land Institute). One way or another, a pluripotent intellect would be essential to our survival and a culture of fast food would very well be undone. And the story doesn't end there: in light of anthropogenic climate change, inter-regional coordination may become increasingly important, as well as a range of efforts from soil management to synthetic biology meant to enable food production despite increasingly volatile and inhospitable growing conditions.

Or what about the lack of plastics that would occur with a shift away from petroleum refining? The array of basic commodities produced out of petroleum-based plastic would need to be entirely reconceptualized, and with it, much of the core social and material relationships that have come to define modern life. Perhaps a material such as Ecovative's mycelium packaging could fill some of the gap, with regional variations taking advantage of whatever agricultural wastes were most readily available as feedstock. In fact, in 2017 Ecovative received a $9 million contract from the Defense Advanced Research Projects Agency (DARPA) to develop mycelium-based living building materials.[36] But even with this and other clean technologies, would we really be able to make so many products in the first place? The most likely result of these transformations would be an incredibly dematerialized standard of living, where reuse and recycling would be essential and many conveniences phased out as no longer socially, economically, or environmentally viable. The net result of all of these reductions would be—we can only imagine—a reduction in total energy demand, making the necessary infrastructure for renewable energy generation that much easier to achieve.

In many ways this exercise simultaneously reveals how impossible the cleantech revolution is, as well as how much more viable a radical energy transformation could be. It reminds us that the most difficult aspect of any energy transition will not be getting renewable infrastructure online, but keeping the existing fossil fuel infrastructure—broadly understood—offline.[37] The sociotechnical—and most likely political, economic and cultural—developments that will be required to keep the fossilized remains of past life from being transformed into fuel are urgently needed, perhaps even more so than the incremental gains of clean technologies as currently approached. Discussions around "just transitions" are beginning to make these connections, asking that emphasis shifts to "whole system reconfiguration," in which patterns of everyday life are just as likely to be targeted as the technologies enabling them.[38]

There is very little in first-world consumer lives, especially when it comes to high-tech gadgets, that is capable of being produced fossil free. This means that in a truly post-petroleum world, a majority of the industrial base could not sell its wares, make its profits, or justify its existence within the prevailing socioeconomic system. These are—I think—exciting connections to trace and paths to follow. They lead us toward visions of radically transformed sociotechnical futures. They help reveal which technologies depend on which material and energetic flows, and they help us begin to see that the most crucial issues we face have to do with broader questions: How will we live together? What materials will make our cultures? What energies will we depend upon and put toward what ends? How will we let go and learn to love other worlds?

Critical environmentalists need to take both concrete technological decisions and more abstract sociotechnical imaginaries just as seriously. We need to be able to help shape our societies' collective innovation agendas in radically new ways. While this means fighting for a voice in these conversations, we also need to be careful to make sure that that voice is nuanced, thoughtful, and not simply an endorsement of clean technologies and the industries ready and willing to roll them out as an augmentation of the status quo. We need to be able to shift the terms of these conversations, to make sure that they are not just about which technologies—but about which uses, which purposes: what we want to do with technologies and most importantly, what lives we want to live.

If we are ever going to escape this reality, this petroculture, we will need to believe that other worlds are possible, and that we don't have to go to Mars to create one. Instead, we have to fight to make this place so radically different that it will feel like we are on another planet.

Final Words From the Funders Forum: Gaming the System

MQ, one of the investors who regularly attended the Funders Forum, was intrigued by Eric Lerner's presentation about LPP's aneutronic fusion reactor. He eventually scheduled a private meeting at Lerner's lab, though he ultimately declined to get involved. Over the course of my research, I had a number of long philosophical conversations with MQ. After a Funders Forum presentation we would sometimes leave together and walk across town, toward his apartment on the Upper East Side. Often he would have us stop in at Christie's auction house or pause to look in the windows. He collected watches, or at least he *had* collected watches, during one of the less austere periods in his life. One afternoon over coffee, we ended up discussing some of the problems inherent in the waste-making economy, from disposability and pollution to his interest in pharmaceuticals. Discussing the pharmaceutical industry, we addressed its preference for developing maintenance drugs to procure a lifelong-patient customer base, as opposed to developing one-time cures. Frustrating as this may be, I suggested, it is hard to deny that from a business standpoint this seems to be a good tactic. MQ disagreed vehemently:

MQ: It isn't good business. If you can cure somebody that's a better thing than simply maintaining them.
JG: According to whose standards?
MQ: My standards. Any human standards.
JG: But it's not good business.
MQ: Doesn't matter. Good business is what eventually does the best for the world. There's a moral standard to it. There's a total moral standard. We don't do things that are wrong.
JG: We don't?
MQ: We do but we shouldn't. It's not a model; it's not a paradigm. Money will go there, but gaming the system and getting money is not what we're on earth for.

It's not a good way to be. And you're not going to be happy with yourself, you're not going to be happy with your family, and you're not going to happy with others around you.

JG: So is this just about greed?

MQ: You have to earn a living. That's the other side. And if you don't have the ability to go out and create something, you're going to have to game the system in some way, shape, or form.

With that, MQ chuckled. He liked this idea a lot. "I can see this as a doctoral thesis: gaming the system."

Despite the fact that he was a lifelong investor who began his career on Wall Street, MQ identified with the entrepreneurs he helped finance. He was contributing to the innovation economy, to his definition of "good business" as opposed to those just seeking to make money any way possible.

I didn't end up taking MQ's suggestion for the title of my dissertation or this book based on it, but I do want to highlight the importance of his conclusions. If someone is not capable of producing something meaningful, but they still need to feed their family, then they will need to find some other way to make some money. So long as we are structurally excluded from producing in meaningful ways, we will have no choice but to "game the system," or, I would add, to contribute to that "boring," waste-making economy.

This is important. It reminds us that our spirit—by which I mean our desire to be impactful, our vision of how and in what ways we could potentially improve the human condition—is often far more noble, far more adventurous, far more creative and innovative and virtuous, then most of us are readily given the ability to act upon. And here, with this final use of "we," I do not simply mean me and you or any specific set of individuals—but a more general *we*—a collectively laboring and thinking social body, largely, but not entirely, patterned by capitalist social relationships. Capital's rhythms are powerful, but they are not all-encompassing. It is important to remember this. The pluripotent intellect will always exceed these bounds; it will always remain creative and innovative and capable of producing, thinking, and transforming a world that capital could never dream of, or survive within.

Notes

Introduction

1. To further protect the anonymity of those I interviewed and identified by initials, and to respect the privacy of the event itself, I created a fictitious name for these gatherings.

2. "About," Vegawatt, retrieved April 12, 2016, http://vegawattchp.com/about/. As of July 2017, the site claims monthly utility savings of up to $3,000.

3. See Raj Patel, *Stuffed and Starved: The Hidden Battle for the World Food System* (Brooklyn: Melville House Books, 2012); Eric Schlosser, *Fast Food Nation: The Dark Side of the All-American Meal* (Boston: Houghton Mifflin Harcourt, 2001).

4. See, for example, Sheldon Rampton and John C. Stauber, *Toxic Sludge Is Good for You: Lies, Damn Lies, and the Public Relations Industry* (Monroe, NY: Common Courage Press, 2002); Ozzie Zehner, *Green Illusions: The Dirty Secrets of Clean Energy and the Future of Environmentalism* (Lincoln: University of Nebraska Press, 2012); and Subhabrata Bobby Banerjee, "Corporate Social Responsibility: The Good, the Bad and the Ugly," *Critical Sociology* 34, no. 1 (2008): 51–79.

5. Antonio Regalado, "Innovation Clusters and the Dream of Being the Next Silicon Valley," *MIT Technology Review*, July 1, 2013, http://www.technology review.com/news/516501/in-innovation-quest-regions-seek-critical-mass. In terms of cleantech-specific venture investing, San Francisco, San Jose, Boston, and Los Angeles, together account for 54% of the capital flows from 2011 through 2016. During this time, the New York metro area accounted for 3% of the total market, making it the eighth-largest venture capital market in cleantech, with just over $1 billion invested. See Devasree Saha and Mark Muro, "Cleantech Venture Capital: Continued Declines and Narrow Geography Limits Prospects," *Brookings Report*, May 16, 2017, https://www.brookings.edu/research/cleantech-venture-capital-continued-declines-and-narrow-geography-limit-prospects.

6. NEXUS-NY Blog, "A Grand Unified Theory of Tech Startups, October 1, 2015, http://nexus-ny.org/recent-news/page/11/.

7. As of February 2016, the event was forced to once again find a new location, as the host at this most recent law firm took a new job. Without him, the firm was not interested in continuing to sponsor the sessions.

8. Federico Caprotti, "The Cultural Economy of Cleantech: Environmental Discourse and the Emergence of a New Technology Sector," *Transactions of the Institute of British Geographers* 37, no. 3 (2012): 370–385.

Chapter 1

1. *Bloomberg* forecasters anticipate a 58% increase in global energy demand by 2040, and while they also predict a peak in energy sector (not total) emissions by 2026, they go on to say that this very gradual decline "is not nearly enough for the climate." See "New Energy Outlook 2017: Executive Summary," *Bloomberg New Energy Finance* (June 15, 2017).

2. Intergovernmental Panel on Climate Change, *Climate Change 2014—Impacts, Adaptation and Vulnerability: Regional Aspects* (Cambridge: Cambridge University Press, 2014).

3. Aaron M. McCright and Riley E. Dunlap, "Anti-reflexivity the American Conservative Movement's Success in Undermining Climate Science and Policy," *Theory, Culture & Society* 27, no. 2–3 (2010): 100–133.

4. There are far too many texts about the greening of society to cite here, but for a representative sampling of this diversity of perspectives see: Ron Pernick and Clint Wilder, *The Clean Tech Revolution: Winning and Profiting from Clean Energy* (New York: HarperCollins e-Books, 2014); David J. Hess, *Good Green Jobs in a Global Economy: Making and Keeping New Industries in the United States*, (Cambridge, MA: MIT Press, 2012); Giacomo D'Alisa, Federico Demaria, and Giorgos Kallis, eds., *Degrowth: A Vocabulary for a New Era* (London: Routledge, 2014); Michael Löwy, "Ecosocialism: Putting on the Brakes Before Going Over the Cliff," *New Politics* 14, no. 4 (2014): 24. Olivia Bina offers a succinct overview of the various types of green economy proposals in "The Green Economy and Sustainable Development: An Uneasy Balance?," *Environment and Planning C: Government and Policy*, 31, no. 6 (2013): 1023–1047.

5. Leo Marx, "The Idea of 'Technology' and Postmodern Pessimism," in *Does Technology Drive History,* ed. Leo Marx and Merritt Roe Smith (Cambridge, MA: MIT Press, 1994), 237–258.

6. See Lester R. Brown, *Plan B 4.0: Mobilizing to Save Civilization* (New York: W. W. Norton, 2009); Thomas L. Friedman, *Hot, Flat, and Crowded: Why We Need a Green Revolution, and How It Can Renew America* (New York: Farrar, Straus and Giroux, 2008); Paul Hawken, Amory B. Lovins, and L. Hunter Lovins, *Natural Capitalism: Creating the Next Industrial Revolution* (Boston: Little, Brown, 1999); Fred Krupp and Miriam Horn, *Earth: The Sequel: The Race to Reinvent Energy and Stop Global Warming*

(New York: W. W. Norton, 2008); Jonathon Porritt, *Capitalism as if the World Matters* (London: Earthscan, 2007); James Gustave Speth, *The Bridge at the Edge of the World: Capitalism, the Environment, and Crossing from Crisis to Sustainability* (New Haven, CT: Yale University Press, 2008).

7. Mike Berners-Lee, *How Bad Are Bananas? The Carbon Footprint of Everything* (Vancouver: Greystone Books, 2012).

8. Andrew Szasz, *Shopping Our Way to Safety: How We Changed From Protecting the Environment to Protecting Ourselves* (Minneapolis: University of Minnesota Press, 2007).

9. Travis Bradford, *Solar Revolution: The Economic Transformation of the Global Energy Industry* (Cambridge, MA: MIT Press 2006); Bill Reed, *The Integrative Design Guide to Green Building: Redefining the Practice of Sustainability.* (Hoboken, NJ: John Wiley & Sons, 2009).

10. Murray Bookchin offers a classic perspective on the ways in which "liberatory technologies" can anchor a post-capitalist world in *Post-scarcity Anarchism* (Berkeley: Ramparts Press, 1971). For an example of the green-growth paradigm, see Paul Ekins, *Economic Growth and Environmental Sustainability: The Prospects for Green Growth* (New York: Routledge, 2002).

11. For classical examples of ecological modernization theory, see Arthur Mol, "Ecological Modernisation and Institutional Reflexivity: Environmental Reform in the Late Modern Age," *Environmental Politics* 5, no. 2 (1996): 302–323; Gert Spaargaren, *The Ecological Modernization of Production and Consumption: Essays in Environmental Sociology* (Wageningen: Landbouw Universiteit Wageningen, 1997). It is worth noting that more recent forms of ecological modernization coming out of the Breakthrough Institute support ongoing growth, albeit with the faith that the trajectory of this growth can and should be asymptotic, eventually leveling off into a steady-state economy sometime in the future. See for instance, Harry Saunders, "Does Capitalism Require Endless Growth? Marx and Malthus Reconsidered," *The Breakthrough Journal* 6 (2016), http://thebreakthrough.org/index.php/journal/issue-6/does-capitalism-require-endless-growth. This perspective depends on the possibility that advanced industrial economies can "decouple" their economic growth from their environmental footprint. For a succinct critique of this perspective, see Robert Fletcher, "Decoupling, A Dangerous Fantasy," *Entitle* (May 10, 2016), https://entitleblog.org/2016/05/10/decoupling-a-dangerous-fantasy.

12. For an overview of these hybrid approaches, see Damian White, Alan Rudy, and Brian Gareau, *Environments, Natures, and Social Theory: Toward A Critical Hybridity* (London: Palgrave, 2015). Also, in Olivia Bina's typology of green economy proposals, she considers a number of hybrid categories; see Bina, *The Green Economy*. Despite the nuance in many of these proposals, Goldstein and Tyfield argue that these proposals represent a form of green Keynesianism that ultimately seeks to save

civilization by saving capitalism and with it, the very forms of modern industrial life that are the primary source of our climate crisis. See Jesse Goldstein and David Tyfield, "Green Keynesianism: Bringing the Entrepreneurial State Back in(to Question)?," *Science as Culture*, July 7, 2017, http://www.tandfonline.com/doi/abs/10.1080 /09505431.2017.1346598?journalCode=csac20. Geoff Mann describes Keynesianism as a rejoinder to liberalism, an approach to governance that is willing to take illiberal actions if they are necessary to avert crisis in the short term. These actions are understood as part of an effort to save civilization from capital's tendencies toward crisis without descending into the chaos and violence of revolutionary disruptions. See Geoff Mann, *In The Long Run, We Are All Dead: Keynesianism, Political Economy and Revolution* (New York: Verso, 2017).

13. Brian Dumaine, "Why Jeff Bezos, Peter Thiel, and Others Are Betting on Fusion," *Fortune*, September 28, 2015, http://fortune.com/2015/09/28/jeff-bezos-peter-thiel -fusion/. Peter Thiel has had a more complicated relationship with cleantech, emerging early on as a strong advocate, and then in 2011 proclaiming that cleantech was all but dead primarily due to failures in the venture capital funding model—only to then continue to support clean energy projects, including Helion. Nicole Perlroth, "PayPal Founders: Innovation Is Dead," *Forbes.com*, http://www.forbes.com/sites /nicoleperlroth/2011/09/12/paypal-founders-innovation-is-dead/#17fb38e96d87.

14. Ted Nordhaus and Michael Shellenberger, "The Long Death of Environmentalism," *The Breakthrough Institute*, http://thebreakthrough.org/archive/the_long_death _of_environmenta. See also Nordhaus and Shellenberger, *Break Through: From the Death of Environmentalism to the Politics of Possibility* (Boston: Houghton Mifflin, 2007).

15. *An Ecomodernist Manifesto*, http://www.ecomodernism.org. A series of excellent critiques of the manifesto can be found in *Environmental Humanities* 7, no. 15 (2015). These essays each focus, in different ways, on the "amnesias" and omissions of the manifesto; from a history of struggle that is effaced in the celebration of modernity's successes, to entanglements with the more-than-human world, whose plight, along with that of colonized and other non-modern subjects, is largely left out of consideration. See from this series Rosemary-Claire Collard, Jessica Dempsey, and Juanita Sundberg, "The Moderns' Amnesia in Two Registers," (227–232), and Eileen Crist, "The Reaches of Freedom" (245–254). Latour and Szerszynski both explore narratives of progress implied by their use of modernism, and the temporalities that this implies; see Bruno Latour, "Fifty Shades of Green" (219–225), and Bronislaw Szerszynski, "Getting Hitched and Unhitched with the Ecomodernists," (239–244). As Szerszynski writes, "These textual 'chronotropes' serve to reassure us that, through the 'noise' of historical accident, the clear 'signal' of progress can nevertheless be discerned" (242). Clive Hamilton's contribution argues that the manifesto is structured as "The Theodicy of the 'Good Anthropocene'" (233–238).

16. Fred Block and Matthew Keller, *State of Innovation: The U.S. Government's Role in Technology Development* (Boulder, CO: Paradigm Publishers, 2011).

17. Jesse Jenkins and Sara Mansur, *A Clean Energy Deployment Administration* (Oakland, CA: The Breakthrough Institute, 2011), http://thebreakthrough.org/blog/CEDA .pdf; Shellenberger and Nordhaus, *Break Through.*

18. Goldstein and Tyfield, "Green Keynesianism"; David Tyfield, "A Cultural Political Economy of Research and Innovation in an Age of Crisis," *Minerva* 50, no. 2 (2012): 149–167.

19. Herbert Marcuse, *One-Dimensional Man: Studies in the Ideology of Advanced Industrial Society* (Boston: Beacon Press, 1991); Harry Braverman, *Labor and Monopoly Capital: The Degradation of Work in the Twentieth Century* (New York: NYU Press, 1998); David F. Noble, *America by Design: Science, Technology, and the Rise of Corporate Capitalism* (Oxford: Oxford University Press, 1979). For an examination of Marx's views, see Regina Roth, "Marx on Technical Change in the Critical Edition," *The European Journal of the History of Economic Thought* 17, no. 5 (2010). Victor Wallis offers an overview of the concept of innovation in "Historical Critical Dictionary of Marxism: Innovation," *Historical Materialism* 16, no. 3 (2008): 227–232.

20. Philip Mirowski, *Science-Mart* (Cambridge, MA: Harvard University Press, 2011); David Tyfield, *The Economics of Science: A Critical Realist Overview: Volume 2: Toward a Synthesis of Political Economy and Science and Technology Studies* (London: Routledge, 2014).

21. Benjamin Gaddy, Varun Sivaram, and Francis O'Sullivan, "Venture Capital and Cleantech: The Wrong Model for Clean Innovation," *MIT Energy Initiative* 77, July 2016. See also Louise Story, "An Oracle of Oil Predicts $200-a-Barrel Crude," *New York Times*, May 21, 2005.

22. Federico Caprotti, "The Cultural Economy of Cleantech: Environmental Discourse and the Emergence of a New Technology Sector," *Transactions of the Institute of British Geographers* 37, no. 3 (2012): 370–385.

23. James LoGerfo, "Cleantech Venture Investing: Patterns and Performance," Vortex Energy LLC, March 6, 2005, http://s3.amazonaws.com/lyro-production/e2aa 2dc59cc7692bdb63a47c5f49a561%2FMarkDonohuePerformance-File2.pdf.

24. Neal Dikeman, "What is Cleantech," *The Cleantech Group,* http://www.cleantech .org/what-is-cleantech/. Dikeman reports in this article how, in 2006, John Doerr of the venture capital firm Kleiner Perkins attempted to shift terminology back to greentech. His justification: "The word 'green' means money is to be made."

25. LoGerfo, "Cleantech Venture Investing."

26. Daniel Gross, "The Dot-Com Energy Boost," *Washington Post*, July 23, 2006, http://www.washingtonpost.com/wp-dyn/content/article/2006/07/21/AR200 6072101367.html.

27. Caprotti, "Cultural Economy of Cleantech."

28. Amy Cortese, "Business: Can Energy Ventures Pick Up Where Tech Left Off?," *New York Times*, February 9, 2009, http://www.nytimes.com/2003/02/09/business /business-can-energy-ventures-pick-up-where-tech-left-off.html.

29. Terrence Chea, "Betting on a Green Future," *Wired*, February 22, 2006, http:// www.wired.com/science/discoveries/news/2006/04/70641.

30. Frank Davies, "Silicon Valley Leaders: Political Climate Right for 'Green Tech,'" *San Jose Mercury News*, retrieved February 22, 2015, http://www.mercurynews.com /search/ci_5440875.

31. LoGerfo, "Cleantech Venture Investing."

32. Ibid., 15.

33. Gary Rivlin, "Green Tinge Is Attracting Seed Money to Ventures," *New York Times*, June 22, 2005, http://www.nytimes.com/2005/06/22/business/22clean.html.

34. Juliet Eilperin, "Why the Cleantech Boom Went Bust," *Wired*, January 2012, http://www.wired.com/2012/01/ff_solyndra/. See also Gaddy et al. "Venture Capital and Cleantech."

35. See, for instance, Gaddy et al., "Venture Capital and Cleantech"; and Brian Nese, Parissa Florez, and Kimberly Hellwig, "A Handy List of Energy-Related Bills Advancing in California," *Greentech Media*, June 14, 2017, https://www.greentech media.com/articles/read/a-handy-list-of-energy-related-bills-advancing-in-california.

36. Bill Gates, "Beating Nature at Its Own Game," *Gates Notes*, March 14, 2017, https://www.gatesnotes.com/Energy/Beating-Nature. I discuss Gates's "energy mira-cles" again in chapter 3.

37. Thaya Brook Knight, "A Walk Through the JOBS Act of 2012: Deregulation in the Wake of Financial Crisis," *Cato Institute*, July 14, 2016, https://www.brookings.edu /research/cleantech-venture-capital-continued-declines-and-narrow-geography-limit -prospects/. For an example of a super-connector organization, see http://primecoali tion.org/ and http://www.cato.org/publications/policy-analysis/walk-through-jobs -act-2012-deregulation-wake-financial-crisis.

38. Rob Day, "Cleantech is Dead! Long Live Cleantech!," *TechCrunch*, April 2015, https://techcrunch.com/2015/04/18/cleantech-is-dead-long-live-cleantech/.

39. Gates, *Beating Nature*.

40. Clayton Christensen, *The Innovator's Dilemma: When New Technologies Cause Great Firms to Fail* (Boston: Harvard Business Press, 1997).

41. See for instance, Brian Tokar, *Earth for Sale: Reclaiming Ecology in the Age of Corpo-rate Greenwash* (Boston: South End Press, 1999) and Heather Rogers, *Green Gone Wrong* (New York: Verso, 2013). Mackenzie Funk, in *Windfall* (New York: Penguin,

2015), offers a window into the many ways that climate change is being turned into opportunities for profit beyond cleantech.

42. Kenneth Gould, David N. Pellow, and Allan Schnaiberg, *The Treadmill of Production: Injustice and Unsustainability in the Global Economy* (London: Routledge, 2008); Cindi Katz, "Whose Nature, Whose Culture?: Private Productions of Space and the 'Preservation' of Nature," in *Remaking Reality: Nature at the Millennium*, ed. Bruce Braun and Noel Castree (London: Routledge, 1998), 46–63; Neil Smith, "Nature at the Millennium: Production and Re-enchantment," in *Remaking Reality: Nature at the Millennium*, 271–285; John Bellamy Foster, *Marx's Ecology: Materialism and Nature* (New York: Monthly Review Press, 2000).

43. Richard Smith, *Green Capitalism. The God That Failed* (London: College Publications, 2016); Joel Kovel, *The Enemy of Nature: The End of Capitalism or the End of the World?* (London: Zed Books, 2002); Jason W. Moore, *Capitalism in the Web of Life: Ecology and the Accumulation of Capital* (New York: Verso, 2015); James O'Connor, *Natural Causes: Essays in Ecological Marxism* (New York: Guilford Press, 1998).

44. Brett Clark and Richard York, "Dialectical Materialism and Nature: An Alternative to Economism and Deep Ecology," *Organization & Environment* 18, no. 3 (2005): 318–337.

45. For treadmill of production see Allan Schnaiberg, *The Environment, from Surplus to Scarcity* (New York: Oxford University Press, 1980). O'Connor, *Natural Causes*; John Bellamy Foster and Brett Clark, "Ecological Imperialism: The Curse of Capitalism," in *Socialist Register 2004: The New Imperial Challenge*, ed. Leo Panitch and Colin Leys (New York: Monthly Review Press, 2003), 186–201.

46. Max Weber, *The Protestant Ethic and the Spirit of Capitalism,* trans. Stephen Kalberg (Chicago: Fitzroy Dearborn, 2001); Albert O. Hirschman, *The Passions and the Interests: Political Arguments for Capitalism Before Its Triumph,* (Princeton. NJ: Princeton University Press, 1977).

47. Weber's thesis, central as it is to the discipline of sociology, has precipitated wide-ranging debates. Issues include whether and to what extent Protestantism and other religious beliefs actually influenced the development of capitalism as well as the question of whether capitalism requires an external morality or legitimizing force at all. See Ellen Meiksins Wood, *Democracy Against Capitalism* (Cambridge: Cambridge University Press, 1995) and Hartmut Lehmann and Guenther Roth, *Weber's Protestant Ethic: Origins, Evidence, Contexts* (Cambridge: Cambridge University Press, 1995).

48. Boltanski and Chiapello's work focuses on the transformations of French culture, but the story has a clear analog in the US. For example, Fred Turner's history of the *Whole Earth Catalog* presents a convincing account of the seamless transformation of 1970s counterculture and (some of) those committed to developing appropriate

technologies into what would eventually become a technophilic entrepreneurialism aimed at creating radical transformations within, as opposed to of, the capitalist economy. Fred Turner, *From Counterculture to Cyberculture: Stewart Brand, the Whole Earth Network, and the Rise of Digital Utopianism* (Chicago: University of Chicago Press, 2008). See also Mark Dowie, *Losing Ground: American Environmentalism at the Close of the Twentieth Century* (Cambridge, MA: MIT Press, 1995) and Andrew Dobson, *Green Political Thought* (London: Routledge, 2007).

49. Dowie, *Losing Ground*; and Leigh Glover, "From Love-Ins to Logos: Charting the Demise of Renewable Energy as a Social Movement," in *Transforming Power: Energy, Environment and Society in Conflict* (New Brunswick, NJ: Transaction Publishers, 2006), 249–270.

50. Hawken, Lovins, and Lovins, *Natural Capitalism*.

51. Naomi Klein, *This Changes Everything: Capitalism vs. the Climate* (New York: Simon & Schuster, 2014).

52. Ellen Meiksins Wood, *The Origin of Capitalism: A Longer View* (New York: Verso, 2002); Jesse Goldstein, "Terra Economica: Waste and the Production of Enclosed Nature," *Antipode* 45, no. 2 (2013): 357–375; David McNally, *Political Economy and the Rise of Capitalism: A Reinterpretation* (Berkeley: University of California Press, 1990).

53. Goldstein, "Terra Economica"; McNally, *Political Economy*; Ellen Meiksins Wood, *Empire of Capital* (London: Verso, 2003).

54. John Locke and C. B. Macpherson, chapter 5, section 37 in *Second Treatise of Government* (Indianapolis, IN: Hackett Publishing Company, 1980).

55. Goldstein, "Terra Economica"; J. M. Neeson, *Commoners: Common Right, Enclosure and Social Change in England, 1700–1820* (Cambridge: Cambridge University Press, 1996).

56. Wood, *Origins of Capitalism*; George C. Comninel, "English Feudalism and the Origins of Capitalism," *Journal of Peasant Studies* 27, no. 4 (2000): 1–53.

57. Nicholas Blomley, "Making Private Property: Enclosure, Common Right and the Work of Hedges," *Rural History* 18, no.1 (2007): 1–21; R. W. Bushaway, *By Rite: Custom, Ceremony and Community in England, 1700–1880* (London: Junction Books, 1983).

58. Wood, *Origins of Capitalism*.

59. Marx writes of this community of money in *Grundrisse; Foundations of the Critique of Political Economy (Rough Draft)*, trans. Martin Nicolaus (London: Pelican Marx Library, in association with *New Left Review*, 1973). Capital dissolves community, and in its place arises a community of money instead. The latter is of course pre-

sented somewhat facetiously, as an alienated world where relations between people and between people and the more than human world are all mediated by capital.

60. See Goldstein, "Terra Economica." Neil Smith developed the concept of the production of nature via his reading of Lefebvre. See Neil Smith, *Uneven Development: Nature, Capital, and the Production of Space, 3rd ed.* (Athens: University of Georgia Press, 2008).

61. See for instance E. P. Thompson, "Time, Work, Discipline and Industrial Capitalism," in *Customs in Common* (New York: New Press, 1990); Braverman, *Labor and Monopoly Capital.*

62. Martin Melosi, *Garbage in the Cities: Refuse, Reform and the Environment* (Pittsburgh, PA: University of Pittsburgh Press, 2004); Daniel Burnstein, *Next to Godliness: Confronting Dirt and Despair in Progressive-Era New York City* (Urbana: University of Illinois Press, 2006; Susan Strasser, *Waste and Want: A Social History of Trash* (New York: Metropolitan Books, 1999).

63. Susan Strasser, *Satisfaction Guaranteed: The Making of the American Mass Market* (New York: Pantheon Books, 1999); Stewart Ewen, *Captains of Consciousness: Advertising and the Social Roots of the Consumer Culture* (New York: Basic Books, 2001).

64. Karen Ho, *Liquidated: An Ethnography of Wall Street* (Durham, NC: Duke University Press, 2009).

65. John Sinclair, *The First Report from the Select Committee* (London: John Stockdale, 1796).

66. Krupp and Horn, *Earth: The Sequel*, 248.

67. Friedman, *Hot, Flat, and Crowded*, 289. In another example, Hawken, Lovins, and Lovins (*Natural Capitalism*, 1999) discuss Walmart's experiment with creating an eco-store in Lawrence, Kansas. To the extent this store is successful, it means that their other thousands of box stores represent an "untapped source of potential savings" (89). Walmart is simply not-yet green.

68. Peter Barnes, *Capitalism 3.0: A Guide to Reclaiming the Commons* (San Francisco: Berrett-Koehler, 2006), 26.

69. Max Weber's thesis regarding the spirit of capitalism investigated some of the central actors involved in this process—such as the yeoman farmers working to transform their privately held or rented lands into maximally profitable businesses. Instead of focusing on the market imperatives compelling such small businesspeople to operate at the highest standards of efficiency (so as to generate enough revenue to pay market rates for rent, labor, and supplies), Weber focused on the ways in which Protestant asceticism could, after the fact, serve to legitimize the pecuniary and efficiency-maximizing logic that had come to subsume productive life. We must interpret any new green spirit of capitalism in a similar vein—not as harbinger of a new

economic logic, but as a new way to make sense of, promote, and legitimize processes already underway. See Stephen Kalberg, "Introduction to the Protestant Ethic," introduction to Max Weber, *The Protestant Ethic and the Spirit of Capitalism* (Chicago: Fitzroy Dearborn, 2001), xi–xxvi.

Chapter 2

1. Christos Kalantaridis, *Understanding the Entrepreneur: An Institutionalist Perspective* (Aldershot: Ashgate Publishing, 2004); Christos Kalantaridis, "Veblen and the Entrepreneur," *International Review of Sociology* 14, no. 3 (2004): 487–501; Israel M. Kirzner, *Perception, Opportunity, and Profit: Studies in the Theory of Entrepreneurship* (Chicago: University of Chicago Press, 1979); Sven Ripsas, "Towards an Interdisciplinary Theory of Entrepreneurship," *Small Business Economics* 10, no. 2 (1998): 103–115.

2. Mark Blaug, "Entrepreneurship Before and After Schumpeter," in *Entrepreneurship: The Social Science View*, ed. Richard Swedberg (Oxford: Oxford University Press, 2000). The Austrian economist Ludwig von Mises and his student Kirzner argued that entrepreneurship is simply market arbitrage that is ultimately beholden to consumer preferences, whose tastes and wants ultimately determine which entrepreneurs succeed and which do not. The entrepreneur can only introduce a new or innovative product to the extent that consumers will pay for it.

3. Richard Swedberg, "The Social Science View of Entrepreneurship: Introduction and Practical Applications," in *Entrepreneurship: The Social Science View* (Oxford: Oxford University Press, 2000); Blaug, "Entrepreneurship Before and After Schumpeter"; Joseph Schumpeter, *The Economics and Sociology of Capitalism* (Princeton, NJ: Princeton University Press, 1991).

4. Swedberg, "The Social Science View of Entrepreneurship."

5. Emery Kay Hunt and Mark Lautzenheiser, *History of Economic Thought: A Critical Perspective*, 3rd ed. (Abingdon, UK: Routledge, 2011).

6. Joseph A. Schumpeter, *The Theory of Economic Development: An Inquiry Into Profits, Capital, Credit, Interest, and the Business Cycle* (Piscataway, NJ: Transaction Publishers, 1934).

7. Swedberg, "The Social Science View of Entrepreneurship."

8. Schumpeter, *The Theory of Economic Development*, 93.

9. Ibid.

10. Luc Boltanski and Eve Chiapello, *The New Spirit of Capitalism*, trans. Gregory Elliott (London: Verso, 2007).

11. Ibid.

12. Assessing one's impact, by no means unique to cleantech, operates throughout neoliberal culture, often deployed in managerial efforts meant to measure performance (and discipline the labor of) a wide range of knowledge workers. See for instance, Ruth Evans, "Achieving and Evidencing Research 'Impact'?: Tensions and Dilemmas from an Ethic of Care Perspective," *Area* 48, no. 2 (2016): 213–221.

13. According to Domenico Losurdo, in *Liberalism: A Counter-History* (Brooklyn: Verso Books, 2014) the inclusivity of liberal concepts such as equality and freedom are built upon the decidedly illiberal grounds of racialized exclusions and slavery; we can consider a critique of liberal environmentalism in a similar vein. See Kathleen McAfee, "Green Economy and Carbon Markets for Conservation and Development: A Critical View, *International Environmental Agreements: Politics, Law and Economics* 16, no. 3 (2015): 333–353. Also see Sanjay Chaturvedi and Timothy Doyle, *Climate Terror: A Critical Geopolitics of Climate Change* (New York: Palgrave Macmillan, 2015). It should go without question that "saving the planet" is likely to look quite different from the perspective of a first-world cleantech entrepreneur than it might from the "subsistence perspective" of women and men trying to survive in far less materially and energetically intensive ways. See Maria Mies and Vandana Shiva, "Subsistence Perspective," in *The Feminist Standpoint Theory Reader: Intellectual and Political Controversies,* ed. Sandra Harding (London: Routledge, 2004).

14. Jeremy Walker and Melinda Cooper, "Genealogies of Resilience From Systems Ecology to the Political Economy of Crisis Adaptation," *Security Dialogue* 42, no. 2 (2011): 143–160; Michael Redclift, *Sustainable Development: Exploring the Contradictions* (London: Routledge, 2002).

15. "Impact Investing," 2014. *Wikipedia,* which quotes the definition of the Global Impact Investing Network, retrieved June 2014: http://en.wikipedia.org/w/index .php?title=Impact_investing&oldid=597295146.

16. Maximilian Martin, "Dr. Maximilian Martin," *Toniic,* July 5, 2012, http://www .toniic.com/blog.

17. "About," *GIIRS,* retrieved March 9, 2014, http://giirs.org/about-giirs/about. GIIRS has since become a subsidiary of B Analytics, which has integrated the GIIRS system into their free to use, impact assessment platform (http://bimpactassessment .net). See http://globaldevincubator.org/global-impact-investing-rating-system.

18. These visions of planetary improvement most often presume, often uncritically, that the requisite material and energetic inputs required for the planetary expansion of good green technologies will be readily available at a scale that can cater to prevailing patterns of consumption and industrial growth. For a notable exception, see David MacKay, *Sustainable Energy—Without the Hot Air* (Cambridge: Cambridge University Press, 2008).

19. Lewis Mumford, *Technics and Civilization*, with a new foreword by Langdon Winner (Chicago: University of Chicago Press, 2010 [orig. New York: Harcourt, 1934]), 385.

20. See Thorstein Veblen, *The Theory of the Leisure Class* (Oxford: Oxford University Press, 2009 [orig. London: Macmillan, 1899]) and *The Engineers and the Price System* (Eastman, CT: Martino Fine Books, 2012 [orig. New York: Viking, 1921]). See also David Riesman, *Thorstein Veblen: A Critical Interpretation* (New York: Seabury Press, 1975).

21. Alexander Wilson, *The Culture of Nature: North American Landscape from Disney to the Exxon Valdez* (Toronto: Between the Lines, 1991).

22. Allan Schnaiberg and Kenneth A. Gould, *Environment and Society: The Enduring Conflict* (New York: St. Martin's Press, 1994).

23. Matthew Huber, *Lifeblood: Oil, Freedom, and the Forces of Capital* (Minneapolis: University of Minnesota Press, 2013); John Urry, *Societies Beyond Oil: Oil Dregs and Social Futures* (London: Zed Books, 2013).

24. Vance Packard, *The Waste Makers* (New York: D. McKay Co., 1960).

25. Woody Tasch, *Inquiries into the Nature of Slow Money: Investing as if Food, Farms, and Fertility Mattered* (White River Junction, VT: Chelsea Green Publishing, 2008), 46. Like Veblen, Tasch is enamored with the entrepreneurial productivity of Henry Ford, who eschewed throwaway culture by producing well-made, durable, yet basic cars for a mass market. For the connection between Ford and Veblen see Riesman, *Thorstein Veblen*.

26. Anderson's company is profiled in a number of texts. See for instance, Paul Hawken, Amory B. Lovins, and L. Hunter Lovins, *Natural Capitalism: Creating the Next Industrial Revolution* (Boston: Little, Brown, 1999).

27. E. F. Schumacher, *Small Is Beautiful: Economics as if People Mattered: 25 Years Later...with Commentaries* (Point Roberts, WA: Hartley & Marks Publishers, 1995). See also Witold Rybczynski, *Paper Heroes: Appropriate Technology: Panacea or Pipedream?* (London: Penguin Books, 1991).

28. Andrew Jamison, *The Making of Green Knowledge: Environmental Politics and Cultural Transformation*, (Cambridge: Cambridge University Press, 2001), 66. See also Andrew Jamison and Ron Eyerman, *Seeds of the Sixties* (Berkeley: University of California Press: 1995). A paradigmatic example comes from the social ecologist Murray Bookchin, "Towards a Liberatory Technology," in *Post-scarcity Anarchism* (Berkeley: Ramparts Press, 1971).

29. Mumford, *Technics and Civilization*; Jamison, *The Making of Green Knowledge*.

30. Lewis Mumford, *Interpretations and Forecasts, 1922–1972: Studies in Literature, History, Biography, Technics, and Contemporary Society* (New York: Harcourt Brace Jovanovich, 1979), cited in Jamison, *The Making of Green Knowledge*, 67.

31. Bookchin, "Towards a Liberatory Technology."

32. Fred Turner, *From Counterculture to Cyberculture: Stewart Brand, the Whole Earth Network, and the Rise of Digital Utopianism* (Chicago: University of Chicago Press, 2008).

33. Carroll Pursell, "The Rise and Fall of the Appropriate Technology Movement in the United States, 1965–1985," *Technology and Culture* 34 (1993): 629–637. Marilyn Carr, *The AT Reader: Theory and Practice in Appropriate Technology* (London: Intermediate Technology Publications, 1985), http://www.cabdirect.org/abstracts/19856700772 .html; Malcolm Hollick, "The Appropriate Technology Movement and Its Literature: A Retrospective," *Technology in Society* 4, no. 3 (1982): 213–229; Denton E. Morrison, "Soft, Cutting Edge of Environmentalism: Why and How the Appropriate Technology Notion Is Changing the Movement." *The Natural Resources Journal* 20 (1980): 275–296.

34. *Bulletin of the New Alchemists*, Fall 1970, quoted in "About," The Green Center, https://newalchemists.net/about/.

35. Fred Turner, *From Counterculture to Cyberculture: Stewart Brand, the Whole Earth Network, and the Rise of Digital Utopianism* (Chicago: University of Chicago Press, 2008).

36. Tasch, *Inquiries into the Adventures of Slow Money*; Bill McKibben, *Deep Economy: The Wealth of Communities and the Durable Future* (New York: Henry Holt, 2007) and *Eaarth: Making a Life on a Tough New Planet* (New York: Henry Holt, 2011); Robert Hopkins, *The Transition Handbook: From Oil Dependency to Local Resilience* (White River Junction, VT: Chelsea Green Publishers, 2008). Much of the work that is associated with the degrowth movement might also fit here. However, this movement and the work associated with it is decidedly more critical of capitalism as a potential agent of positive environmental transformation, aligning it more with the post-capitalist politics of activist-scholars such as J. K. Gibson-Graham. See J. K. Gibson-Graham, *The End of Capitalism (As We Knew It)* (Minneapolis: University of Minnesota Press, 2006); and Giacomo D'Alisa, Federico Demaria, and Giorgos Kallis, eds., *Degrowth: A Vocabulary for a New Era* (London: Routledge, 2014). For a critique of these various localisms, see Greg Sharzer, *No Local: Why Small-Scale Alternatives Won't Change the World* (Hampshire, UK: John Hunt Publishing, 2012). It is worth noting that in the conclusion of his work, Sharzer ends up leaning on Murray Bookchin's work, in particular his conception of "libertarian municipalism," as an alternative to what he dismisses as ineffectual, petty-bourgeois localisms.

37. Gary Hirshberg, *Stirring It Up: How to Make Money and Save the World.* (New York: Hyperion, 2008), http://www.loc.gov/catdir/enhancements/fyl204/2009282329-d .html.

38. David Goodman, "Culture Change," *Mother Jones*, January 2003, http://www .motherjones.com/politics/2003/01/culture-change. For the sale to Lactalis, see http://www.masslive.com/business-news/index.ssf/2017/07/new_hampshire_ yogurt_maker_stonyfield_fa.html.

39. Ibid.

40. Hirshberg, *Stirring It Up,* 2.

41. Ibid., 3.

42. Ibid., 185.

43. See Heather Rogers, *Green Gone Wrong: Dispatches from the Frontlines of Ecocapitalism* (London: Verso Books, 2013).

44. Daniel Yergin, *The Prize: The Epic Quest for Oil, Money, & Power* (New York: Free Press, 2009).

45. Paul R. Ehrlich and David Brower, *The Population Bomb, 13th ed.* (New York: Ballantine Books, 1978 [1968]); Donella Meadows, *Limits to Growth.* (New York: Signet, 1972).

46. Yergin, *The Prize.*

47. Ibid., 527. Also during this time, the anti-nuclear movement was at its prime, presenting a trenchant critique of the technological industrial complex and engaged in direct actions and the largest mass protests of the post-Vietnam era. See Christian Joppke, *Mobilizing against Nuclear Energy: A Comparison of Germany and the United States* (Berkeley: University of California Press, 1993).

48. Yergin, *The Prize.*

49. Daniel Bell, *The Coming of Post-industrial Society* (New York: Basic Books, 2008 [1976]).

50. Julian Lincoln Simon, *The Ultimate Resource 2* (Princeton, NJ: Princeton University Press, 1996 [1981]), 66.

51. Mark Dowie, *Losing Ground: American Environmentalism at the Close of the Twentieth Century* (Cambridge, MA: MIT Press, 1995).

52. Hirshberg, *Stirring It Up,* xiii.

53. Tasch, *Inquiries into the Adventures of Slow Money,* 44.

54. Auden Schendler, *Getting Green Done: Hard Truths from the Front Lines of the Sustainability Revolution* (New York: PublicAffairs, 2009), 115.

55. Ibid.

56. There are numerous statistics to support this. The Bureau of Labor Statistics reports that after five years, only half of new businesses are still in operation (http://www.bls .gov/bdm/entrepreneurship/bdm_chart3.htm). The odds for a venture-funded business, or those aspiring to become one, are decidedly worse, with success estimated at anywhere from 1 out of 200 to 1 out of 10. See for instance Deborah Gage, "The Ven-

ture Capital Secret: 3 out of 4 Start-Ups Fail," *Wall Street Journal*, September 20, 2012, https://www.wsj.com/articles/SB10000872396390443720204578004980476429190; Henry Blodget, "A Startup's Odds of Success Are Very Low," *Business Insider*, May 28, 2013, http://www.businessinsider.com/startup-odds-of-success-2013-5.

57. Karen Ho, *Liquidated: An Ethnography of Wall Street* (Durham, NC: Duke University Press, 2009).

58. Trish Ruebottom, "The Microstructures of Rhetorical Strategy in Social Entrepreneurship: Building Legitimacy through Heroes and Villains," *Journal of Business Venturing* 28, no.1 (2013): 98–116; Alistair R. Anderson and Lorraine Warren, "The Entrepreneur as Hero and Jester: Enacting the Entrepreneurial Discourse," *International Small Business Journal* 29, no. 6 (2011): 589–609.

59. Eric Schurenberg, "Letter from the Editor," *Inc.*, June 2015.

60. Imre Szeman, "Entrepreneurship as the New Common Sense," *South Atlantic Quarterly* 114, no. 3 (2015): 231–244.

61. This emerges as a popular theme in green capitalist literature, which rails against the short-termism of Wall Street and financialized logics. See for instance, Tasch, *Inquiries into the Adventures of Slow Money*; Peter Barnes, *Capitalism 3.0: A Guide to Reclaiming the Commons* (San Francisco: Berrett-Koehler, 2006), 26; and Frances Moore Lappé, *EcoMind: Changing the Way We Think, to Create the World We Want* (New York: Nation Books, 2013).

62. Veblen, *Engineers and the Price System.*

63. See two works by David Harvey: "Space as a Keyword," chapter 3 in *Spaces of Global Capitalism: A Theory of Uneven Geographical Development* (London: Verso, 2006) and *The Condition of Postmodernity: An Enquiry into the Origins of Cultural Change* (Oxford: Wiley-Blackwell, 1991). In these works Harvey is building on the ideas presented in Henri Lefebvre's *The Production of Space* (Oxford: Wiley-Blackwell, 1992). Of course in actual fact Silicon Valley is deeply embroiled in networks of financialized capital, and therefore by extension so too is the entrepreneurship that it promotes and supports. Yet even still, the idea of Silicon Valley, and the way it operates as a relational space-time, is more closely associated with innovation than it is with financialization. Perhaps in lay terms we could say that innovation is its brand.

64. Karen Ho does a remarkable job explaining the culture of investment banking—and the self-conception of investment bankers as masters of the universe—in *Liquidated*. For the Silicon Valley focus on libertarian productivism, see Richard Barbrook and Andy Cameron, "The Californian Ideology," *Science as Culture* 6, no. 1 (1996): 44–72.

65. JQ's model is called an energy-saving corporation, or ESCO.

66. Cleantech investors, not just entrepreneurs, also distinguish themselves from the crass profiteering of Wall Street. They see themselves as "impact investors"—not the sort that self-define as such, but investors who choose the sectors in which they invest and the projects they fund with intention. This has a lot to do with the self-perpetuated narrative of venture capital as a space for entrepreneurial investment. Venture capital does not just invest in entrepreneurs—but they are themselves entrepreneurial. The most famous venture capitalists were all formerly founders of startups that made it big—or at least early employees in these efforts. They see their transition to becoming an investor as a maturation and graduation of sorts—they proved themselves as entrepreneurs and so now they will function as the masters of the entrepreneurial universe—choosing which companies are worthy of investment, mentorship, and support.

67. Robert Fine, "The Marx-Hegel Relationship: Revisionist Interpretations," *Capital and Class* 75 (2001): 71–81.

Chapter 3

1. Christophe Bonneuil and Jean-Baptiste Fressoz, *The Shock of the Anthropocene*, trans. David Fernbach (New York: Verso, 2017). Bonneuil and Fressoz trace the development of geopower through the rise of cybernetically informed earth system science during the 20th century, as evidenced in texts such as the Brundtland Report (1987), which suggest that first seeing the world from outer space precipitated a "Copernican revolution" making visible a "new reality, from which there is no escape, [that] must be recognized—and managed." United Nations Commission on Environment and Development, *Our Common Future* (Oxford: Oxford University Press, 1987), quoted in *Shock of the Anthropocene*, 90. Bonneuil and Fressoz see geoengineering as the penultimate expression of geopower, a planetary experiment to be conducted by "geocratic experts" while leaving a passive public behind. The term *geopower* first gained popularity with the work of Elizabeth Grosz. See Grosz, *Chaos, Territory, Art: Deleuze and the Framing of the Earth* (Durham, NC: Duke University Press, 2008). Whereas Bonneuil and Fressoz interpret geopower as an expansion of Foucault's concept of biopower (as a power over) into the nonhuman, Grosz actually takes a somewhat different tact: "Biopower is, for Foucault, the power over life that regulates it from outside; but geopower has no outside, no 'place' or 'time' before or beyond it: it is the force, the forces, of the earth itself: forces which we as technical humans have tried to organize, render consistent and predictable, but which we can never fully accomplish insofar as the earth remains the literal ground and condition for every human, and non-human, action." Quoted in Elizabeth Grosz, Kathryn Yusoff, and Nigel Clark, "An Interview with Elizabeth Grosz: Geopower, Inhumanism and the Biopolitical," *Theory, Culture and Society* 34, no. 2–3 (2017): 135.

2. Friedman, *Hot, Flat and Crowded: Why We Need a Green Revolution, and How It Can Renew America* (New York: Farrar, Straus and Giroux, 2008), 244: "There is only one

thing bigger than Mother Nature, and that is Father Profit, and we have not even begun to enlist him in this struggle."

3. Schendler, *Getting Green Done: Hard Truths from the Front Lines of the Sustainability Revolution* (New York: PublicAffairs, 2009), 6.

4. Ibid., 18–19.

5. Bonneuil and Fressoz, *Shock of the Anthropocene*, 95.

6. Breakthrough Energy Coalition, "Introducing the Breakthrough Energy Coalition." http://www.breakthroughenergycoalition.com. Gate's project puts the creative dexterity of tech billionaires and investors on display: as it becomes clear that small, incremental improvements to the status quo might not be proceeding at a pace fast enough to meaningfully address the climate crisis, their answer is simply to look for bigger increments, "energy miracles" instead of mere cleantech improvements.

7. Larry Lohmann and Nicholas Hildyard, *Energy, Work and Finance* (Manchester, UK: The Corner House, 2014), 19.

8. Along these lines, Marx himself was seemingly optimistic about the "civilizing influence of capital." In a portion of the *Grundrisse* known as the Fragment on Machines, he expresses a vision of technoscience's radically emancipatory potential, "call[ing] to life all the powers of science and of nature, as of social combination and of social intercourse." See Marx, *Grundrisse; Foundations of the Critique of Political Economy (Rough Draft)*, trans. Martin Nicolaus (London: Pelican Marx Library, in association with *New Left Review*, 1973), 409, 706.

9. For a thorough engagement with the complexities and "hybridities" of this dynamic, see Damian White, Alan Rudy, and Brian Gareau, *Environments, Natures and Social Theory: Towards a Critical Hybridity* (London: Palgrave, 2015). The Soviet experiment discovered these complexities in painful ways; simply expanding the productive base through industrial technology and labor practices developed in the capitalist core could not build toward a liberated society; alienation and ultimately "state capitalism" prevailed. See Peter Hudis, *Marx's Concept of the Alternative to Capitalism* (Leiden: Brill, 2012).

10. Alistair R. Anderson and Lorraine Warren, "The Entrepreneur as Hero and Jester: Enacting the Entrepreneurial Discourse," *International Small Business Journal* 29, no. 6 (2011): 589–609.

11. Imre Szeman, "Entrepreneurship as the New Common Sense," *South Atlantic Quarterly* 114, no. 3 (2015): 231–244.

12. Luc Boltanski and Eva Chiapello, *The New Spirit of Capitalism*, trans. Gregory Elliott (London: Verso, 2007).

13. Noam Wasserman, *The Founder's Dilemmas: Anticipating and Avoiding the Pitfalls That Can Sink a Startup* (Princeton, NJ: Princeton University Press, 2013).

14. Lester Spence makes this argument in a different context, that of African American culture and its embrace of the "hustle." Lester Spence, *Knocking The Hustle: Against The Neoliberal Turn in Black Politics* (Brooklyn: Punctum Books, 2015).

15. Joseph A. Schumpeter, *The Theory of Economic Development: An Inquiry Into Profits, Capital, Credit, Interest, and the Business Cycle* (Piscataway, NJ: Transaction Publishers, 1934), 93.

16. See for instance Fred Block and Matthew R. Keller, *State of Innovation: The U.S. Government's Role in Technology Development* (New York: Paradigm, 2011); Tom Nicholas, "The Role of Independent Invention in U.S. Technological Development, 1880–1930," *Journal of Economic History* 70, no. 1 (2010): 57–82. When it comes to spaces such as universities, it is important to be clear on the encroachment of capital and its investment logic. See for instance Phillip Mirowski, *Science-Mart* (Cambridge, MA: Harvard University Press, 2011).

17. William Janeway, *Doing Capitalism in the Innovation Economy* (Cambridge: Cambridge University Press, 2012).

18. Support for public investment in early stage cleantech development is becoming a common theme. Bill Gates and the Breakthrough Institute both advocate for this sort of state-financed (though importantly, not state-led) innovation ecosystem. The economist Mariana Mazzucato, on the other hand, advocates for a state-financed and somewhat more state-led innovation ecosystem—though she never questions the ways in which the state she hopes to do the leading may itself already be captured by the logic of venture investing. Jason Pontin, "What Bill Gates Has Up His Sleeve for Investing in Energy Technology," *MIT Technology Review* (April 25, 2016); Michael Shellenberger, Ted Nordhaus, Alex Trembath, and Jesse Jenkins, "Where the Shale Gas Revolution Came From," *Breakthrough Institute* (2012), http://thebreak through.org/images/main_image/Where_the_Shale_Gas_Revolution_Came_From2 .pdf; Mariana Mazzucato, *The Entrepreneurial State: Debunking Public vs. Private Sector Myths* (London: Anthem Press, 2013). For a summary of these arguments and their differences, see Jesse Goldstein and David Tyfield, "Green Keynesianism: Bringing the Entrepreneurial State Back in(to Question)?" *Science as Culture* (July 7, 2017), http://www.tandfonline.com/doi/abs/10.1080/09505431.2017.1346598?journal Code=csac20.

19. Friedman, *Hot, Flat and Crowded*, 243–244.

20. Ibid., 244, 246.

21. For a brief history of dressage, see United States Dressage Federation, "History of Dressage," http://www.usdf.org/about/about-dressage/history.asp. The modern practice is primarily associated with competition at horse shows, and has evolved into an art of "horse dancing." Prior to this, however, dressage was primarily associated with cavalries and the discipline, composure, and agility of military horses.

This earlier history of dressage traces its roots to the 4th-century BCE treatise *On Horsemanship* written by Xenophon, as well as to the Roman military, for whom the process entailed preparing warhorses to remain composed during battle. See Richard Berenger, *The History and Art of Horsemanship ... in Two Volumes* (London: T. Davies and T. Cadell, 1771).

22. Henri Lefebvre, *Rhythmanalysis: Space, Time, and Everyday Life* (London: Continuum, 2004, 39).

23. Donna Landry, *Noble Brutes: How Eastern Horses Transformed English Culture* (Baltimore: Johns Hopkins University Press, 2009), 26.

24. Philip Sidney, *An Apologie for Poetry*, ed. Evelyn S. Shuckburgh (Cambridge: Cambridge University Press, 2011 [1905]). Quoted by Landry, *Noble Brutes*, 26–27.

25. Foucault briefly mentions the term *dressage* in the beginning of his chapter on docile bodies in *Discipline and Punish: The Birth of the Prison* (New York: Random House, 1977). His focus is on the rise of modern institutions of military discipline, schooling, and work—all institutional spaces in which the bodies of the working class were increasingly seen as available to be molded, able to be remade as obedient, docile subjects.

26. Landry, *Noble Brutes*, 26.

27. This is a well-established theme in entrepreneurship. See for instance Wasserman, *The Founder's Dilemma*.

28. Janeway, *Doing Innovation,* 78.

29. Ibid., 53.

30. Thomas Hellman and Manju Puri, "Venture Capital and the Professionalization of Startup Firms: Empirical Evidence," *The Journal of Finance* 57, no.1 (2002): 169–197.

31. William Sahlman, "The Structure and Governance of Venture-Capital Organizations" *Journal of Financial Economics* 27, no. 2 (1990): 473–521; John Freeman, "Venture Capital and Modern Capitalism," *The Economic Sociology of Capitalism*, ed. Victor Nee and Richard Swedberg (Princeton, NJ: Princeton University Press, 2005), 144–167.

32. See http://www.khoslaventures.com.

33. See http://www.chrysalix.com/about.

34. Jesse M. Fried and Mira Ganor, "Agency Costs of Venture Capitalist Control in Startups," *New York University Law Review* 81, no. 3 (2006): 967–1025.

35. Manuel Utset, "Reciprocal Fairness, Strategic Behavior & Venture Survival: A Theory of Venture Capital-Financed Firms," *Wisconsin Law Review* 45, no. 1 (2002): 45–168.

36. Utset, "Reciprocal Fairness"; Darwin Neher, "Staged Financing: An Agency Perspective," *The Review of Economic Studies* 66, no. 2 (1999): 255–274.

37. Paul Gompers, "Optimal Investment, Monitoring, and the Staging of Venture Capital," *The Journal of Finance* 50, no. 5 (1995): 1461–1489.

38. Keith C. Brown, "Opaque Financial Contracting and Toxic Term Sheets in Venture Capital," *Journal of Applied Corporate Finance* 28, no. 1 (2016): 72–85.

39. Utset, "Reciprocal Fairness."

40. Gordon D. Smith, "The Exit Structure of Venture Capital," *UCLA Law Review* 53 (2005): 315–356.

41. National Venture Capital Association's standard legal documents can be found at http://nvca.org/resources/model-legal-documents.

42. Ibid.

43. Utset, "Reciprocal Fairness," 96.

44. Noam Wasserman, "Founder-CEO Succession and the Paradox of Entrepreneurial Success," *Organization Science* 14, no. 2 (March–April 2003): 149–172.

45. One example is Michel Ferrary and Mark Granovetter, "The Role of Venture Capital Firms in Silicon Valley's Complex Innovation Network," *Economy and Society* 38, no. 2 (2009): 326–359. In their analysis of venture capital's role in Silicon Valley's innovation ecosystem, they present a picture of symbiotic network relationships; Silicon Valley is a success, and venture capital is a large part of that success. Any sense of power imbalances, conflicts, domination, or exploitation in the innovation ecosystem are downplayed and even erased.

46. Fried and Ganor, "Agency Costs of Venture Capital Control."

47. Ibid.

48. The presumption that a founder will not be able to successfully transition to become a manager and CEO of a growing firm (once the "innovation" is largely complete) has been referred to as "founder's disease." See George C. Rubenson, and Anil K. Gupta, "The Founder's Disease: A Critical Re-Examination," in *Frontiers of Entrepreneurship Research* (Wellesley, MA: Babson College, 1990), 167–183. However, a "diseased" founder cannot be replaced until the investors are confident that any unique intellectual knowledge and capacities held by the founder have been successfully transferred to the firm. This creates a set of perverse incentives for an entrepreneurial founder, which Utset (in "Reciprocal Fairness") terms the *innovator's dilemma*: "The faster that she transfers that knowledge, the faster that she will become expendable" (54). This becomes a somewhat self-fulfilling prophesy—entrepreneurs have it in their best interest to avoid delegation of responsibilities when

this will entail loosening their grip on information asymmetries (and therefore job security), but then as a result they become a paranoid, controlling "mad entrepreneurs" who are unfit for the duties of managerial control—and therefore investors are justified in wanting to replace them. If founders try to hold on to control, they will be seen as recalcitrant or untamable and therefore opportunistic and inefficient managers. But if they do as they are supposed to, and become docile and responsive and open, then they will be good entrepreneurs, though increasingly expendable as such.

49. Utset, "Reciprocal Fairness," 131.

50. Ibid.

51. Many entrepreneurs seeking funds are well aware of this. As one inventor-entrepreneur we will meet in the next chapter explained to me: "The venture capitalists are pretty much hopeless for our purposes. I mean a venture capitalist first of all wants control. As you are well aware, most scientists refer to them as vulture capitalists, because of their persistent tendency to take the company and pick it clean and get rid of scientific initiators. I have wasted time talking to them, I think it is a waste of time."

52. Karl Marx, *Capital, Vol. 1* (London: Penguin, 1991) and *Grundrisse*. See also Massimo De Angelis, "Marx and Primitive Accumulation: The Continuous Character of Capital's Enclosures," *The Commoner* 2 (September 2001); Werner Bonefeld, "The Permanence of Primitive Accumulation: Commodity Fetishism and Social Constitution," *The Commoner* 2 (September 2001); Werner Bonefeld, "Primitive Accumulation and Capitalist Accumulation: Notes on Social Constitution and Expropriation," *Science and Society* 75, no. 3 (2011): 379.

53. Here, the distinctions between market and extra-market discipline begin to blur, as much of this violence comes to be internalized by capital and its everyday manifestations. In the workplace this manifests in technologies of labor control, from de-skilling and disempowering technologies to forms of legitimized precarity (de-unionization, contingency, toxicities) that render workers disposable. The other side of this process is found in the consumer marketplace, where we see a different array of technologies of control; an infrastructure of mass consumption, suburbanization, and disposability that increasingly shapes a way of life built upon the proliferation of commodified desires.

54. This sets up what Utset calls the innovator's dilemma. Basically, it is in the interests of entrepreneur-innovators to stall the process of transferring all of their knowledge to the firm, as this puts them at risk of becoming expendable, even if the health of the startup as well as the likelihood of optimally developing their innovation requires just this sort of free exchange of technical knowledge. As a result, entrepreneur-innovators have an incentive to refuse to disseminate and make

openly available all of the necessary technical details of a project, reinforcing the idea that they are "mad entrepreneurs" who make for bad managers. See Utset, "Reciprocal Fairness."

55. Wasserman, "Founder-CEO Succession," 155.

56. Joseph A. Schumpeter, "Entrepreneurship as Innovation" and Richard Swedberg, "The Social Science View of Entrepreneurship: Introduction and Practical Applications," in *Entrepreneurship: The Social Science View*, ed. Richard Swedberg (Oxford: Oxford University Press, 2000). For Marx's view on the matter, see for instance the chapter on cooperation in *Capital, Vol. 1*.

57. Blaug, "Entrepreneurship Before and After Schumpeter."

58. Ibid., 79.

59. Marx, *Grundrisse*.

60. Ibid.

61. Karl Marx, *Capital, Vol. 3* (London: Penguin, 1991), 199. Marx was not the only theorist to develop this idea. A half century later Thorstein Veblen wrote: "The state of the industrial art is a joint stock of knowledge derived from past experience, and is held and passed on as an indivisible possession of the community at large. It is the indispensible foundation of all productive industry, of course, but except for certain minute fragments covered by patent rights or trade secrets, this joint stock is no man's individual property." See Veblen, *The Engineers and the Price System* (Eastman, CT: Martino Fine Books, 2012 [orig. New York: Viking, 1921]), 28. And Lewis Mumford explains: "In actuality, the claim to a livelihood rests upon the fact that, like the child in a family, one is a member of a community: the energy, the technical knowledge, the social heritage of a community belongs equally to every member of it, since in the large the individual contributions and differences are completely insignificant." See Mumford, *Technics and Civilization*, with a new foreword by Langdon Winner (Chicago: University of Chicago Press, 2010 [orig. New York: Harcourt, 1934]), 403.

62. Marx, *Capital, Vol. 3*, 199.

63. Janeway, *Doing Capitalism*, 168.

64. Vinay K. Gidwani, *Capital, Interrupted: Agrarian Development and the Politics of Work in India* (Minneapolis: University of Minnesota Press, 2008), xxi; Jesse Goldstein, "Terra Economica: Waste and the Production of Enclosed Nature," *Antipode* 45, no. 2 (2013): 357–375.

65. Goldstein, "Terra Economica."

66. See for instance Mirowski, *Science-Mart,* and Tyfield, *The Economics of Science.*

Chapter 4

1. Scott Prudham, "Pimping Climate Change: Richard Branson, Global Warming, and the Performance of Green Capitalism," *Environment and Planning A* 41 (2009): 1594–1613.

2. Imre Szeman, "Entrepreneurship as the New Common Sense," *South Atlantic Quarterly* 114, no. 3 (2015): 231–244.

3. Ronald Burt, "The Network Entrepreneur," in *Entrepreneurship: The Social Science View*, ed. Richard Swedberg (Oxford: Oxford University Press, 2000), 281–307.

4. For discussion of *cultural field* see Pierre Bourdieu, *Distinction: A Social Critique of the Judgment of Taste* (Cambridge, MA: Harvard University Press, 1983). For discussion of *common sense* see Antonio Gramsci, *Prison Notebooks* (New York: International Publishers, 1971), and for discussion of *everyday rhythms* see Henri Lefebvre, *Critique of Everyday Life, Vol. 2: Foundations for a Sociology of the Everyday*, trans. Michel Trebitsch (London: Verso, 2008).

5. Moishe Postone, *Time, Labor, and Social Domination: A Reinterpretation of Marx's Critical Theory* (Cambridge: Cambridge University Press, 1993).

6. John Doerr, "Salvation (and Profit) in Greentech," *TED* (2007) https://www.ted.com/talks/john_doerr_sees_salvation_and_profit_in_greentech?language=en. See also Alex Madrigal, *Powering the Dream: The History and Promise of Green Technology* (Cambridge, MA: Da Capo Press, 2011).

7. Prudham, "Pimping Climate Change."

8. Ibid., 1605. Prudham's critique focuses on the performative green entrepreneurialism of Richard Branson. For an updated critique of Branson, see Naomi Klein, *This Changes Everything: Capitalism vs. the Climate* (New York: Simon and Schuster, 2015).

9. See for instance, Tad Friend. "Tomorrow's Advance Man," *New Yorker*, May 18, 2015.

10. Phillip Mirowski, *The Road from Mont Pèlerin: The Making of the Neoliberal Thought Collective* (Cambridge, MA: Harvard University Press, 2009); Wendy Brown, *Undoing the Demos: Neoliberalism's Stealth Revolution* (Brooklyn: Zone Books, 2015).

11. Kean Birch, "Rethinking Value in the Bio-economy Finance, Assetization, and the Management of Value," *Science Technology and Human Values* 42, no. 3 (2017), http://sth.sagepub.com/content/early/2016/08/10/0162243916661633.abstract.

12. The differentiation between different types of potential investment capital is reminiscent of Viviana Zelizer's work on the social meaning of money. Zelizer, *The Social Meaning of Money: Pin Money, Paychecks, Poor Relief, and Other Currencies* (New York: Basic Books, 1994).

13. Michel Ferrary and Mark Granovetter, "The Role of Venture Capital Firms in Silicon Valley's Complex Innovation Network," *Economy and Society* 38, no. 2 (2009): 326–359.

14. Karen Ho, *Liquidated: An Ethnography of Wall Street* (Durham, NC: Duke University Press, 2009).

15. See for instance, Friend, *Tomorrow's Advance Man*. Peter Theil, Vinod Khosla, and John Doerr all made their fortunes as founders or early employees of tech startups.

16. Ferrary and Granovetter, "The Role of Venture Capital Firms"; Richard Florida and Marin Kenney, "Venture Capital–Financed Innovation and Technological Change in the USA," *Research Policy* 17, no. 3 (1998): 119–137; Paul Gompers and Josh Lerner, *The Money of Invention: How Venture Capital Creates New Wealth* (Cambridge, MA: Harvard Business Press, 2001).

17. Paul Gompers, "The Rise and Fall of Venture Capital," *Business and Economic History* 23, no. 2 (1994): 1–26; Martha Reiner, "Innovation and the Creation of Venture Capital Organizations," *Business and Economic History* 20 (1991): 200–209.

18. Reiner, "Innovation."

19. Freeman, "Venture Capital and Modern Capitalism."

20. Bevis Longstreth, *Modern Investment Management and the Prudent Man Rule* (New York: Oxford University Press, 1986).

21. Gompers, "The Rise and Fall of Venture Capital."

22. Longstreth, *Modern Investment Management*, 5.

23. In 1992 the prudent investor rule was codified in the Uniform Prudent Investor Act (UPIA). See John Langbein, "Uniform Prudent Investor Act and the Future of Trust Investing," *Iowa Law Review* 81 (1995), 641.

24. Gompers, "The Rise and Fall of Venture Capital."

25. Ibid.

26. Many smaller investment banks went out of business or were consolidated into larger banks over the first decade of the 21st century. This consolidation of the industry negatively effected the startup market, as the larger banks would only consider managing much more substantial public offerings—leaving venture funded startups with far fewer options for their eventual "exit."

27. The term comes from the Russian linguist Valentin Voloshinov. See David McNally, *Bodies of Meaning* (Albany: State University of New York Press, 2001).

28. Hirschman, *The Passions and the Interests*.

29. Michael Perelman, *The Invention of Capitalism: Classical Political Economy and the Secret History of Primitive Accumulation* (Durham, NC: Duke University Press, 2000); Ellen Meiksins Wood, *The Origin of Capitalism: A Longer View* (New York: Verso, 2002). There are different ways to make sense of these ideologies. For Michael Perelman they entail a level of conscious and deliberate deceit; he scours the private correspondences of figures like Adam Smith and James Steuart to reveal a very intentional revisionist and sanitizing account of capital accumulation—propaganda in the most basic sense. Yet for Albert Hirschman these same narratives are instead read as a more honest and straightforward attempt to make sense of a changing world—to articulate the laws of the market that were on the ascent, along with the economic system that was developing around them. In other words, they were not meant to falsely label what one knew to not actually exist, but to accurately name what one perceived to be really developing—an expression of the very real market forces animating economic life.

30. Postone, *Time, Labor, and Social Domination*, 30.

31. Mike Hawkins, *Social Darwinism in European and American Thought, 1860–1945: Nature as Model and Nature as Threat* (Cambridge: Cambridge University Press, 1997); Simon Clarke, *Marx, Marginalism and Modern Sociology: From Adam Smith to Max Weber* (London: Palgrave Macmillan, 1982); Samuel Bowles and Herbert Gintis, "The Revenge of Homo Economicus: Contested Exchange and the Revival of Political Economy," *Journal of Economic Perspectives* 7 (1993): 83.

32. Nathan Schneider, *Thank You, Anarchy: Notes from the Occupy Apocalypse*. (Oakland: University of California Press, 2013).

33. Geoff Mann, *In the Long Run We Are All Dead* (Brooklyn: Verso, 2017).

34. United Nations Framework Convention on Climate Change, *Paris Agreement: Essential Elements* (UNFCCC, November 2016), http://unfccc.int/paris_agreement/items /9485.php.

35. Paul Hawken, ed. *Drawdown: The Most Comprehensive Plan Ever Proposed to Reverse Global Warming*, (New York: Penguin Books, 2017); "Top Venture Deals and Corporate Investors," 2016 Innovation Monitor Presentation; Cleantech Group, 2016, https://www.cleantech.com/wp-content/uploads/2016/05/1Q16-Innovation -Monitor_Slides.pdf.

36. Pilita Clark, "The Big Green Bang: How Renewable Energy Became Unstoppable," *Financial Times*, May 18, 2017; Leslie Hook, "Uber," *Financial Times*, October 5, 2017.

37. Karl Marx, *Early Writings* (New York: Penguin, 1992), 375.

38. Ibid., 377.

39. Jason W. Moore, *Capitalism in the Web of Life: Ecology and the Accumulation of Capital* (New York: Verso, 2015). Extending well-established arguments in materialist

feminism, Moore argues that the production of capitalist value is inseparable from the appropriation (and production) of cheap natures—labor-power, energy, raw materials, and food—whose availability, use, and exhaustion are all integral to the capitalist economy.

Chapter 5

1. Lester Russell Brown, *Plan B 3.0: Mobilizing to Save Civilization* (New York: W. W. Norton, 2008); Fred Krupp and Miriam Horn, *Earth, the Sequel: The Race to Reinvent Energy and Stop Global Warming* (New York: W. W. Norton, 2008); Joel Makower, *Strategies for the Green Economy: Opportunities and Challenges in the New World of Business* (New York: McGraw Hill, 2009).

2. Eric Ries, *The Lean Startup: How Today's Entrepreneurs Use Continuous Innovation to Create Radically Successful Businesses* (New York: Crown Business, 2011); Steve Blank and Bob Dorf, *The Startup Owner's Manual: The Step-by-Step Guide for Building a Great Company* (Pescadero, CA: K&S Ranch, 2012).

3. Krupp and Horn, *Earth: The Sequel*, 3.

4. Ibid.

5. Teju Cole writes of a White Savior Industrial Complex, and although he references a different sort of racialized, humanitarian intervention, the concept and critique hold quite well in relation to cleantech entrepreneurship. Cole argues that much first-world humanitarian relief can be more about the affective needs of the aid-givers than about any direct assessment of the self-assessed needs of those being aided. He writes: "There is much more to doing good work than 'making a difference.' There is the principle of first do no harm. There is the idea that those who are being helped ought to be consulted over the matters that concern them." See Teju Cole, "The White-Savior Industrial Complex," *Atlantic*, March 21, 2012, https://www.theatlantic.com/international/archive/2012/03/the-white-savior-industrial-complex/254843/.

6. Stanley Cohen, *States of Denial: Knowing About Atrocities and Suffering.* (Hoboken, NJ: John Wiley & Sons, 2013), quoted by Kari Norgaard, *Living in Denial: Climate Change, Emotions, and Everyday Life* (Cambridge, MA: MIT Press, 2011), 60. Norgaard quotes Cohen, who describes denial emerging in the space between knowing and not-knowing: "We are vaguely aware of choosing not to look at the facts, but not quite conscious of just what it is that we are evading. We know, but at the same time we don't know."

7. Kari Norgaard, *Living in Denial: Climate Change, Emotions, and Everyday Life* (Cambridge, MA: MIT Press), 2011.

8. Ibid., 5.

9. Samantha MacBride, *Recycling Reconsidered: The Present Failure and Future Promise of Environmental Action in the United States* (Cambridge, MA: MIT Press, 2013).

10. Rogers, *Gone Tomorrow: The Hidden Life of Garbage* (New York: New Press, 2005).

11. Ibid.

12. MacBride, *Recycling Reconsidered.*

13. On the last point in particular, see Susan Strasser, *Waste and Want: A Social History of Trash* (New York: Metropolitan Books, 1999).

14. The seventh-generation principle from the Haudenosaunee Nation states: "Look and listen for the welfare of the whole people and have always in view not only the present but also the coming generations, even those whose faces are yet beneath the surface of the ground—the unborn of the future Nation." See *The Great Binding Lawn (Gayanashagowa)* http://www.indigenouspeople.net/iroqcon.htm.

15. Andrew Szasz, *Shopping Our Way to Safety: How We Changed From Protecting the Environment to Protecting Ourselves* (Minneapolis: University of Minnesota Press, 2007).

16. There is a well-established literature making sense of the measurement, quantification, and ultimately financialization of natural systems and climatological effects. See, for instance, Morgan Robertson, "Measurement and Alienation: Making a World of Ecosystem Services," *Transactions of the Institute of British Geographers* 37, no. 3 (2012): 386–401; Jessica Dempsey, *Enterprising Nature: Economics, Markets, and Finance and Biodiversity Politics* (Hoboken, NJ: John Wiley & Sons, 2016); Neil Smith, "Nature as an Accumulation Strategy," *Socialist Register* 43 (2007): 16–36.

17. Dempsey, *Enterprising Nature.*

18. Norgaard, *Living in Denial.*

19. Jon A. Krosnic et al., "The Origins and Consequences of Democratic Citizens' Policy Agendas: A Study of Popular Concern about Global Warming," *Climatic Change* 77, no. 1–2 (2006): 7–43; John Immerwahr, *Waiting for a Signal: Public Attitudes Toward Global Warming, the Environment and Geophysical Research* (Washington, DC: American Geophysical Union, 1999).

20. Peder Anker offers a history of this "Imperial Ecology" as developed in the 20th century by the British Empire. See Peder Anker, *Imperial Ecology: Environmental Order in the British Empire, 1895–1945,* (Cambridge, MA: Harvard University Press, 2001). Sian Sullivan revives this concept to discuss payments for ecosystem services as a new imperial ecology. See Sian Sullivan, "A New 'Imperial Ecology'?," *New Formations* 69 (2010): 111–128.

21. Rob Nixon, *Slow Violence and the Environmentalism of the Poor* (Cambridge, MA: Harvard University Press, 2011), 8.

22. John Urry, *Societies Beyond Oil: Oil Dregs and Social Futures* (London: Zed Books, 2013).

23. Matthew T. Huber traces the historic connections between petroleum use and the hyper-individuality of entrepreneurial culture in *Lifeblood: Oil, Freedom, and the Forces of Capital* (Minneapolis: University of Minnesota Press, 2013.

24. Oxfam, "Extreme Carbon Inequality," *OXFAM Media Briefing*, December 2, 2015, https://www.oxfam.org/sites/www.oxfam.org/files/file_attachments/mb-extreme -carbon-inequality-021215-en.pdf.

25. Lucas Chancel and Thomas Piketty, "Carbon and Inequality: From Kyoto to Paris," *Paris School of Economics* (November, 2015). http://piketty.pse.ens.fr/files/Chan celPiketty2015.pdf.

26. Schendler, *Getting Green Done: Hard Truths from the Front Lines of the Sustainability Revolution* (New York: PublicAffairs, 2009), 48.

27. Ibid.

28. Ibid., 81–82.

29. Susan Opotow and Leah Weiss, "New Ways of Thinking About Environmentalism: Denial and the Process of Moral Exclusion in Environmental Conflict," *Journal of Social Issues* 56, no. 3 (2000): 475–490, quoted in Norgaard, *Living in Denial*.

30. Erik Swyngedouw, "Apocalypse Forever? Post-Political Populism and the Spectre of Climate Change," *Theory, Culture & Society* 27, no. 2–3 (2010): 213–232; Erik Swyngedouw, "Impossible Sustainability and the Post-Political Condition," in *The Sustainable Development Paradox: Urban Political Economy in the United States and Europe*, ed. D. Gibbs and R. Kreuger (2007), 13–40; Chantal Mouffe, *On the Political* (New York: Taylor and Francis, 2005).

31. Norgaard, (quoting Arendt) *Living in Denial*, 53.

32. Norgaard, *Living in Denial*, 76.

33. Joseph Lacob quoted in Matt Richtel, "Green Energy Enthusiasts Are Also Betting on Fossil Fuels," *New York Times*, March 16, 2007.

34. Leo Marx, "Technology: The Emergence of a Hazardous Concept," *Technology and Culture* 51, no. 3 (2010): 561–577.

35. Ibid., 576.

36. Ibid., 577.

37. David Pellow, Allan Schnaiberg, and Adam Weinberg, "Advanced Industrial Countries: Putting the Ecological Modernisation Thesis to the Test: The Promises and Performances of Urban Recycling," *Environmental Politics* 9, no. 1 (2000): 109–137.

38. Swyngedouw, "Apocalypse Forever."

39. Norgaard, *Living in Denial,* 61.

40. Anthony Giddens, *Modernity and Self-Identity: Self and Society in the Late Modern Age* (Hoboken, NJ: John Wiley & Sons, 2013).

41. Immerwahr, "Waiting for a Signal," 24–25. Quoted in Norgaard, *Living in Denial,* 191–192.

42. Robert D. Putnam, *Bowling Alone: The Collapse and Revival of American Community* (New York: Simon and Schuster, 2001).

43. Norgaard, *Living in Denial.*

44. Walter Benjamin, "Theses on the Philosophy of History," in *Illuminations,* ed. Hannah Arendt (New York: Schocken, 1969).

Chapter 6

1. Arthur Neslen, "Portugal Runs for Four Days Straight on Renewable Energy Alone," *Guardian,* May 18, 2016, http://www.theguardian.com/environment/2016/may/18 /portugal-runs-for-four-days-straight-on-renewable-energy-alone?CMP=share _btn_fb.

2. Pilita Clark, "The Big Green Bang: How Renewable Energy Became Unstoppable," *Financial Times,* May 18, 2017.

3. Benjamin Gaddy, Varun Sivaram, and Francis O'Sullivan, "Venture Capital and Cleantech: The Wrong Model for Clean Innovation," *MIT Energy Initiative* 77, July 2016.

4. Clark, "The Big Green Bang."

5. Ibid.

6. Renewable Energy Policy Network for the 21st Century. *Renewables 2015: Global Status Report,* http://www.ren21.net/wp-content/uploads/2015/07/REN12-GSR2015 _Onlinebook_low1.pdf.

7. Clark, "The Big Green Bang."

8. David Graeber, *The Utopia of Rules: On Technology, Stupidity, and the Secret Joys of Bureaucracy* (Brooklyn: Melville House, 2015), 147.

9. Ibid., 88. Graeber uses the term "ontology" with hesitation, but describes what he means by political ontology with the following example: "When one says "let's be realistic here," what reality is it we're referring to? What is the hidden reality, the underlying forces, assumed to be moving below the surface of political events?" (245, n.70)

10. Ana Isla, "Conservation as Enclosure: An Ecofeminist Perspective on Sustainable Development and Biopiracy in Costa Rica," *Capitalism Nature Socialism* 16, no. 3 (2005): 49–61; Nik Heynen, James McCarthy, Scott Prudham, and Paul Robbins, eds., *Neoliberal Environments: False Promises and Unnatural Consequences* (London: Routledge, 2007).

11. Cindi Katz, "Whose Nature, Whose Culture?: Private Productions of Space and the 'Preservation' of Nature," in *Remaking Reality: Nature at the Millennium*, ed. Bruce Braun and Noel Castree (London: Routledge, 1998), 46. A number of feminist science studies scholars have also posed similar questions. For instance, Sandra Harding asks "Whose Science? Whose Knowledge?" in *Whose Science? Whose Knowledge?: Thinking from Women's Lives* (New York: Cornell, 1991) and Donna Harraway asks "what counts as nature, for whom, and at what cost?" in Modest_Witness @Second_Millenium.Female-Man_Meets_ONcoMouse: *Feminism and Technoscience* (New York: Routledge, 1997), 104.

12. Geoff Mann, *In the Long Run, We Are All Dead: Keynesianism, Political Economy and Revolution* (New York: Verso, 2017).

13. I've borrowed this way of framing the uneven landscape of social reproduction, as a question of peoples differentially enabled and disabled, from the feminist science studies scholar Martha Kenney.

14. Mann, *In the Long Run We Are All Dead*, 356.

15. Mann, *In the Long Run We Are All Dead*.

16. Brian Dumaine, "Why Jeff Bezos, Peter Thiel, and Others Are Betting," *Fortune*, September 28, 2015, http://fortune.com/2015/09/28/jeff-bezos-peter-thiel-fusion/.

17. Eric Lerner, *The Big Bang Never Happened: A Startling Refutation of the Dominant Theory of the Origin of the Universe* (New York: Vintage, 1992).

18. These fears are substantiated by the US military's current efforts to deploy alternative energy as part of its strategic preparedness. See Patrick Bigger and Benjamin D. Neimark, "Weaponizing Nature: The Geopolitical Ecology of the U.S. Navy's Biofuel Program," *Political Geography* 60 (2017): 13–22.

19. With the JOBS Act of 2012, crowdfunding platforms have been made available to venture investing. Initially, this provision was governed by the same restrictions that apply to all private investment, limiting investment to accredited investors, meaning individuals with at least $250K annual income or $1 million in assets. This meant that Lerner was not able to offer equity through his first crowdfunding campaign, and instead relied upon other rewards. For instance, the seven individuals who donated more than $2,500 had their names engraved on a small plaque, hanging on a thick metal door separating Lerner's lab from the back room housing his focused fusion reactor. As of May 2016, these rules have changed, allowing anyone

to purchase equity through a crowdfunding site (up to a maximum of $100,000 annually), with limitations on annual investment for people whose net worth or annual income is less than $100,000. See Financial Industry Regulatory Authority, "Crowdfunding and the JOBS Act: What Investors Should Know," http://www.finra .org/investors/alerts/crowdfunding-and-jobs-act-what-investors-should-know.

20. Gaddy, Sivaram, and O'Sullivan, "Venture Capital and Cleantech."

21. Devasree Saha and Mark Muro, "Cleantech Venture Capital: Continued Declines and Narrow Geography Limits Prospects," *Brookings Report*, May 16, 2017, https:// www.brookings.edu/research/cleantech-venture-capital-continued-declines-and -narrow-geography-limit-prospects.

22. Issie Lapowsky, "Tech Billionaires Team Up to Take on Climate Change," *Wired*, November 30, 2015, https://www.wired.com/2015/11/zuckerberg-gates-climate-change -breakthrough-energy-coalition. See also http://www.breakthroughenergycoalition .com/en/index.html.

23. Lapowsky, "Tech Billionaires."

24. Ibid.

25. David Brancaccio, "Bill Gates on Getting Billionaires Behind Clean Energy," http://www.marketplace.org/2016/02/22/world/bill-gates.

26. Mariana Mazzucato, *The Entrepreneurial State: Debunking Public vs. Private Sector Myths* (London: Anthem Press, 2013). The connection between Gates and Mazzucato was actually confirmed via a twitter conversation, shared with me by Daniel Aldana-Cohen. On October 26, 2015, he tweeted, "Bill Gates on ineptitude of private sector, need 4 state climate action. Or is it @MazzucatoM?" Mazzucato replies, "@aldatweets @patrickmbigger Yup. He read 1st version of Entrepreneurial State (US ed out this wk) & visiting him this wk to discuss further."

27. John Asafu-Adjaye et al., *Ecomodernist Manifesto*, April 2015, https://static1.square space.com/static/5515d9f9e4b04d5c3198b7bb/t/552d37bbe4b07a7dd69fcdbb /1429026747046/An+Ecomodernist+Manifesto.pdf.

28. Philip Mirowski, *Science-Mart* (Cambridge, MA: Harvard University Press, 2011), 25. Mirowski argues that the rise of information science, and subsequently the computer as a "machine that thinks" provided social scientists—notably economists— with cybernetic metaphors for how the market economy can and should work. The market was no longer simply a means for moving goods from one place to another, but was seen as a computational machine, able to make decisions regarding the optimally efficient allocation of goods and services in ways that were far superior to any analogous attempt by mere humans and the institutions they administer. Neoliberalism was, then, a rejoinder to and defense against any interest in the planned economy—whether that of the World War II economy or the Soviet Union's scientific

and industrial machine. The market, and not the state—not any state—was to be empowered to make decisions about economic life. Accordingly, the state was tasked with actively producing the conditions of possibility for this market-hegemony.

29. For a discussion of Green New Deal proposals and the entrepreneurial state, see Jesse Goldstein and David Tyfield, "Green Keynesianism: Bringing the Entrepreneurial State Back in(to Question)?" *Science as Culture* (July 7, 2017), http://www.tandfonline .com/doi/abs/10.1080/09505431.2017.1346598?journalCode=csac20.

30. Friedman agrees, and ends his book *Hot, Flat and Crowded*, with a call for the US to become "China for a day." Just one day though—just long enough to put some policies in place and chart a course for cleantech innovation, and then we should turn back to our free-market democracy, to which Friedman goes to every length to prove his allegiance.

31. See Regenerative Finance, "About," http://regenerativefinance.com. Other similar projects include the RSF Social Finance, http://rsfsocialfinance.org, and Slow Money Investing Network, https://slowmoney.org. Most of these projects focus on supporting local food systems, and still—despite their best intentions—maintain a position of authority and control for the wealthy investors who ultimately control the purse strings.

32. Mark Z. Jacobson and Mark A. Delucchi, "Providing All Global Energy With Wind, Water, and Solar Power. Part I: Technologies, Energy Resources, Quantities and Areas of Infrastructure, and Materials," *Energy Policy* 39, no. 3 (2011): 1154–1169; Mark A. Delucchi and Mark Z. Jacobson, "Providing All Global Energy With Wind, Water, and Solar Power. Part II: Reliability, System and Transmission Costs, and Policies," *Energy Policy* 39, no. 3 (2011): 1170–1190. Though they predicate their plan on proposing only already proven technologies, they do discuss a few material limitations—such as rare earth minerals, silver and platinum, which will require new innovations in photovoltaic cells and hydrogen fuel cells. Their work was subsequently critiqued on technical grounds in Ted Trainer, "A Critique of Jacobson and Delucchi's Proposals for a World Renewable Energy Supply," *Energy Policy* 44 (2012): 476–481.

33. Mark Z. Jacobson and Mark A. Delucchi, "A Plan to Power 100 Percent of the Planet With Renewables," *Scientific American* 26 (2009): 58, 59.

34. See for instance Bill McKibben, "A World at War," *New Republic*, August 15, 2016, https://newrepublic.com/article/135684/declare-war-climate-change-mobilize -wwii.

35. See www.thesolutionsproject.org. Cofounders include the actor Mark Ruffalo, the businessman Marco Krapels, and the activist Josh Fox. Presidential candidate Bernie Sanders also supported this plan, in his impassioned calls to take climate change seriously as an immediate and pressing threat.

36. Asafu-Adjaye et al., *Ecomodernist Manifesto*.

37. John Baudrillard, *Simulations*, trans. Paul Foss (New York: Semiotext(e), 1983).

38. Petrocultures Research Group, *After Oil* (Edmonton, Alberta: Petrocultures Research Group, 2016), 27. The term *petromodernity* was first introduced by Stephanie LeMenager. See Stephanie LeMenager, *Living Oil: Petroleum Culture in the American Century* (Oxford: Oxford University Press, 2014).

39. Laura Pulido, "Geographies of Race And Ethnicity II: Environmental Racism, Racial Capitalism and State-Sanctioned Violence," *Progress in Human Geography*, 1–10, doi: 10.1177/0309132516646495.

40. Daniel Yergin, *The Quest: Energy Security and the Remaking of the Modern World* (New York: Penguin, 2011).

41. Matthew T. Huber, *Lifeblood: Oil, Freedom, and the Forces of Capital* (Minneapolis: University of Minnesota Press, 2013. Along these lines, Andreas Malm argues that fossil fuel consumption and specifically the petroleum-based commodities regularly purchased (from fuel at the gas station to plastic packaging at the store) function as an ideological apparatus, "interpolating" or "hailing" individuals as petrosubjects. The problem, then, is that were these "fossil subjects" to rise up against the petroeconomy, "[they] could lose themselves in the process." Andreas Malm, *Fossil Capital: The Rise of Steam Power and the Roots of Global Warming* (New York: Verso Books, 2016), 365.

42. Petrocultures Research Group, *After Oil*, 68.

43. Lauren Gail Berlant, *Cruel Optimism* (Durham, NC: Duke University Press, 2011).

44. Tony Fry, *Design Futuring* (Oxford: Berg, 2009).

45. In this way, cleantech anchors a powerful narrative of technological salvation, or what Evgeny Morozov calls technological solutionism, a computational world-view in which all problems can be addressed with technological—as opposed to social or political—advance; so long as the market, or "father profit" is available to commercialize and deploy these technological fixes to the furthest reaches of the globe. Evgeny Morozov, *To Save Everything, Click Here: The Folly of Technological Solutionism* (New York: PublicAffairs, 2014).

46. Larry Lohmann and Nicholas Hildyard, *Energy, Work, and Finance* (The Corner House, 2014), http://www.thecornerhouse.org.uk/resource/energy-work-and-finance.

Coda

1. Ian Angus, *Facing the Anthropocene: Fossil Capitalism and the Crisis of the Earth System* (New York: New York University Press, 2016).

2. Lauren Gail Berlant, *Cruel Optimism* (Durham, NC: Duke University Press, 2011).

3. Rory Rowan, "Extinction as Usual?: Geo-social Futures and Left Optimism," *e-flux journal*, July 31, 2015, http://supercommunity.e-flux.com/texts/extinction-as-usual -geo-social-futures-and-left-optimism.

4. Ibid.

5. Roy Scranton, "Learning How to Die in the Anthropocene," *New York Times*, November 10, 2013, http://opinionator.blogs.nytimes.com/2013/11/10/learning -how-to-die-in-the-anthropocene/?_r=0.

6. Ibid.

7. See William Cronon, "The Trouble With Wilderness; or, Getting Back to the Wrong Nature," in William Cronon, ed., *Uncommon Ground: Rethinking the Human Place in Nature* (New York: W. W. Norton & Co., 1995), 69–90; and Jennifer Peoples, "Toxic Sublime: Imaging Contaminated Landscapes," *Environmental Communication: A Journal of Nature and Culture* 5, no. 4 (2011): 373–392.

8. Scranton, "Learning How to Die." Compare Scranton's argument with Theodore Roosevelt, who writes, "There he passes his days, there he does his life-work, there, when he meets death, he faces it as he has faced many other evils, with quiet, uncomplaining fortitude. Brave, hospitable, hardy, and adventurous, he is the grim pioneer of our race; he prepares the way for the civilization from before whose face he must himself disappear. Hard and dangerous though his existence is, it has yet a wild attraction that strongly draws to it his bold, free spirit." Quoted in Cronon, "The Trouble with Wilderness," 80.

9. For this latter observation, about the need to develop the humility to understand that we may not even know how to ask the right questions, I am indebted to my student Camila Grez-Messina, who made this point as part of our public research symposium, *Geofuturism: Learning to Let Go and Love Other Worlds* (Virginia Commonwealth University, December 2016).

10. Giacomo D'Alisa, Federico Demaria, and Giorgos Kallis, eds., *Degrowth: A Vocabulary for a New Era* (London: Routledge, 2014).

11. Eduardo Gudynas, "Buen Vivir: Today's Tomorrow," *Development* 54, no. 4 (2011): 441–447; Ashish Kothari, Federico Demaria, and Alberto Acosta, "Buen Vivir, Degrowth and Ecological Swaraj: Alternatives to Sustainable Development and the Green Economy," *Development* 57, no. 3–4 (2014): 362–375; Juliet Schor and Karen Elizabeth White, *Plenitude: The New Economics of True Wealth* (New York: Penguin Press, 2010); Tim Jackson. *Prosperity Without Growth: Economics for a Finite Planet* (London: Routledge, 2011).

12. For an excellent critique of one libertarian strain of this sort of environmentalism, see Matthew Schneider-Mayerson, *Peak Oil: Apocalyptic Environmentalism and Libertarian Political Culture.* (Chicago: University of Chicago Press, 2015).

13. Geoff Mann, *In The Long Run, We Are All Dead: Keynesianism, Political Economy and Revolution* (New York: Verso, 2017).

14. Ozzie Zehner, *Green Illusions: The Dirty Secrets of Clean Energy and the Future of Environmentalism* (Lincoln: University of Nebraska Press, 2012)

15. Walter Mignolo, *The Darker Side of Western Modernity: Global Futures, Decolonial Options* (Durham, NC: Duke University Press, 2011).

16. Feenberg asks for a democratization of technology in Andrew Feenberg, *Transforming Technology: A Critical Theory Revisited* (Oxford: Oxford University Press, 2002).

17. Karl Marx, *Grundrisse; Foundations of the Critique of Political Economy (Rough Draft)*, trans. Martin Nicolaus (London: Pelican Marx Library, in association with *New Left Review*, 1973), 410.

18. William E. Connolly, *The Fragility of Things: Self-Organizing Processes, Neoliberal Fantasies, and Democratic Activism* (Durham, NC: Duke University Press, 2013); Elizabeth R. Johnson and Jesse Goldstein, "Biomimetic Futures: Life, Death, and the Enclosure of a More-than-Human Intellect," *Annals of the Association of American Geographers* 105, no. 2 (2015): 387–396.

19. Lewis Mumford, *Technics and Civilization*, with a new foreword by Langdon Winner (Chicago: University of Chicago Press, 2010 [orig. New York: Harcourt, 1934]). Here Mumford's work is in direct contrast to that of his predecessor, Thorstein Veblen, who exonerated the engineer and forms of expert-driven technocracy. See Veblen, *The Engineers and the Price System* (Eastmn, CT: Martino Fine Books, 2012 [orig. New York: Viking, 1921]).

20. Mumford, *Technics and Civilization*, 410.

21. Galeano, "A Few First Questions for the Sciences and Their Consciences," December 26, 2016, http://enlacezapatista.ezln.org.mx/2017/01/17/a-few-first-questions-for-the-sciences-and-their-consciences/.

22. Frantz Fanon, *The Wretched of the Earth*, trans. Richard Philcox (New York: Grove Press, 1963), 141.

23. Galeano, "A Few First Questions."

24. Nick Srnicek and Alex Williams, *Inventing the Future: Postcapitalism and a World Without Work* (New York: Verso Books, 2015).

25. Decreases in human labor have historically been accomplished via increases in other, non-human forms of material, energetic and lively inputs. See Jason W. Moore, *Capitalism in the Web of Life: Ecology and the Accumulation of Capital* (New York: Verso, 2015).

26. Petrocultures Research Group, *After Oil* (Edmonton, AB: Petrocultures Research Group, 2016), 68.

27. Including Harraway's work here is one way to more generously read her call for "making kin," which has otherwise been critiqued as a resurgence of left-Malthusianism. Donna Harraway, *Staying With The Trouble: Making Kin in the Cthulucene* (Durham, NC: Duke University Press, 2016). For a critique of Harraway, see Sophie Lewis, "Cthulhu Plays No Role For Me," *Viewpoint Magazine*, May 8, 2017, https://www.viewpointmag.com/2017/05/08/cthulhu-plays-no-role-for-me/.

28. Maria Mies and Vandana Shiva, *Ecofeminism* (Halifax: Fernwood Press, 1993).

29. Elizabeth Johnson and I have, in this regard, taken inspiration from Wes Jackson's Land Institute, and their attempts to create a grain-yielding prairie ecosystem, a perennial polyculture that might eventually be capable of superseding prevailing forms of monocropped agriculture. Johnson and Goldstein, "Biomimetic Futures." It is also worth noting that Paul Hawken, one of the earliest champions of green capitalism, is currently exploring a diverse range of sociotechnical strategies for addressing the need to dramatically curtail fossil fuel consumption. While the book's sociopolitical imaginary may still be lacking, it does provide an encouraging resource. Paul Hawken, ed., *Drawdown: The Most Comprehensive Plan Ever Proposed to Reverse Global Warming* (New York: Penguin, 2017).

30. "Kernza Grain: Towards a Perennial Agriculture," *The Land Institute*, https://landinstitute.org/our-work/perennial-crops/kernza/.

31. "Our Work," *The Land Institute*, https://landinstitute.org/our-work/.

32. Johnson and Goldstein, "Biomimetic Futures," 394.

33. Wes Jackson, *Altars of Unhewn Stone* (Wooster, OH: Wooster Book Company, 2006), 23. Quoted in Johnson and Goldstein, "Biomimetic Futures," 394.

34. Donna Haraway, "Anthropocene, Capitalocene, Plantationocene, Cthulucene: Making Kin, *Environmental Humanities* 6 (2015), 159–165, 160.

35. Sandra Harding, *Objectivity and Diversity: Another Logic of Scientific Research* (Chicago: University of Chicago, 2015).

36. Mirianna Limas, "Ecovative Design Awarded $9.1 Million U.S. Department of Defense Research Contract to Develop and Scale a New Generation of Living Building Materials," *SynBioBeta*, June 28, 2017, https://synbiobeta.com/ecovative-design-awarded-9-1-million-u-s-department-defense-research-contract-develop-scale-new-generation-living-building-materials/. The role of DARPA funding in clean technologies is a contentious topic in its own right. While figures such as Mazzucato and the Breakthrough Institute celebrate these sorts of funding programs for their track record of bringing important technologies into existence (television, the internet), it is also important to remain critical of the ways in which the US military, the single

largest institutional contributor to global warming on the planet, considers its "green" initiatives as a means of sustaining itself (and all that it does to destabilize the climate) in the face of climate change. See Patrick Bigger and Benjamin D. Neimark, "Weaponizing Nature: The Geopolitical Ecology of the U.S. Navy's Biofuel Program," *Political Geography* 60 (2017): 13–22.

37. See for instance David Tyfield, "'King Coal is Dead! Long Live the King!': The Paradoxes of Coal's Resurgence in the Emergence of Global Low-Carbon Societies," *Theory, Culture & Society* 31, no. 5 (2014): 59–81; Bill McKibben, "Global Warming's Terrifying New Math," *Rolling Stone*, July 19, 2012, http://www.rollingstone.com /politics/news/global-warmings-terrifying-new-math-20120719.

38. On just transitions, see Peter Newell and Dustin Mulvaney, "The Political Economy of the 'Just Transition,'" *The Geographical Journal* 179, no. 2 (2013): 132–134; Damian White, "Critical Design, Hybrid Labor, Just Transitions: Moving beyond Technocratic Ecomoderisms and the It's-Too-Late-O-Cene, in Manuel Arias-Maldonado and Zev Trachtenberg (eds.), *Rethinking the Environment for the Anthropocene: Political Theory and Socio-Natural Relations for a New Geological Age*, London: Routledge, 2018.

Index